M000188321

Being Born

All human beings are born and all human beings die. In these two ways we are finite: our lives begin and our lives come to an end. Historically philosophers have concentrated attention on our mortality, and comparatively little has been said about being born and how it shapes our existence. Alison Stone sets out to overcome this oversight by providing a systematic philosophical account of how being born shapes our condition as human beings. Drawing on both feminist philosophy and existentialist concerns about the structure of meaningful human existence, Stone offers an original perspective on human existence. She explores how human existence is shaped by the way that we are born. Taking natality into account transforms our view of human existence and illuminates how many of its aspects are connected with our birth. These aspects include dependency, the relationality of the self, vulnerability, reception and inheritance of culture and history, embeddedness in social power, situatedness, and radical contingency. Considering natality also sheds new light on anxiety, mortality, and the temporality of human life. This book therefore bears on death and the meaning of life, as well as many debates in feminist and continental philosophy.

Studies in Feminist Philosophy is designed to showcase cutting-edge monographs and collections that display the full range of feminist approaches to philosophy, that push feminist thought in important new directions, and that display the outstanding quality of feminist philosophical thought.

STUDIES IN FEMINIST PHILOSOPHY

Published in the Series:

Being Born

Birth and Philosophy

ALISON STONE

OXFORD
UNIVERSITY PRESS

OXFORD
UNIVERSITY PRESS

Great Clarendon Street, Oxford, OX2 6DP,
United Kingdom

Oxford University Press is a department of the University of Oxford.
It furthers the University's objective of excellence in research, scholarship,
and education by publishing worldwide. Oxford is a registered trade mark of
Oxford University Press in the UK and in certain other countries

First published 2019
First published in paperback 2022

Published in the United States of America by Oxford University Press
198 Madison Avenue, New York, NY 10016, United States of America

British Library Cataloguing in Publication Data
Data available

Library of Congress Cataloging in Publication Data
Data available

ISBN 978-0-19-884578-2 (Hbk.)
ISBN 978-0-19-287230-2 (Pbk.)

DOI: 10.1093/oso/9780198845782.001.0001

Contents

Acknowledgements

I am very grateful to the Leverhulme Trust for awarding me a Major Research Fellowship, which funded two years of research leave (2017–19) during which I wrote this book.

I am also grateful to many people who have commented on earlier drafts of this material or discussed its ideas with me, including Anu Aneja, Victoria Browne, Lewis Coyne, Simon Gillham, Stephen Houlgate, Kate Kirkpatrick, Clare Palmer, Chakravarthi Ram-Prasad, Christina Schües, Fanny Söderbäck, Bob Stern, Bron Szerzynski, Angus Taylor, Veronica Vasterling, Jon Webber, Steve Wilkinson, and Kate Withy. I particularly want to thank Tanja Staehler, for reading several draft chapters, and the two anonymous referees for Oxford University Press, whose extremely helpful, detailed, and constructive comments enabled me to make many improvements to the book. I thank Peter Momtchiloff at Oxford University Press for his support for this project. Above all, my thanks to John Varty for his help and support.

I put forward much earlier versions of some of the ideas in Chapter 6 in 'Natality and Mortality: Rethinking Death with Cavarero', in *Continental Philosophy Review* (2010) 43: 353–72, and 'The Relationality of Death', in *On the Feminist Philosophy of Gillian Howie*, ed. Daniel Whistler and Victoria Browne (Bloomsbury, 2016).

This book is dedicated to my daughter Elinor Varty Stone and to the memory of my parents, Hannah and Patrick Stone.

Introduction

Towards a Philosophy of Being Born

I. Main Themes

All human beings begin life by being born, and all human beings die. In these two ways we are finite: our lives are not endless, but they begin and they come to an end. Historically, however, philosophers have concentrated their attention on only one of these two ways in which we are finite: our mortality. Philosophers have asked whether death is bad; how one might die well; how our existence is shaped by our mortality; whether there is life after death and what it might be like; whether immortality is possible or desirable; and much more besides. In contrast, philosophers have said little about being born and how *that* shapes our existence. There are exceptions to this neglect of birth, notably in some recent work in feminist philosophy. But even here attention to being born has often been overshadowed by a focus on the experience and politics of giving birth and the maternal body.

My aim in this book is to contribute to overcoming the neglect of being born by philosophers. To this end I draw on feminist philosophy. I also take up the existentialist project of inquiring into the structure of meaningful human existence, but unlike other existentialists I explore how human existence is *natal,* that is, is as it is because we are born. I use the terms *natality* and *being born* as synonyms: to be born is to be natal, and our existence is natal in that we exist as beings that are born.[1] Taking natality into account transforms our view of human existence. It sheds new light on our mortality, foregrounds the extent and depth of our dependency on one another, and brings additional phenomena—such as our relatedness to others and the temporal shape of human life—together in a new way.

What does being born consist in? For a human being, to be born is (i) to begin to exist at a certain point in time, by (ii) coming into the world with and as a specific body, and in a given place, set of relationships, and situation in society, culture, and history, while (iii) doing so by way of being conceived and gestated in and then exiting from the womb. Historically, this has

Being born: Birth and Philosophy. Alison Stone, Oxford University Press (2019). © Alison Stone.
DOI: 10.1093/oso/9780198845782.001.0001

almost always been the maternal womb, although this is changing with the rise of transgender pregnancies and it is becoming complicated by new reproductive technologies and practices such as surrogacy.

Regarding (iii) particularly, we can distinguish narrow and broader senses in which the expressions 'birth' and 'being born' are normally used. Most narrowly, to be born is just to exit the womb of the person who gestated me. More broadly, to be born is to be conceived and gestated in that person's womb and finally exit it. A still broader view treats the process of birth as continuing into psychological birth during the infant's earliest years. I favour the middle, broad but not maximally broad, understanding, as I think that talk of 'psychological birth' over-extends the concept. But as one cannot exit the womb without having first been formed and grown within it, it is helpful to grasp this process as a whole, thus under the (broad) concept *birth*.[2]

To examine how we exist as natals is to explore how our being born in aspects (i) to (iii) gives rise to some structuring features of our existence and affects others, so that our existence is the way it is only because we are born. In exploring these features, we at the same time clarify what it is to be born in the first place; for instance, when we explore what it is to be situated, we shed light reciprocally on what it is to begin existence in a particular socio-cultural-historical situation. Thus, our inquiry is at once into what being born consists in and into what follows about human existence from our being born, in mutually informing ways.

In particular, when we take into account that we are natals, beings that enter the world by being born, the following features of our existence are thrown into relief. One is *dependency*. The initially acute helplessness of human babies and infants, and children's prolonged need for care and education, mean that we begin life profoundly dependent on the other people who care for us physically and emotionally. By social convention, this care is often given by children's mothers, usually their biological mothers. We become more independent over time, but never completely or permanently so: dependency on others persists throughout human life to varying degrees.[3] We depend on others, for instance, for much of our means of subsistence, by virtue of the organization of work and the division of labour, and through processes of collective administration that supply us with such goods as clean water, electricity, and sanitation. The depth and extent of our dependency have been underestimated in much mainstream philosophy, which has foregrounded the figure of the autonomous rational agent—although our dependency is recognized within recent work in care ethics (e.g. Kittay 1999), on vulnerability (e.g. Mackenzie, Rogers, and Dodds 2014a), and by MacIntyre (1999). Building on this work, I aim specifically to show how dependency is connected with natality. We are most deeply dependent on others in our infancy and childhood, but, in addition, many of the ways in which we remain dependent on others in later life retain continuities with our childhood dependency. For example, we depend on language, which is communally shared—it organizes our thought and experience, the world of meaning in which we operate, and our communicative relations with others—but we first acquire language in infancy, and the language we speak retains a wealth of connections with this childhood context. Not all the elements of our dependency derive directly from our being born, but some do, while others remain connected with birth in various ways. Reciprocally, part of what it is to be born is to come into existence in a state of deep dependency which has life-long ramifications.

Another feature of our existence as beings that are born is our *relationality*. Informed by psychoanalytic thought about the formative impact of our early relationships with our first care-givers, I will argue that these relationships constitute a person's basic sense of self as well as their concrete personality structure. To have a sense of self is, however implicitly, to ascribe all one's experiences and acts to a single locus and so experience them as being one's own. According to Jessica Benjamin (1988) and Daniel Stern (1985/1998), babies form a first, rudimentary sense of self over their first few months through their interactions and constant 'being-with' their central care-givers; thus, the self is constituted all along as a self-with-this-other. Personality structure is more concrete, including emotional dispositions and character traits, and taking shape over our first years of life as we internalize aspects of our relationships with those who give us care. Thus, our early relationships constitute and do not merely qualify who we are. In turn, the relationality of our early lives shapes the nature of our subsequent relationality: throughout our lives, we are open to later relationships in ways patterned by our previous relationships. Furthermore, our first relationships impact on us so heavily because of our acute dependency as infants and children; thus, relationality, dependency, and natality are intertwined.

To be born is also to be inescapably *situated*. In being born one arrives in a situation—historical, social, ethnic, geographical, etc.—which is unique for each individual, because in each case it is comprised of a unique convergence of factors transmitted through that individual's birth, for instance through their parents' religious allegiance and place of residence.[4] One's *natal situation*, then, comprises the specific set of circumstances and relationships into which one arrives by birth. How far this aspect of our natality affects our entire lives may be debated. Everyone can agree that by birth we all begin life in specific situations, some more advantageous than others. But some may argue that by exercising our innate freedom we can transcend whatever disadvantages we started with—or, conversely, fritter away any advantages. In this book I defend an alternative view of situatedness, informed by Jean-Paul Sartre and Martin Heidegger: that individuals only ever make choices from within their pre-given situations, without which they would not be presented with the particular possibilities they face, under the meanings those possibilities carry. One's situation thus infuses every choice one makes, and each new situation that results from a choice carries the stamp of both one's previous choice *and* one's previous situation; likewise, with one's next situation, and so on. Consequently, situatedness—and with it the initial situating force of one's birth—remain ever-operative in one's life, across the series of choices one makes, which would not be this particular series were it not for the specificities of one's natal situation, and of the situation that arose out of one's response to that situation, and so on.

One important factor with respect to which we are situated, by birth and subsequently, is *social power relations*. These include power relations of gender, race, class and economic position, age, and disability, to mention just a few. These power relations begin straightaway to be transmitted to us, however obliquely, through our relationships with our first care-givers—for example, the language they speak may be the dominant one in our country of residence or a minority language, and may be spoken in the country's standard, 'official' style or in a minority variant or dialect. To be born is to be always embedded in social power, from the outset, so that power relations affect us before we have any possibility of or capacity for criticizing or questioning them. Once we take being born into account, then, we come to see power as a normal and constitutive rather than aberrant or accidental feature of human life. This does not mean that criticism of power relations is impossible, but that such criticism is always dependent on and made possible by power relations, even perhaps the same ones against which it is directed.

Dependency, relationality, situatedness, and embeddedness in social power—all these features of our existence have been scrutinized before, but more-or-less separately from one another, respectively by feminist care ethicists, psychoanalytic and feminist theorists of the self, existentialists such as Sartre and Heidegger, and Foucauldian and feminist theorists of power.[5] My aim here is to show that all these features are connected with our being born, and that these connections affect how these features manifest themselves in our lives.

In addition, to be born is to be *vulnerable* in various ways. We begin life helpless and vulnerable to distress and harm if or when our care-givers do not meet our needs; as relational beings, we are vulnerable to being damaged by failures of care in our very selves and personalities; and because we arrive in existence within natal situations, we are vulnerable to coming into more-or-less adverse, disadvantageous, and even disastrous ones. We remain vulnerable to all sorts of harms throughout our lives; nonetheless, I'll suggest that the kinds of vulnerability to which we are subject as adults retain continuities with our vulnerability in infancy and childhood.

To be natal is also for it to be *radically contingent* who one is in each case. There is a root contingency to my being born as this particular embodied individual, and in turn my living this particular life as it unfolds out of a specific natal situation. One can ask, 'Why is this the life I am leading?' or 'Why am I this individual?' Such questions are genuine, I believe, and do not merely reflect metaphysical or grammatical confusion. A variety of answers come from Western and Eastern religious traditions: for instance, that God created the soul that I essentially am and infused it, at or soon after conception, into a particular body. I submit instead that there is no explanation of why we are each born the particular individuals we are; this is just a fact—an ultimate fact for which no explanatory grounds can be supplied. This is the *facticity* of my existence. 'Facticity', a concept of Sartre's, partly encompasses the reality that my being me and my arriving in the world in my particular situation within it are, for each of us, ultimate facts behind which we can penetrate no further. Insofar as there is no explanation for my being born the individual I am, this is a radically contingent event, and one that is *groundless*. Moreover, because each subsequent situation of mine flows down from the one before it, and because it is radically contingent what my original natal situation was, a thread of radical contingency and groundlessness runs through my entire life. Likewise, my life always has an aspect of givenness (this is facticity's other meaning for Sartre): the givenness of all that I inherit at each moment from my past, and ultimately from my birth. In this way facticity is also bound up with our natality, as are inheritance and reception.

The fact that there is no explanation for who I am, or why I am leading the life I am, can be a source of existential anxiety, because there is an element of impenetrable mystery about my own life. This, I suggest, is one of several forms of *natal anxiety* to which we are disposed: anxiety about discomforting and troubling features that our existence has insofar as it is natal. Another of these features is that we cannot remember the formative years and events of our lives—the phenomenon of 'infantile amnesia'—but, because those years were formative, we are left opaque to ourselves in important ways. Often, we simply do not know why we act and feel as we do. We are not masters in our own houses and this is, in part, because of our natality.

As I've stated, I want to help to correct the historic imbalance within Western attitudes to death and birth. But it is not my intention to argue that being born and not being mortal is central to our existence—my aim is to re-balance, not reverse, our attitudes. On this I disagree with some feminist thinkers of natality—such as Adriana Cavarero and Grace Jantzen, considered below—who favour a cultural re-orientation towards birth rather than death. Instead I take it that birth and death structure human existence, and in ways affected by one another. Although I focus on birth because it has been the more neglected pole, I also discuss mortality, suggesting that it looks different once we take natality into account. Thus, I address the interdependence of death and birth from the side of birth. Admittedly, some might dispute my claim that birth has been the more neglected of our two 'ends', given the trend in Western modernity since the nineteenth century to deny or repress our awareness of death (a trend documented in particular by Ariès 1974). Perhaps birth was once neglected compared to death, but now death has succumbed to repression too. Even if so, we need not react to this undesirable trend by re-emphasizing death and not birth. Instead, by attending to natality, we can pave the way for an honest, as well as more balanced, approach to mortality.

More specifically, taking natality into account shows, I believe, that our condition is one of *relational mortality*. Because our selves and personalities are relational through and through—because we are born—our deaths, too, are relational and shade into one another continuously. A more individualistic view is that my own death and the deaths of others are radically different; one version of that view is found in Heidegger's *Being and Time*. I argue instead that each individual's death is bound up with the deaths of the others with whom that individual has had close relationships—so that if one of these others dies, then part of me dies, while when I die, part of those others dies too: death is always shared. Consequently, my death and those of others are to be feared because these deaths spell the end of our relationships, the point when we will be separated forever. In disagreement with Heidegger, then, I argue that facing the prospect of our deaths does not 'individualize' me but 'relationalizes' me, bringing into relief the fundamental importance for me of the relationships that I care about.[6]

The *temporal direction* of our lives is involved in many of these preceding aspects of our natality. My birth and death both shape the temporal character of my lived experience. As my starting-point, my birth is the organizing pole towards which my past runs back, while my death is the organizing pole towards which my future runs forwards. For instance, the succession of situations in which I find myself over the course of my life runs back to my initial natal situation, and my earliest relationships provide the template for my history of subsequent ones. But, although my life-history runs back to my birth, I cannot remember being born or my early childhood, so that my birth structures the temporal shape of my life as an absence or vanishing point. Nonetheless, my birth and my past are inescapably linked, so that in attending to birth we see how the past is just as fundamental as the other temporal dimensions—contrary to Sartre, who accords ultimate priority to the present, and Heidegger, who assigns ultimate priority to the future.

My exploration of these aspects of natality throws up ethical issues. I am critical of the central value placed on autonomy and independence in much Western moral and political thought. I also believe that features of our natal condition generate a case for equality: for natal equality as an ideal goal, admittedly a very broad and general one. At present we are born into natal situations that are not only very different but also very unequal, especially on a worldwide scale. Whereas death is, to an extent, an equalizer—for it is a fate we will all suffer—birth is an unequalizer—such benefits as we enjoy by birth are very unevenly distributed.[7] But, given our radical contingency, there is no reason why anyone arrives by birth in the particular situation they do. For while there is in each case a chain of causal factors that explains why a given embodied individual is born in a certain situation, there is no reason why I am this individual, why you are that individual, and so on. Nothing therefore justifies its being me who enjoys benefits by birth compared to others, if I do, or conversely who shares in very few of these benefits, if not. This is where a case for natal equality arises.

As I hope this preliminary summary makes apparent, I shall not attempt to derive every aspect of our existence from birth in a linear way. Rather, the features of our existence that I consider—such as dependency, relationality, facticity, situatedness, contingency—are connected with birth along manifold paths. By taking birth into account, we discern a web of connections amongst these features where the ramifications of birth run through and imbue the whole web in complex ways. In this interwoven and circuitous, rather than linear way, we exist as beings that are born.

To complicate this picture a little further, let's recall that for a human being to be born is (i) to begin to exist at a certain point in time, by (ii) coming into the world with and as a specific body, and in a given place, set of relationships, and socio-cultural location, while (iii) doing so by way of being conceived and gestated in, and then leaving, someone's womb. To exist as someone who is born, or who is natal, is for a wide range of structuring features of how we exist to be shaped or affected, however circuitously, by our being born in senses (i) to (iii). But some features are affected more by aspect (i); others by aspect (ii) or (iii) or their combinations. For example, our first relationships impact upon us so formatively, partly just because they come first, which they do because we have beginnings (from i); partly because we come into these relationships straightaway (from ii) before we have formed any ability to criticize or stand back from them; and partly because of our acute dependency and helplessness as babies and infants, which derives from (iii) in the particular shape that being conceived, gestated, and expelled from the womb takes in the human species. Namely, because of the obstetric dilemma—the combination of big brains and narrow pelvises due to bipedalism—human babies need to be born very immature to pass through their mothers' birth canals. Hence human babies begin life as acutely dependent as they are.[8] The fact that being born is internally multifaceted, then, complicates how it affects other features of our existence.

I can now clarify two further aspects of this inquiry. First, I am concerned with birth as it figures in human existence. Yet features (i) to (iii) of birth might seem to apply equally well to other viviparous species, albeit that we might wonder whether non-human animals are ever born into 'socio-cultural-historical' locations (other than humanly produced ones). However, as I've just indicated, (iii) is realized in a particular way in the human species, such that we are born extremely immature, with very unformed bodies and brains. In consequence, we are specially open and receptive to our initial, and in turn subsequent, surroundings: we are specially cultural beings who, being at first peculiarly unformed, become correspondingly deeply formed by what others around us do, doings that we transmit to others in turn. Humanity therefore comes to revise and rework its shared ways of life over time in an ongoing process of collective self-alteration and self-making. The resulting phenomena—culture, open-endedness, and with them collectively shared and shifting horizons of meaning—are thus characteristically human phenomena that pervade how we exist. Therefore, numerous elements of our natality—such as situatedness, relationality, beginning, and coming into the world—obtain in our lives in particular ways that are bound up with their meaningfulness. So, whereas features (i) to (iii) apply beyond humanity when viewed in very abstract terms, in their concrete, lived character they are particular to human beings.[9]

Second, concerning aspect (iii) of being born, I spoke of 'being conceived and gestated in, and then leaving, someone's womb'. But 'someone's' sounds vague and evasive. To date, almost all people have been born to women, their mothers. So perhaps being born should be defined with reference to gestation in and departure from the maternal womb. However, that would make invisible the pregnancies of trans fathers and the complications introduced into maternity by adoption, surrogacy, and new reproductive technologies (see Chapter 2, Section I, of this volume). One solution might be to talk of gestating bodies (with Fanny Söderbäck 2018) and so the gestator's womb. But sometimes the resulting locutions would be clumsy, for instance if being born were said to involve 'gestation in the gestator's womb'. Moreover, historically and culturally, women, mothers, and gestation have been profoundly linked and these links should be remembered. Given that there is no perfect solution, then, I speak of sometimes 'the gestator's womb' and sometimes 'the maternal womb'. Sometimes, too, I use neutral talk of 'the womb'. Such talk is also imperfect (and so I don't use it all the time). It abstracts the womb from both the whole body of which it is part and from the living person who has and is that body, and this seems implicitly to reduce those persons to support-functions for the babies that they gestate and bear. That kind of reduction of mothers as embodied meaning-making subjects to mere supports for babies has been widespread in Western culture (a reduction that I criticized in Stone 2011): ultrasound images of foetuses *in utero* are a graphic instance, in which the maternal body containing the foetus is reduced to empty space (see Rothman 1986: 114). Even so, neutral talk of 'the womb' sometimes works best, firstly because it sidesteps the choice between 'mothers' and 'gestators', and secondly because it helps us to focus on being born from the perspective of the one undergoing it, not that of the one gestating and giving birth.

II. Intellectual Sources and Location of this Inquiry

In developing the themes of this book, I will be building on work in several intellectual traditions, amongst them feminist philosophy, especially those authors within it who have sought to 'give birth to a new philosophy of birth', in Mary O'Brien's words (1981: 13). They include Christine Battersby (1998), Cavarero ([1990] 1995) and ([1997] 2000), Lisa Guenther (2006), Luce Irigaray [1987] (1993b), Alison Martin (2002), Anne O'Byrne (2010), Robin May Schott (2010a, 2010b), Christina Schües (1997, 2008), Söderbäck (2014a, 2018 and forthcoming), and many others.[10] Irigaray and Cavarero deserve mention first, because their ideas on birth and being born motivated and inspired my inquiry here.

Irigaray and Cavarero address birth within their broad and ambitious projects in regard to sexual difference. They believe that the Western symbolic order has precluded any possibility of a positive female or feminine identity. Irigaray holds that this order is matricidal—not literally but symbolically, in that it insists, usually tacitly but at times overtly, that individuals must break psychically from their mothers and from the maternal, bodily realm of infancy to enter into language and communal life. Consequently, for Irigaray, we generally suffer from unresolved psychical difficulties in relation to our mothers. We have broken away from them without mourning or emotionally processing this break, and we tend to push these unresolved issues away defensively, resulting in a culture that shores up its boundaries against the maternal realm by glorifying death, violence, and war. One of Irigaray's goals, in contrast, is to try to remember our maternal and uterine origins and explore how our unresolved preoccupations with them reverberate in philosophical texts. She wants to remind us that we have been born, and to prompt us to grapple with the emotional ramifications of this, rather than pushing these matters aside as we are accustomed to do, including when we concentrate philosophically on death and not birth.

Developing Irigaray's ideas further, Cavarero argues that the Western symbolic order has foregrounded death rather than birth—as in its slogan 'all men are mortal'—and that this reflects a fear and rejection of maternal power. Regarding birth's positive significance, Cavarero maintains that we each have narratable life-stories that begin when we are born and constitute who we are as unique individuals. In setting out these ideas, Cavarero draws heavily on Hannah Arendt's work (esp. 1958). Indeed, as it is Arendt who introduced the concept *natality* into philosophy, it may have seemed curious that I have not mentioned her already. For Arendt, however, being natal means at times being born, at times being unique and new by virtue of being born, and at other times being able to initiate new acts and words in the political realm. As a result, natality has only an ambiguous connection with physical birth for Arendt, as I'll argue in Chapter 1 of this volume (and as other feminist philosophers have already argued; for example, Schott 2010b: 52–7, Söderbäck 2018). My account of natality is therefore different from Arendt's, notwithstanding her importance in naming the phenomenon, identifying some of the ways that being born shapes our condition, and influencing Cavarero and other feminists concerned with birth.

Although Irigaray's and Cavarero's work raises many questions, it forms my starting-point. And it has already occasioned other feminist engagements with birth. For one, the philosopher of religion Grace Jantzen pursues Irigaray's and Cavarero's critique of the Western symbolic order as focused on death and violence. Jantzen recommends a socio-cultural turn towards natality as a way of recovering possibilities for leading peaceful and flourishing lives (1998, 2005).

Natality also figures into Christine Battersby's project, which is to rethink personal and individual identity, taking female embodiment to be normal rather than anomalous. Asking what follows about the self if giving birth is a constant, normal possibility (1998: 2, 9–11), Battersby answers, first, that we are natals: beings who are born, who do not appear in the world out of nowhere but from the bodies of our mothers. Second, because we are natals, we are dependent beings: we begin life dependent on our first care-givers. This dependency is asymmetrical, so that we are from the outset embedded in power relations and inequalities. Power relations are thus normal and constitutive of human existence, not a deviation from a supposed normal condition of equality. Third, because we begin life radically dependent upon and entwined with our carers, we only gradually become fully distinct individuals. There is no sharp self/other division. Rather, each self is in a continuous process of emergence from the 'intersecting force-fields' of its power-laden relations with others. Fourth, the self is embodied, and specifically emerges from this field of 'fleshly continuity' with others. Fifth, the self is 'monstrous', in a productive rather than horrific sense: crossing over and blurring the boundaries between autonomy and dependence, self-containment and relatedness, agency and passivity, mind and body.

To mention a few of the others who have written about birth, Bracha Ettinger (2006) suggests that pregnancy exemplifies how the self is always-already in relation with others, relations that are constitutive of and not merely accidental to who we are—as the embryo is, from the very first, in relation with the maternal body. Pregnancy has also been described—for instance by Tanja Staehler (2016a, 2016b), within the emerging field of phenomenology of pregnancy[11]—in terms of the mother's tactile encounter with an other who is irreducibly different from her, unknown to her, and exceeds her horizon of thought and all her imaginings and anticipations regarding them. For Lisa Baraitser (2008), something similar extends into post-natal maternity: a mother is oriented towards a child whose temporality is oriented away from her, towards the child's own future, which lies beyond the mother's horizons.[12]

Whereas for Irigaray, Cavarero, Battersby and others reflection on being born remains partly enfolded within reflection on birth-giving, Christina Schües distinguishes as I do between giving birth (*Gebären*) and being born (*Geborensein*), and concentrates on the latter (2016). Schües starts with the fact that nobody can remember being born. She argues that this is because birth (taken narrowly as the exit from the womb) is the condition of possibility for experience in the first place. To be born is to make an absolute transition, and come into the world and relations with others. Schües takes the 'world' to be not primarily a bare physical realm but rather the context of interrelated involvements, meanings, and values which is shared with other people, every element of which is interwoven—such that the world is a whole, and one in which we always-already find ourselves, prior to any possibilities for individual meaning-making. She is informed by Heidegger, for whom the world is constituted as a world of 'the context of references [*Verweisungszusammenhang*]...as significance [*Bedeutsamkeit*]' ([1927] 1962: 121/88).[13] It is only by abstraction from the lived, meaningful, shared world that we come to conceive of the bare physical world that subtends it, whereas in everyday life the physical is always-already imbued with meaning. Schües's argument, then, is that intentional experience, which is directed towards items in the world *as* specific items picked out against the background of a total set of meaningful relations, first becomes possible through being born as the transition by which we enter the world. Being the necessary precondition *of* experience, birth cannot itself figure directly *in* experience (Schües 2016: 214). This, Schües concludes, is why being gestated and born necessarily cannot be remembered afterwards. Here birth, for Schües, forms a conduit into a number of ways in which our experience as individuals is pervaded, shaped, and framed by conditions that we nonetheless cannot take up or incorporate explicitly within that experience. Central amongst these, for Schües, are our 'generative' relations with others, which are both intergenerational and with our rough contemporaries: we always come from somewhere and from someone, and are delivered by birth into a given time along with our co-generationists. Thus, no subject is self-constituting; rather, we are constituted by a wealth of prior generative relations.

I find Schües's conception of generative relations important and insightful, but I am not convinced that (narrow) birth is the precondition of experience. During the later stages of gestation, foetuses in the womb already have sentient experience: for example, they respond to music and voices, and they can detect changes in levels of light and noise in the outer world. Indeed, Schües herself accepts that late-stage foetuses have experience, within the womb and whilst leaving it; thus, she acknowledges, 'The one born was necessarily present at their birth' (2016: 12). But she preserves her view that exiting the womb is the precondition of experience by characterizing pre-natal existence as being-towards-being-in-the-world, being-towards-intentionality, and being-towards-being-there, whereas post-natal existence is intentional and in the world, properly so (1997: 246). Now, certainly, after leaving the womb I am more fully in the shared world in my own right, rather than only through the mediation of the person gestating me. Yet given the extent of our neonatal and infantile dependency, one's post-birth participation in the world is still very heavily mediated through one's care-givers. Conversely, something approximating intentional experience already begins during late gestation, for instance in that the mother's voice stands out as a particular and especially salient one. That is evidenced in that three-day-old newborns prefer their mother's to other voices; these 'perceptual preferences... are profoundly affected by auditory experience before birth' (DeCasper and Fifer 1980: 1176). So, dividing pre- and post-natal existence into being-towards-being-there versus (fully) being-there makes too sharp a cut. What remains true is that being born in the broad sense that includes conception and gestation is the precondition of experience; obvious as this may sound, it is still worth remarking.

Moving away from feminist work on birth as such, I also draw on care ethics, in which authors such as Eva Kittay (1999) have highlighted our dependency on one another, in and beyond infancy, and how dependency precedes and outstrips interdependency. Feminist theorists have also had much to say about power, its ever-presence in our lives, and how it constitutes our mental and bodily powers, even our powers to criticize the same workings of power which have formed us (see, especially, Butler 1997). And in philosophy of mind, feminists have argued in various ways that the self is constitutively, not accidentally, relational (Brison 2017); they have insisted that we all begin life as children and that this bears on the nature of the self (Baier 1985); and they have largely eschewed the abstraction of much philosophy of mind, instead attending to how our early and later relationships and experiences, and their social settings, shape our selves in the concrete.

Another intellectual tradition by which I am guided is psychoanalysis, because of its attention to the key formative impact of our earliest relationships and experiences in infancy and early childhood. Psychoanalysis is commonly seen as foregrounding the role of unconscious forces and motivations throughout our lives. But it equally foregrounds the fact that we all begin life as children and we never entirely leave our childhood behind—it continues to shape us, even when we cannot remember it. Freud originally focused, of course, on the Oedipus complex: our relations with 'the father', a figure as much imaginary and symbolic as real and empirical, and virtually equivalent to basic laws that regulate social life. Subsequent psychoanalysts, especially in the object–relations tradition, have re-emphasized the importance of the mother and of our actual, empirical care-givers. But on either view, our early relationships with parental figures are central for our lives, and they indelibly stamp our characters as individuals. Thus, much of what psychoanalysis examines—how our earliest relationships get inside and shape us—in fact pertains to our condition as beings that are born and so whose lives begin—as they continue—under the formative aegis of our first care-givers.

The third principal tradition to guide this book is existentialism, especially that of Sartre, Camus, and Beauvoir, but also Heidegger in *Being and Time*—whom we can include under the existentialist heading so long as we construe it broadly enough.[14] I take up the existentialist inquiry into what makes for a meaningful life and into the structure of human existence as a whole and, to some extent, I follow such existentialists as Sartre, Beauvoir, and Camus in looking to fictional characters and their situations to illuminate, concretely, our ways of navigating our lives.[15] However, most authors in the existentialist tradition see human existence as being fundamentally structured by mortality rather than natality. This is true, in different ways, of Beauvoir, Camus, and Heidegger. For instance, Beauvoir argues that, while death may be bad, being mortal is the condition of a meaningful life, so that immortality would be worse. To this extent, existentialism adheres to the Western philosophical vision in which 'all men are mortal' rather than 'all human beings are born'. Death does not figure so prominently for Sartre, yet he believes in radical individual freedom construed as autonomy: one's freedom to choose one's own values and commitments, choices that over time shape the self—who I am is who I make myself through my freely undertaken commitments. This view underestimates such aspects of natality as the formative force of our early relationships and our dependency on others (even though Sartre can also help us think about those phenomena). While I am informed by existentialism, then, I try to re-orientate it to take account not only of death and endings but also of birth and beginnings, and thereby also to accommodate dependency, relationality, and the weight of the past alongside freedom, individuality, and the lightness of the future.

The sources that inform my analysis of being born—recent feminist thought, psychoanalysis, and existentialism—may now seem so numerous as to tell against my claim that the Western tradition has overlooked or marginalized birth, and to suggest that the tradition is more variegated than I've claimed.[16] Certainly, the Western tradition is variegated.[17] Nevertheless, it is possible to identify dominant currents in Western thought, and a focus on mortality rather than being born is amongst these. Even those authors whose work sheds light on being born, such as Sartre and Freud, generally do not put birth at the centre of their frameworks or conceive themselves to be investigating birth—being born instead comes into their frameworks sideways-on. And in, say, Heidegger's case, he illuminates being born despite explicitly arguing that mortality has priority over how one 'exists as born' (*existiert gebürtig*; 1962: 425/373). Whereas death has had an explicit and central presence in Western thought and culture and has been the direct subject of a flood of writings philosophical, literary, and religious, then, birth's presence has been more indirect and oblique. Not altogether absent, it has nonetheless been in the background, behind death in the foreground. That said, and as I've indicated, there has been a growing trend to bring birth into the open, with feminist philosophers at its forefront; it is this trend that I wish to take further.

One might ask why feminists have spearheaded the attention to birth. Part of the answer is that feminists try to articulate women's experience, and women tend to have a relatively vivid awareness that all human beings are born; that other people bear them; that infants are dependent and need care; and that our earliest relationships shape us very deeply. This is not primarily because of women's biological capacity for child-bearing but because of their social position as the presumed, and often actual, main carers for children. However, in feminist reflection—as we saw from my brief account of some of its currents above—there has been a tendency to run exploration of being born together with exploration of birth-*giving* along with the experience and politics of reproduction, pregnancy, maternity, and child-care.[18] One reason is that, for feminists, to be born is not to pop into the world out of nowhere, or pull oneself into life by one's own bootstraps, but to be gestated and born *from* the mother's body. Here, though, I shall consider maternal and gestating bodies solely as they bear on being born rather than in respect of birth-giving.

Another question arises here. If our existence is structured by our being born, then how can we possibly have neglected our birth? If its role in our existence is so central then surely it must force itself on our notice, we might think. Yet there are cases when, as Hegel remarks, 'the familiar as such, because it is familiar, is not known' ([1807] 1977: 18; my translation). Sometimes it is just when something has a pervasive role in our experience that we take it for granted to the point of overlooking it. This is the case with our being born. Moreover, arguably we also have emotional reasons for shying away from birth: Irigaray and Cavarero argue that we are motivated to avoid birth because of unresolved difficulties with our mothers and fears of maternal bodily powers. The result, for Irigaray, is that we live in denial of our natal condition even though it nonetheless shapes our lives.

Let me indicate some neighbouring fields of inquiry from which this book stands aside. I won't directly engage in feminist debates about the experiences or politics of pregnancy, motherhood, and parenting. Nor do I enter into debates about parental rights and obligations or the pros and cons of assisted reproductive technologies.[19] I bracket all this because it pertains more to giving birth than being born—to what birth-givers are obliged to do or refrain from doing and what further (especially parental) obligations their birth-giving creates for them. I will, however, criticize David Benatar's anti-natalism (2006), the view that it would always be better for one not to have been born. This is a new manifestation of a longer-running stream of anti-natal pessimism distilled in the 'wisdom of Silenus' which Nietzsche reports in *The Birth of Tragedy*. King Midas hunts down Dionysus's companion Silenus to ask him what is best for human beings, and Silenus replies:

Wretched ephemeral race . . . why do you force me to tell you the very thing which it would be most profitable for you *not* to hear? The very best thing is utterly beyond your reach, not to have been born, not to *be*, to be *nothing*. However, the second best thing for you is: to die soon.

(Nietzsche [1872] 1999: 23)

We could reverse this slogan: 'the best thing is to be born, the next best is to die as late as possible'—although I'll argue that this would overstate matters. On the other hand, taking another saying, 'as soon as a man comes to life, he is at once old enough to die',[20] we can reverse it to yield a slogan that I do endorse: 'right up until a person dies, she is young enough to have been born'. That is, right through one's life, one's birth and its ramifications are still with one, shaping where one is each step of the way—and this remains true for however long one's life continues.

It might seem surprising that I do not discuss debates about genetic enhancement or *ex utero* gestation.[21] For some critics, these both threaten to transform for the worse the very character of human existence. Although such feminists as Shulamith Firestone (1970) and Marge Piercy (1975) championed ectogenesis as liberating women from their gestational powers and their exploitation, others fear that ectogenesis would take away the relational and affective context in which gestation occurs within the womb of a mother or some other person. (As I noted above, for human beings, intra-uterine gestation—under aspect iii of being born—is already a way of coming into a specific set of relationships—under aspect ii.)

My reasons for not discussing such issues are several. First, even should ectogenesis became widespread (which is doubtful, given its resource-intensiveness and the value many parents place on intra-uterine gestation), parents would surely still maintain relationships with their externally developing foetuses—by watching them, talking to them, playing them music, and so on. At least in ways such as this, foetuses would continue to be held in and inducted into relational, emotional, and meaning-laden settings. Aldous Huxley in *Brave New World* ([1932] 1994) imagined a wholly ectogenetic society in which foetuses are grown in bottles and decanted rather than born, under a mass-production system that removes foetuses, infants, and children from any intimate relationships. The family has been eliminated; the words *mother* and *father* have become obscenities. *That* system might well transform our condition radically—for Huxley, it yielded people 'blissfully ignorant of passion ... plagued with no mothers or fathers; they've not got wives, or children, or lovers to feel strongly about' (194). But ectogenesis in reality would be unlikely to take that form and have that effect, for human beings are deeply attached to gestation's relational significance and would surely preserve and adapt it to *ex utero* circumstances.[22]

Second, as regards genetic enhancement, if selection for certain traits in embryos became widespread or even if traits began to be modified directly, it is not obvious that this would strip us of our natality as, notably, Habermas argues (2003). He understands natality on broadly Arendtian lines, as our being born as in each case someone radically new relative to everything that has happened before, such that we have a capacity for initiating new actions. Habermas grasps these two kinds of newness together under the idea that as natals we have 'open futures'. But, he claims, genetic enhancement eliminates this by encoding specific parental expectations into the child's biological body and so preventing the child from being able to see herself as unique by birth such that she can act autonomously vis-à-vis society. Rather, she sees herself as inherently a product of society, as mediated through parental expectations and the technologies that have shaped her.[23] I'll argue, however, that part of the newness of each child arises from the irreducibility of their first-person existence to its causes and conditions viewed third-personally. It is not clear that that irreducibility can be affected by any technological developments and so, contra Habermas, I am more hopeful that the newness of the natal is here to stay.[24]

Third and most importantly, to assess how far genetic enhancement, ectogenesis, or any other actual or potential reproductive technologies might transform our existence, we first need some understanding of how being born has shaped and continues to shape that existence so far. I'll refrain from assessing the possible impact of reproductive techniques on our existence as natals, then, because we cannot assess that impact until we already have some understanding of that existence and how it is natal—an understanding which it is my aim to develop.

Lastly, I bracket religious perspectives on birth and death. This is not to say that I think the only viable approach to birth, or death, must be secular or atheistic. At the same time, I want neither to offer a theology of birth nor to attempt a rational evaluation of different religious perspectives on birth, on the doubtful presupposition that reason can arbitrate neutrally here. To do justice to questions of birth and religion they would need to be tackled in their own right, and, worthwhile as such an undertaking would be, it is not my project here.[25]

III. Chapter Synopsis

In Chapter 1 of this volume, I explain how Irigaray and Cavarero bring birth into philosophy, including through Cavarero's engagement with Arendt on natality. I also explain how Jantzen takes forward these views on birth and being born. In Chapter 2 of this volume, I consider some objections that might be raised to the whole family of approaches to being born which emerge from Chapter 1. While considering these objections, I introduce two aspects of our existence which are connected with our being born: vulnerability and inheritance. Through Chapters 1 and 2 together, then, I aim to motivate this project and establish its scope, to bring on stage some of its key intellectual inspirations, and to start to discuss some aspects of what it is to be born.

In Chapter 3 of this volume, I explore dependency, the relationality of the self, and situatedness, including situatedness within social power relations. In Chapter 4 of this volume, I turn to the contingency of one's being born the particular individual that one is. As I outlined earlier, although we can each ask, 'Why am I me?', I could not possibly have been leading any other life, so that the question is unanswerable, and the contingency of my being born in my unique situation is fundamental. As a result, a dimension of contingency flows down through our entire lives. To understand this radical contingency along with two related aspects of natality, groundlessness and facticity (roughly, givenness), I use Sartre's *Nausea* and *Being and Nothingness*. His work also shows how situatedness is transmitted down at each step in our lives from our initial (natal) situations. However, I reject his strong conception of individual freedom, and forward in its place an idea of *sedimented sense-making*: in how we respond to our circumstances, we are always taking forward inherited horizons of meaning and value.

The radical contingency of my being born the individual I am, in whatever unique situation I find myself, can provoke deep anxiety, because it exposes a dimension of mystery at the heart of my existence. This is one of a number of forms of birth anxiety which I explore in Chapter 5 of this volume. Psychoanalytic theorists—notably Otto Rank, author of the 1924 work *The Trauma of Birth*, and Freud himself—connected birth with anxiety on the grounds that being born is traumatic. I'll examine these psychoanalytic views somewhat critically, but I'll take from them an insight into the lasting power in our lives of a kind of separation anxiety. Because the people whom we love and on whom we depend are different individuals from us, with minds of their own, they can always hurt or leave us or thwart our wishes. We register this mixture of dependency and vulnerability, relatedness and difference, in anxiety—in adulthood as in childhood. Overall in this chapter I argue that whereas existentialists—Heidegger particularly—link anxiety with mortality, natal anxiety is real as well.

In Chapter 6 of this volume, I set out my account of relational mortality, against the background of two alternative approaches: Cavarero's impersonal view of death as material re-integration into the cosmos, and Heidegger's prioritization of my own death over those of others. In contrast, drawing on Beauvoir's fiction and memoirs, I explore two ways in which our mortality is relational: our deaths shade into one another, and much of what death will deprive us of matters to us specifically because we share it with others. In this last respect, I focus on how we are attached to the world insofar as it is intrinsically shared and is the medium of our lives together with others.

In Chapter 7 of this volume, I draw out how temporality has figured into the preceding discussions. Temporally, lived human existence is future-oriented towards death and past-oriented towards birth. When we take our natal orientation to the past into account, we see that when we project forward and create meaning we are always extending inherited horizons that we have received in and from the past. I also consider whether birth can rightly be said to be a gift given us by our mothers. Although I am doubtful, thinking of birth as a gift illuminates some connections between our natality and the relational setting of our ethical lives and obligations. Finally, I sum up my main theses about how human existence is shaped by the fact that we are born.

Notes

1. Others use the term *natality* differently. For instance, Grace Jantzen distinguishes the mere fact of being born from natality understood as our entire condition and way of existing insofar as it is shaped by our being born (e.g. 2004: 111). I take it instead that since our natal condition flows out of our being born, and since being born is not a mere physical fact but a way of coming into existence that is consequential for the entire existence that comes out of it, we can equate 'being born' and 'natality'. Another distinction is made by Christina Schües between being born (*Geborensein*) and natality (*Gebürtlichkeit*) understood, following Arendt, as the human capacity to initiate new actions spontaneously and freely (*initium*) (Schües 2016: 14, 401). Arendt calls this capacity 'natality' because it realizes the newness that is inherent in each of us insofar as we are born. But sometimes Arendt instead equates 'natality' simply with 'the fact that human beings appear in the world by . . . birth' (Arendt 1978: 217), and sometimes again she uses 'natality' to pick out our newness by birth or our condition of appearing to plural others in a shared world by birth. That is, for Arendt, 'natality' variably encompasses (i) being born, (ii) arriving new by birth, (iii) our human condition as beings who are born, and (iv) being able, because of (ii) and/or (iii), to initiate actions. I follow Arendt on (i), (ii), and (iii), but not (iv), as will emerge later. I therefore equate *natality* directly with meanings (i) to (iii) without giving it the connotations of political action that Arendt does.

2. Feminist philosophers use 'birth' in all three levels of breadth at different times. For example, *narrowly*: Cavarero says that to be born is to come into the public world and become exposed and appear visibly to others. *Broadly*: Irigaray, whilst exploring the lasting psychological impact on us of being born, includes here the

subtle and hidden impact of our tactile relations with the maternal body in the darkness of the womb. *Maximally broadly*: Irigaray treats post-natal psychological self-differentiation from the mother as the mental continuation of the bodily exit from her womb. On all these, see Chapter 1 of this volume. For myself, although I understand 'birth' broadly I will sometimes use the term in its narrower sense, highlighting this at the time unless it is self-evident.

3. And, of course, some people with disabilities always remain heavily dependent on their care-givers, as Eva Kittay points out (1999). This dependency is not an isolated case, but is indicative of the broader dependency of all human beings.

4. Feminists and critical race philosophers have done much to explore situatedness, and I will draw on their work, including Alcoff (2006). I particularly build on Alcoff's idea of horizons of meaning, for which she in turn is indebted to Gadamer, although I use Alcoff's rendition.

5. See, amongst others: on the self, Barvosa (2008), Baier (1985), Brison (2003) and Meyers (1997); and on power, Allen (1999) and Butler (1997).

6. Throughout, I discuss death in the sense of non-existence, or being dead, rather than of dying. However, one might object that, when we reconsider death in light of being born, the processes by which we die come into view: we die by way of ageing and becoming ill, injured, and incapacitated, and these bring in their wake levels of dependency and vulnerability that parallel those of infancy and childhood. So perhaps a natal view of death should be one in which dying looms larger than non-existence. I focus on non-existence, though, to show how death *as* it has predominantly been considered philosophically—that is, as non-existence—looks different when viewed in light of birth; and how our final 'end'—death as non-existence—looks different when considered, not as exhausting our finitude, but as just one of its two poles, the other being birth.

7. But of course 'death inequalities' exist, within nation states and globally. The worse-off are in general more likely to die early, whether from illness, accidents, or violence, and they are at greater risk for certain causes of death: for example, lower-income Westerners have higher risks of dying from heart disease.

8. The young of many species are, like young humans, 'altricial'—that is, helpless at birth—but they don't remain dependent for as long as young humans, even as a proportion of their overall life-span. This difference arises because young humans have more mental and practical skills to develop, as I explain in Chapter 3 of this volume.

9. I agree to an extent, then, with existentialists such as Kierkegaard, Sartre and Heidegger for whom existing is unique to humans. Existing as meaningful is characteristically human, but culture, meaning, etc., aren't necessarily entirely exclusive to human beings. There may be a higher-altitude, more abstract level of meaningful existence in which other animals share, although identifying it would be well beyond this book's scope. In this connection I should in fairness note Heidegger's remark that Dasein 'names something that is by no means

coterminous with human being' ([1961] 1991: vol. 1, 26). That is: *Dasein* does not mean what *human being* means. The last category is of a universal kind, humankind, to which particular instances (human beings) belong on the basis of their essential properties (reason, speech, sociality). That is, human being is a traditional metaphysical category, as Dasein is not (allegedly). Nonetheless, the scope of the notions Dasein and human being is the same, because non-human animals are, unlike Dasein, 'poor in world' (Heidegger [1929–30] 1996: Chs. 3–5). Thus Dasein is after all a rough proxy for 'human beings'.

10. The above are some of those whose approaches to birth and birth-giving accord most closely with mine. Indicatively, some others include LaChance Adams and Lundquist (2010), Cohen Shabot (2017), Heinämaa (2010), Held (1989), Johnson (2014), Kristeva ([1974] 1984, [1983] 1986a), Mullin (2005), Oksala (2004), Roberts (1993), and Warren (1989). Other relevant authors will be mentioned along the way.

11. See Iris Marion Young's now-classic paper 'Pregnant Embodiment' ([1984] 2005b) and since then, inter alia, Bornemark and Smith (2016), Levesque-Lopman (1983), Lundquist (2008), Lymer (2016), and Svenaeus (2017). There has also been growing and much-needed attention to miscarriage: see Browne (2016), Cahill, Norlock and Stoyles (2015), and Scuro (2017).

12. At times one might worry that feminist explorations of pregnancy and birth are idealized, for example when pregnancy is described in terms of an original hospitality (see, e.g. Gray 2012) or when the placenta is described as a mediating 'third term' that enables foetus and mother to co-exist peaceably (Irigaray 1993c: Ch. 4). At best, though, feminist accounts confront and make sense of the difficulties of mothering (as does, e.g. Baraitser 2008) and the troubling side of pregnancy and giving birth (as does Staehler 2016b). Also, for contrasting views that highlight the conflicts of interest between foetuses/infants/children and mothers/parents, see Trivers (1974), Haig (1993), and (with a feminist inflection) Hrdy (2000).

13. Throughout, when quoting texts originally published in languages other than English, I use standard English translations whenever available, occasionally amended without special notice.

14. And after all Camus denied that he was an existentialist, while Kierkegaard—a central influence on Sartre, Heidegger, and Beauvoir alike—wrote before the label was invented. For a defence of Heidegger's inclusion under the label *existentialism*, see Staehler (2012).

15. Having become unpopular during post-structuralism's heyday, existentialism has since enjoyed rediscovery: see, for example, Farrell Fox (2002) and Webber (2010b). Amongst the manifold reasons for this are the return of philosophers to questions of the 'meaning of life' (e.g. Landau 2017); a growing recognition of Beauvoir as a major philosopher; and the helpfulness of existentialism for understanding racial oppression (e.g. Gordon 1995).

16. And, after all, Schües (2016: pt. 1) traces the history of ideas of birth in Plato and Nietzsche, the Enlightenment, Heidegger, and Husserl; O'Byrne (2010) examines the phenomenological contributions on birth of Heidegger, Dilthey, Arendt and Nancy; and Heinämäa (e.g. 2010) explores those of Levinas, Arendt, and Beauvoir.

17. Not only has this 'tradition' never been 'one', it has never been only 'two'—that is, Graeco-Christian—either: the ancient Greeks already took much from the Egyptians and Phoenicians (Bernal 1987), not to mention such 'other' strands as Judaism and Arabic philosophy. On these issues, see inter alia Goswami (2014) and Stone (2017).

18. Feminist writing on these matters is extensive; classic contributions include Firestone (1970), O'Brien (1981), Rich (1976), Roberts (1997). A focus of criticism has been the medicalization of pregnancy and childbirth (see Stone 2007: Ch. 7). Discussions of mothering specifically include Craddock (2005), LaChance Adams (2012, 2014), O'Reilly (e.g. 2004), Ruddick (1989), Stephens (2012), and Stone (2011).

19. See, inter alia, on procreative and parental rights and obligations, Benatar and Wasserman (2015), Brighouse and Swift (2014), Conly (2016), Gheaus (2012), Hannan, Brennan, and Vernon (2016), Overall (2012), and Weinberg (2016). Philosophical arguments for and against genetic enhancement include those by, again amongst many others, Agar (2004), Buchanan (2011), Sandel (2007), Savulescu (2006), and Wilkinson (2016). Feminist writing on new reproductive technologies is also vast, including Callahan and Roberts (1996), Lublin (1998), McLeod (2002), Nsiah-Jefferson and Hall (1989), Parks (2009) and Roberts (2009). For critics, such technologies: (i) extend patriarchal control over maternal and female bodies; (ii) consolidate a 'reproductive caste system' that values and promotes the reproduction of white women while discouraging that of non-white women (Roberts 2009: 784); (iii) treat reproduction as normal, desirable, and 'natural' for women (or, at least, white women)—that is, 'reinforce the idea that women need to be mothers in order to feel fulfilled' (Strickler 1992: 119); (iv) approach in- or sub-fertility in medical rather than social terms; and more besides. On the 'pro' side: (i) many women have deep-seated desires to mother, which assistive techniques may help them to fulfil; (ii) the availability of ARTs enlarges women's set of reproductive options; (iii) ARTs can be enabling for lesbian, gay, and queer families and trans individuals and have encouraged a diversification of forms of family and kinship.

20. This is how Macquarrie and Robinson translate the saying that Heidegger ([1927] 1962: 289) takes from Johannes von Tepl's late medieval German poem, 'The Ploughman and Death': 'als balde ein mensche geboren wirt, als balde hat es den Leikauf getrunken, das es sterben sol' (Tepl [c1401] 1969: Ch. 20). A *Leikauf* was a contractual drink of wine that brought commitments in its wake.

21. The latest development towards the latter has been the successful bringing to term of very premature lambs in an artificial uterus made of a fluid-filled plastic bag; see Hamzelou (2017).

22. It's worth recalling again here that, under my above definition of being born, the womb in and from which one is born (point iii) need not be maternal; nor does it have to be natural. And, if a foetus gestated *ex utero* were still inducted into relationships, this would satisfy part (ii) of being born (coming into a relational situation in the world). Thus, foetuses gestated *ex utero* would still be born; their existential condition would still be natal; and they would still be dependent and relational in ways that flow out of their births. Huxley, however, purposely stipulates that foetuses are grown, *not* gestated, in bottles, *not* wombs, and are decanted, *not* born (narrowly). Further, they are not inducted into relationships during gestation, thus not satisfying (ii). That is, while in reality *ex utero* foetuses would still be (broadly) born, in *Brave New World* they are not, so that the novel provides useful counterfactual speculation on what would change about our condition if we were not born—for one thing, that we would not be the relational beings we are.

23. For a relatively sympathetic reconstruction and assessment of Habermas's arguments, see Pugh (2015). For other cautionary arguments about genetic enhancement which appeal to our natality, see Reader (2017) and Schües (2014).

24. For other arguments that genetic modification need not deprive us of our newness and originality at birth, see O'Byrne (2010: 148–64) and Oliver (2011).

25. One theologian who discusses being born, interpreting it as indicating the nature of the Resurrection, is Falque ([2004] 2013). Having said that I bracket religion, I will discuss certain religious ideas on birth when they are relevant, such as the idea that each birth is a rebirth. That idea, found in Western and Eastern traditions, might seem to challenge my whole conception of birth as one's beginning; but it need not. For it is only as this particular body with its distinctive powers and history that I can be this psychological individual that I am, with my personality and character traits, continuity of memory and experience, and so on. So even if some core part of me will survive my death and undergo subsequent rebirth in another body, that part cannot be identical with me as a psychological individual: the latter, being essentially embodied, cannot survive my death or precede my birth. Indeed, philosophers of rebirth generally accept this (see Phillips 2009: 110–11, 119–30). Even if we embrace a metaphysics of rebirth, then, my birth is still the beginning of my existence as the concrete psychological individual that I am.

1
Birth and Natality in Feminist Philosophy

In Western thought and culture, birth and being born have been neglected compared to death and mortality. Feminist philosophers have criticized this neglect, rescuing birth from the near-silence in which it was formerly shrouded. Their efforts have resulted in a growing body of feminist thought about birth, which I take further in this book. In this chapter I explain the views on birth and being born of three authors who have contributed greatly to this body of thought: Irigaray, Cavarero, and Jantzen.

In Section I, I trace how Irigaray's feminism of sexual difference and attention to the maternal body lead her to consider birth.[1] In Section II, I reconstruct Irigaray's interpretive approach of tracing how difficulties around birth find expression in canonical works of philosophy. For Irigaray, these expressions help us to piece together what is involved in being born, and to remember our debts to the mothers from whom we are born. In Section III, I appraise Irigaray's views critically. Section IV turns to Cavarero's understanding of natality, which is informed by Arendt as well as Irigaray. Section V looks at how Irigaray, Cavarero, and Jantzen criticize Western culture for its preoccupation with death and mortality at the expense of birth and natality; these criticisms have inspired my attempt here to attend to the importance of birth and not only death for our existence. In Section VI, I sum up the avenues for inquiry into natality which have emerged.

I. Irigaray, Sexual Difference, and Matricide

Irigaray's attention to birth and being born arises within her overarching approach to sexual difference. That difference, she claims, has historically been construed as a hierarchy, with one sex, the female, interpreted on the model of the male sex and not in its own right. Here Irigaray agrees with

Being born: Birth and Philosophy. Alison Stone, Oxford University Press (2019). © Alison Stone.
DOI: 10.1093/oso/9780198845782.001.0001

Simone de Beauvoir that women have been relegated to the status of men's Other:

> The terms *masculine* and *feminine* are used symmetrically only as a matter of form, as on legal papers. In actuality ... *man* represents both the positive and the neutral, as is indicated by the common use of *man* to designate human beings in general; whereas woman represents only the negative.... She is defined and differentiated with reference to man and not he with reference to her; she is the incidental, the inessential as opposed to the essential. He is the Subject, he is the Absolute—she is the Other.
>
> (Beauvoir [1949] 1972: 15)

According to Irigaray, philosophy has led the way by dividing some aspects of human existence—the body, passion and feeling, sex and sexuality, irrationality—from their more highly valued opposites—mind, reason, intellect, action—and aligning the inferior terms with women or 'the female', and the superior ones with men or 'the male' (Irigaray [1974] 1985a). Thus, women have been 'Othered' through the construction of sets of hierarchical or 'binary' (1/0) oppositions running through Western philosophy.[2] What is needed instead, for Irigaray, is a positive female identity, endowed with distinctive meanings and value.[3] No such positive female identity yet exists for Irigaray; it remains to be imagined.

For Irigaray, one set of ways in which women have been 'Othered' historically is by maternity being given negative meaning. Indeed, Irigaray contends that Western culture has been matricidal: 'What is now becoming apparent in the most everyday things and in the whole of our society and culture is that, at a primal level, they function on the basis of a matricide' ([1981] 1991: 36). This may sound exaggerated, but Irigaray's view is that the political, public, and cultural domains have been cast against the maternal realm; it has been assumed that individuals must leave that realm behind to participate in civilization.[4]

For Irigaray, Aeschylus's *Oresteia* (c. 458 BC) illustrates this mindset at work. Orestes murders his mother, Clytemnestra, to avenge his father, Agamemnon, whom Clytemnestra had murdered partly to avenge their daughter Iphigeneia, whom Agamemnon in turn had sacrificed to enable the becalmed Greek fleet to sail to war against Troy. Although the Erinnyes—goddesses who guard maternal blood—hound Orestes in revenge, ultimately an Athenian court acquits him. That verdict establishes that paternal and patrilineal ties take precedence over maternal ones. To placate the Erinnyes they are made protectresses of the household—cementing the divide between paternal polis and maternal hearth. The deciding vote for acquittal comes from the goddess Athena, who admits that she always takes the male side, having been gestated in and born from the head of her father Zeus (who had eaten her mother Metis in a belated attempt to prevent Athena's conception).[5] Insofar as the *Oresteia* reveals the classical Greeks' self-conception, it shows that the polis was understood in opposition to the maternal household, which one must leave behind to become a citizen. To Irigaray's mind, this paradigm of social organization lives on: as Mary Rawlinson puts it, 'This double determination—the assignment of women to the body, to domesticity, and to sexuality, on the one hand, and the absence of women in positions of leadership in public life, on the other—is [still] all too familiar' (2016: xi).

Elsewhere Irigaray writes in a more psychological register that little boys need to make a sharp mental break from their mothers, a break that shapes their emerging psyches and persists right through their adult lives.

> The relation of the little boy to his mother is different from the little girl's relation. The little boy, in order to situate himself vis-à-vis the mother, must have a strategy,... because he finds himself in an extremely difficult situation. He's a little boy. He has come out of a woman who's different from him. He himself will never be able to engender, to give birth. He is therefore in a space of unfathomable mystery. He must invent a strategy to keep himself from being submerged, engulfed. For the little girl it's entirely different. She's a little woman born of another woman. She is able to engender like her mother.   (Irigaray 1995: 107–8)

Allegedly, then, all children find it hard to exit their original, uterine relationship with their mothers and, as the extension of this process, to separate from their mothers in weaning, toilet-training, learning to sleep alone, and so on. Children must negotiate a series of 'separations from the first home... The unavoidable and irreparable wound is the cutting of the umbilical cord' (1991: 40–1). For girls, Irigaray thinks, adapting to these stages in the loss of the mother is in principle easier, because girls will in adulthood be able to gestate babies and so recover a version of their earlier closeness with the mother by becoming mothers themselves. The loss of the mother for boys is more final, and so requires a strategy which, ironically, is that boys re-define themselves as being entirely separate from their mothers. Faced with a potentially devastating loss, boys mentally cut themselves off from what they have to lose, making themselves out to be already so unaffected by and unconnected with their mothers that they lose nothing by separation. The fledgling masculine self is re-imagined in total contrast to how it was when dependent on the mother—that is, as counter-posed to dependency and to the body and emotions, already essentially an independent rational agent.[6]

For Irigaray, these psychological forces and the sort of cultural imaginary presented in the *Oresteia* are mutually reinforcing. That imaginary enshrines a way of making sense of the self and the world towards which boys gravitate because of their natal predicament. Reciprocally, culture and socio-political arrangements communicate and promote the same horizon of meaning towards which boys were leaning anyway. However, the cultural-political order affects girls too, presenting them with a dilemma: to take part in public life, they must recast themselves—like Athena—as surrogate men, 'on the male side'.

II. The Forgetting and Remembering of Maternal Origins

According to Irigaray, traditionally the dominant way to handle being born has been to forget about it. We forget that we have lost our first home, thus making the loss harmless—in effect, as nothing to us. We pretend that we never were attached to our mothers, but were always essentially separate; we deny that any significant loss has occurred. We repress, ignore, look away from our entire infancy, otherwise remembering it would threaten our fantasies of having lost nothing. Or if we do take account of birth, we don't experience *ourselves* to have been born, but treat birth with third-person distance and detachment. We act like Ivan Ilyich, who until recently had never appreciated that the syllogism 'All men are mortal—Caius is a man—Caius is mortal' pertained to him: that *he* will die (Tolstoy [1886] 2012: 32). Alternatively again, birth may be devalued and pushed away as something vulgar, dirty, excessively physical—as when we are said to be 'born between faeces and urine'[7]—or as beneath us, as when mere material birth is adversely contrasted to higher kinds of spiritual and cultural 'birth-giving'.[8]

Irigaray interprets the work of several canonical philosophers as manifesting these mingled strategies of forgetting, distancing ourselves from, and disparaging our birth. In *Speculum*, she gives a detailed reading from this angle of Plato's Cave allegory in the *Republic*. Plato's mouthpiece, Socrates, compares our everyday life to imprisonment in an underground cave modelled on a womb, in which prisoners are tied up like cramped-up foetuses. One of them gets 'dragged forcibly away from there up the rough, steep slope' of the narrow passage—the birth canal—leading out into the sunlit real world (Plato 1993: 515e). The cave is the realm of appearance, illusion, and ignorant everyday opinion; only once emerged into sunlight can one ascend towards genuine knowledge of the Forms. Thus, intra-uterine existence is construed negatively as something best left behind and undesirably mixed up with materiality, generation, change, and illusion.

Now, Irigaray's interpretive approach is more complicated than the preceding summary might suggest. To trace the imaginative and argumentative processes by which birth has been repressed, forgotten, and rejected is to trace how philosophers *have* handled birth, despite themselves. And this is to see how philosophers have responded to the difficulties of being born. We can therefore learn about being born and its difficulties, indirectly, when we trace how birth has been pushed aside. Thus, paradoxically, in interpreting how birth has been forgotten, Irigaray is recalling its impact on us. In the same way, her readings of the philosophical canon—of Plato's Cave allegory, for instance—document the pervasive cultural impact that our relations with birth have surreptitiously had.

After *Speculum*, Irigaray continues to trace philosophers' hidden debts to their maternal origins. For instance, she re-interprets Merleau-Ponty on the flesh—roughly the ambiguous, enfolded, pre-personal field of mutual affection amongst bodies and things which makes it possible for some of them to have experience. Merleau-Ponty refers to flesh as 'the mother' and as 'being by porosity and pregnancy' (Irigaray [1984] 1993a: 149). The implication is that, since we inhabit a milieu of flesh, our existence remains continuous with the 'maternal sojourn' (the pre-natal period). Flesh is a substitute womb (173). But it is an idealized womb, Irigaray suggests, which has been reconstructed intellectually in terms of active/passive, touching/touched, reversible polarities, whereas in the relation between pregnant mother and foetus, both are 'more passive than any passivity taken in a passive–active couple' (154). In any case, Irigaray maintains, we need to leave the womb; in imaginatively reconstituting the womb in the guise of flesh, Merleau-Ponty is refusing to leave the womb, not having adequately resolved his relations to his maternal origins.[9]

From Irigaray's excavations of the hidden role of maternal origins in philosophical texts, she concludes that:

(i)   during the 'maternal sojourn', maternal body and foetus affect one another continuously and intimately, each affecting itself by affecting the other with which it is entangled; nonetheless, the two are different, not fused or merged;

(ii) they inhabit a 'placental economy', following biologist Hélène Rouch: the placenta mediates between them so that neither invades or appropriates the other (Irigaray [1990] 1993c: Ch. 4);[10]

(iii) touch precedes vision in the darkness of the womb;

(iv) to be born (i.e. leave the womb) is to begin to breathe: to enter into the air, which is thus the medium of our post-natal lives together (Irigaray [1983] 1999). In sharing the air, we are still intimately materially entwined with others, but differently than in the pre-natal maternal sojourn;

(v)   to be born is also to enter a realm of silence: 'Before our birth, we hear many things, particularly our mother's heartbeat. But when we are born we are born to light and to...silence' (Irigaray [1987] 1993b: 156). One might think that surely we are born into noise. But Irigaray means that once born one is no longer constantly and automatically surrounded and accompanied by one's mother's heartbeat or the sounds of her voice and movements; while other sounds are no longer muffled by the maternal body. The *sorts* of sounds that surround us and the way they surround us have changed;

(vi) having depended on our mothers *in utero*, we are reluctant ever to leave that dependency; so we try to re-create the uterine realm in our imaginations, for example by interpreting it into the fabric of the world as 'flesh'.

Putting these points together, Irigaray takes it that in leaving the womb we undergo a stark transformation in how we experience: we start to breathe; sight assumes new importance; we arrive in a world that initially is utterly strange to us, presenting a barrage of new sounds, people, colours, and events. This transformation becomes bound up for us with the loss of our complete intra-uterine dependence on the maternal body. We have forgotten all this, yet it has marked us—particularly in that we resist the losses incumbent on being born, and resist separating from the comforting bodies of our first care-givers.

III. Appraising Irigaray's Ideas

To summarize Irigaray's theses overall: (1) There is a need for a positive female identity, something that has scarcely existed since the classical Greek era. (2) That positive female identity needs to include a positive conception of the maternal body and of one's maternal origins. (3) All children have difficulties coming to terms with being born and separating from their mothers. (4) Boys' special difficulties predispose them to mark a sharp mental break from their mothers, a strategy expressed in the dominant currents of Western culture. (5) By remembering and acknowledging what we owe to and how we have been shaped by our maternal origins, we can begin to change this long-standing culture of denial and repression.

Irigaray's stance on sexual difference has thus led her to reflect on how being born affects our lives. Namely: To be born is to arrive in the world by being formed in and then leaving the mother's womb. This is never a bare physical process. Rather, babies experience leaving the womb as a tumultuous transformation, the loss of their first home; being born, for humans at least, is always meaningful as well as biological. In addition, to be born is to be, all along, in relationships with others: our first relationship is with the maternal body, during gestation; and when we leave the womb, we come straight into further relationships, with our mothers and others.

As an experienced transformation, being born has a lasting impact on us. As part of this, exiting the womb throws the baby into a journey involving successive losses of the maternal body. But we can navigate that journey in several ways. Traditionally, the dominant way has been to repudiate the early maternal realm along with dependency, emotion, and the body. Even under that approach, though, our early relations with our mothers affect us long past infancy, for how we handle those early relations shapes how our selves become structured (e.g. oppositionally), structures that stay with us throughout our lives and find expression in, and reinforcement from, culture. In these ways, birth's impact on our lives is deep, lasting, and far-reaching.

We can specify more closely than Irigaray that what undergoes structuration here is not the baby's most basic sense of having a self, a locus of first-person experience. Rather, what gets structured is the infant's more developed sense of having a self different from that of its mother (Benjamin 1988: esp. 18–20). In its first few months a baby acquires the sense of a basic 'core' self (see Stern 1985/1998). But from around eight months onwards the infant begins to appreciate that its mother also has a self and that the two selves are different. This provokes emotional distress and difficulty. Something else that gets structured by the way the infant handles this difficulty is its gender identity as masculine or feminine, and the infant's sense of what this identity consists in. And what also begins to get structured here is the infant's incipient psychical organization—or personality structure—which may, say, involve firm defences against the maternal realm and a self-image of having sharp boundaries from other persons. Infants, then, can negotiate their early relations with their mothers in different ways, which shape how they come to experience and understand their selves and their gender (in infancy and beyond) and what emotional and behavioural traits and dispositions they acquire.

At this point, let's deal with some questions regarding Irigaray's claims. (1) For Irigaray, children need to negotiate a series of separations from the maternal body. That suggests that the series must terminate in separateness. Yet Irigaray is critical of the traditional separate form of self, which for her is part-and-parcel of the West's anti-maternal and matricidal culture. Consistently, then, we should say that children need to *differentiate* themselves from their mothers—that is, come to accept that the two have distinct selves—without thereby necessarily having to *separate* from their mothers—that is, sharply repudiate and deny all connection with them (or with other people approached on the mother's model). Whereas separation means rejecting connectedness, one can have a differentiated self while remaining connected.[11] Unfortunately, much psychoanalytic theory occludes this distinction by using 'separation' ambiguously, sometimes to mean the kind of sharp psychical break that Irigaray condemns as 'matricidal' but sometimes to mean the weaker sort of 'differentiation' commended by Chodorow, Irigaray, and I myself (in Stone 2011). Even if children need only to differentiate and not separate themselves from their mothers, though, they will still face the sorts of difficulties that Irigaray details. For acquiring a sense that one's self differs from that of one's mother will still present emotional problems, given the depth of children's early emotional entwinement with their mothers. And these problems can motivate separation, even though separation is actually neither necessary nor desirable.

(2) Irigaray seems to assume that little boys and girls know almost directly from birth that they are either differently-sexed from or the same-sexed as their mothers, and this in terms of whether they will or will not later be able to give birth. But babies are in no position to know this; and babies and

infants form intense affective relationships with their mothers long before forming any remotely accurate understandings about reproduction. This problem noted, we can still agree with Irigaray that infants and children face a difficult process of undergoing 'separation from that first home, the first nurse' (1991a: 40). We begin life acutely dependent on our mothers, but must gradually come to appreciate that they are different individuals with minds of their own. As Irigaray highlights, this is difficult not only cognitively but also emotionally.

(3) Further difficulties surround the status of the mother here. In focusing on our difficulties separating from our mothers, Irigaray assumes that it is always one and the same woman who gestates, bears, and then looks after a child: children must negotiate their relations with 'the person[s] who bore them', Irigaray says ([1989] 1994: 110). That is, Irigaray amalgamates biological child-bearing and social childcare. She also assumes that those who bear babies are always women: our first home is always the maternal body, for her, never a paternal body. I will return to these difficulties in Chapter 2.

(4) Turning back to the broader cultural claims within which Irigaray's thoughts on birth are embedded, we might question whether one can meaningfully or accurately generalize about 'Western culture' as she does (for a critique of the notion, see Appiah 2016). Irigaray accepts the familiar view that 'Western culture' was born in classical Greece, rather than, say, treating ancient Greek culture as deriving to a considerable extent from Egyptian and Phoenician influences, as Martin Bernal argues in *Black Athena* (1987).[12] Besides which, many extra-European influences have since acted on European culture: for example the Arabic reception of Aristotle's works hugely influenced the later-medieval synthesis of Christian and classical Greek thought. 'Western culture' has always been hybrid. So we should take Irigaray's claims as applying not across the board but specifically to the most dominant strands of an internally complex and variegated culture (or set of cultures).

(5) In its dominant strands Western culture has perhaps, far from effacing maternity, tended to reduce female identity to maternity and to inflate and over-valorize motherhood. After all, its central female icon is a maternal one: the Virgin Mary. However, from Irigaray's perspective, Mary's exalted position is part-and-parcel of the culture of matricide. Mary is valued because she provides the passive, nurturing background from which Jesus springs forth into his central civilizing and spiritual

position. Mary corresponds, so to speak, to the benign Eumenides who contentedly accept a secondary role. Thus, for Irigaray, being female has been reduced to maternity only as construed in merely passive, secondary terms, which is part of Western culture's failure to envision positive female or maternal identities.

These cautions noted, Irigaray has still opened up a hugely generative field of inquiry into how our lives are shaped by our being born. Indeed, she herself turns to write explicitly about the latter in *To Be Born* (2017). Yet here she takes a direction somewhat contrary to her previous work. We *choose* to be born, she says: 'Whatever the unknown factors of our conception, we have wanted to be born. Our existence cannot be the outcome of a mere chance, and our will to live clearly manifested itself at the time of our birth. We were the ones who determined its moment' (2017: 1). But, she continues, we do not find it easy to accept and embrace our autonomous existence. We need guidance in how to cultivate our perceptual capacities and move and grow faithfully to our inner energies and regularities. Unfortunately a manufactured, artificial, alienating culture is imposed on us instead, and adults reduce our needs to physical ones and impose stifling rules and conventions on us, 'cultural constructions extraneous to our original vitality' (75). Sexual relations offer us a chance for *re*birth out of this confining framework, for in them we encounter others who are irreducibly sexually different from us; we thereby reconnect with our own origins, at conception, in the meeting of two, male and female.[13] We do not know about our origins here; rather, we re-experience the mystery of difference out of which we were originally born and can now be reborn.

In Irigaray's latest view, then, to be born is not really to come into the world in an unchosen place within it, acutely dependent on adult care. That last is a conceit of adults, who reduce infants to creatures of physical need. Infants are in fact intrinsically autonomous, right down to their choices to be born. The task bequeathed us by our condition of being born is to remain faithful to our autonomy and solitude, to which we are 'abandoned' by birth but which we shrink from taking up. There is some continuity with Irigaray's earlier thought here, in that she was previously critical of our tendency to imagine ourselves, post-natally, still to be *in utero*, not cast out into independence. But, on the whole, in *To Be Born* she so stresses autonomy and individuality rather than dependency and relationality that she jettisons many of her most valuable earlier insights.

IV. Cavarero on Natality

Cavarero's thought comes out of several influences, including Irigaray's work, that of the Italian philosophical group Diotima to which Cavarero belonged and which espoused a feminism of sexual difference, and her readings of ancient Greek philosophy, especially Plato. Cavarero's approach to birth and natality as it takes shape from these influences has two aspects: a positive account of natality and a critique of Western culture's preoccupation with death and mortality. I begin with the positive aspect (Sec. IV) then turn to the critique (Sec. V).

Another key influence on Cavarero's conception of natality is Arendt— not surprisingly, for Arendt introduces the concept *natality* into philosophy. To quote two key passages on natality from *The Human Condition* (1958):

> [O]f the three [labour, work and action], action has the closest connection with the human condition of natality; the new beginning inherent in birth can make itself felt in the world only because the newcomer possesses the capacity of beginning something anew, that is, of acting. In this sense of initiative, an element of action, and therefore of natality, is inherent in all human activities. Moreover, since action is the political activity par excellence, natality, and not mortality, may be the central category of political, as distinguished from metaphysical, thought.   (9)

> To act, in its most general sense, means to take an initiative, to begin...Because they are *initium*, newcomers and beginners by virtue of birth, men take initiative, are prompted into action....It is in the nature of beginning that something new is started which cannot be expected from whatever may have happened before....The new always happens against the overwhelming odds of statistical laws and their probability, which for all practical, everyday purposes amounts to certainty; the new therefore always appears in the guise of a miracle. The fact that man is capable of action means that the unexpected can be expected from him, that he is able to perform what is infinitely improbable. And this again is possible only because each man is unique, so that with each birth something uniquely new comes into the world. With respect to this somebody who is unique it can be truly said that nobody was there before....[A]ction as beginning corresponds to the fact of birth, if it is the actualization of the human condition of natality.   (177–8)

These statements permit a range of interpretations of exactly what *natality* means, partly depending on how we situate them in Arendt's broader body of work. But my take on Arendt's core view of natality is this. We are not timeless, eternally existing beings, but rather our lives (a.i) *begin* when we are born. (a.ii) To be born is to arrive as someone *new*, who was not there before. (a.iii) To be born is also to come *into the world*, which is shared, and so (a.iv) to come amongst *others*, in their plurality, where each is 'single…, unique, unexchangeable, and unrepeatable' (97). This plurality is the concomitant of our each being born new, irreducible to anything or anybody that is already given. Also, to be born is (a.v) to begin on an entire *course* of existence which cannot be deduced or predicted from its beginnings. (a.vi) There is something miraculous, in a positive and hopeful way, about this appearance of someone new, irreducible to the causal conditions of their emergence and the whole prior state of the world. This appearance shows that the world can be *renewed* and made better (247).[14]

In all these respects, being born prefigures action specifically conceived as (b.i) our power spontaneously to *begin* or initiate deeds and acts of speech that are (b.ii) *new*, not reducible to any prior conditions or chains of causal determination. These acts are always (b.iii) interventions into the *public world*—the common, political realm—addressed and presented to, and appearing in the eyes of (b.iv) plural *others*, with (b.v) *chains* of ramifications, consequences, and meanings that depend unpredictably on how our acts, as addressed to others, are taken up, construed, and acted upon. (b.vi) In their novelty and unpredictability, our actions have the potential to *renew* the world. (However, hope can be crushed if the socio-political world stifles our power of action; the concept of natality therefore underpins Arendt's critique of totalitarian regimes.)

What does this imply about the meaning of the concept *natality*? In *The Life of the Mind*, Arendt defines natality simply as 'the fact that human beings appear in the world by virtue of birth' (1978: 217; and see 1966: 48). More specifically, natality perhaps picks out our character of absolute newness in virtue of being born. Being 'natal', then, might be synonymous, not with being born as such, but with being unique and new on account of birth—or with being a beginner (again, by virtue of birth)—or existing in the world with others (again, by birth). Either way, arriving in the world through being conceived and gestated in and then exiting the mother's womb does not figure for Arendt. What matters is beginning and appearing in the world, rather than *how* one has come to do so corporeally and through a gestational relationship. To complicate things further, elsewhere Arendt instead identifies natality specifically with our political power to begin or initiate actions (1958: 247), where our being born only prefigures, symbolizes, or enables this power of *initium*, standing to it as first to second birth (176), potential to actuality (177). In that case, although we are new by birth, that newness only becomes fully realized subsequently, when we take up and actualize our capacity for acting. On that view, to be born is to be natal only in the reflected light of the political.[15]

Not surprisingly, many different readings of natality in Arendt exist.[16] But I'll focus solely on Cavarero's account of natality, as she takes up and modifies certain Arendtian ideas. In particular, Cavarero re-emphasizes that we are born *from our mothers*. To be born is not to come into existence from nowhere, out of nothing; rather, it is 'a coming from the mother's womb' (Cavarero [1990] 1995: 6). This means, first, and *pace* Arendt, that the way we enter existence corporeally matters: being born is not just appearing, but appearing *by* being conceived and gestated in then coming out of the maternal womb. Second, to be born is to be in an original relation with someone else: one's gestational mother, in each case. Relation is prior to individuality, and, specifically, relation with the mother is primary (Jones 2012).

That said, for Arendt too we are relational beings through-and-through: to be born is to begin to exist *in the world*, as one shared, *with others*. Cavarero agrees, saying that what it is to exist is to have come *out* of one's mother's body—*ex*-istere (2000: 19–20)—and so to be *ex*-posed to others. One has been put out into a realm in which one perceptibly appears to others who, reciprocally, are now perceptible to the one born. Our condition begins, as it remains, one of reciprocal exposure and appearance. Like Arendt, Cavarero intends no appearance/essence contrast here: who we are is just who we appear to be, bodily, to others; the only existence is one of mutual appearance, and the only existence is a bodily one.

However, we see an important equivocation in Cavarero's views here. Often, she understands being born in the narrow sense of leaving the womb, whereby one enters the shared world amongst others; here 'the world' means the world outside the mother's womb. But in fact—and this is implied by Cavarero's recognition of the primacy and originality of the existent's relations with the other who gestates her—we are already in relation with others and start to be in the world during intra-uterine life. Inside the womb we begin to have tactile, auditory, and other sensations; to detect changes in levels of light; to hear the relative quiet of night and the sounds of day-time; to hear our mothers' voices, most regularly, and other voices, more inter-mittently. And even before a foetus has experience, she begins to appear to others: mothers are aware of their foetuses inside them; in the past this was from the 'quickening' onwards, but now it tends to begin much earlier via ultrasound. The mother can feel the late-stage foetus moving and others can sometimes perceive these movements too, perhaps seeing or feeling the baby's kicks stretching the mother's belly. The protagonist of Atwood's *The Handmaid's Tale*, known as Offred, remembers her pregnancy:

> Lying in bed, with Luke, his hand on my rounded belly. The three of us, in bed, she kicking, turning over within me. Thunderstorm outside the windows, that's why she's awake, they can hear, they sleep, they can be startled, even there in the soothing of the heart.   (1985: 113)

In these ways the foetus begins to be in the world, exposed to others, from conception onwards.

Nonetheless the exit from the mother's womb is a caesura of sorts, as Cavarero marks. The question is how to characterize this transition. Perhaps what distinguishes intra-uterine participation and appearance in the shared world is that they are completely mediated by the maternal body. But a newborn baby's participation is also very heavily mediated through her care-givers; if there is a caesura here, there is also continuity.[17] Let's just say, then, that after leaving our mothers' wombs we are more fully and completely in the world amongst others, whereas in the intra-uterine period we were so relatively partially and ambiguously.[18] The overall point is that we come to be in the world with others through birth taken broadly as beginning at conception, not only through birth in the narrow sense.

The same equivocation about whether birth is taken broadly or narrowly reappears when Cavarero insists that 'maternity is the matrix of the arrival of humans into the world' (1995: 59), hence that we do not come into existence from nowhere. We come *from someone*, she insists, objecting to Arendt's statement that, of everyone who is born, it can be truly said that they were not there before (1958: 178). Yet Cavarero in fact agrees with Arendt that every new existent is unique, not the same as anyone else who ever lived or will live. That very uniqueness seems to entail, though, that the individual cannot have been there in existence before their birth. To that extent the individual *has* after all arisen from nowhere. The problem is that 'birth' is functioning sometimes broadly and sometimes narrowly. I was already a unique being before I left the womb (i.e. was born narrowly), for it was from conception onwards that the unique physical configuration that I am took shape. And, taking it that I am also unique in having my particular first-person stream of experience, I began to have experience in some rudimentary form during gestation—again, before leaving the womb.

I started to be a unique being during gestation, then, not only when I left my mother's womb.

Elsewhere, though, Cavarero takes a stronger view that even before conception the individual already had a kind of existence. She elaborates with reference to Clarice Lispector's novel *The Passion According to G. H.* Having tried to kill a cockroach, and watched with revulsion as its insides oozed out, the main character G. H. feels drawn into (what she now sees as) the single immemorial process of life going on within and through the cockroach. Embracing this life-process, G. H. says:

> The narrow passage had been the daunting cockroach . . . And I had ended up, all impure myself, embarking, through it, upon my past, which was my continuous present and my continuous future . . . and my fifteen million daughters, from that time down to myself, were also there. My life had been as continuous as death. Life is so continuous that we divide it into stages and call one of them death . . . . I had always been in life.
>
> (Lispector 1988: 57)

I have 'always been in life', then, just insofar as the broader process of life in which I participate has always been unfolding. Even so, the unique bodily and psychical configuration that is me, this individual, has not always been in existence. Cavarero is right to remind us that our individual existence has causal and material antecedents and conditions in much broader, anonymous, species-wide and trans-species life-processes, running back to time immemorial, processes that leave their traces and residues in us as their products, including in our genetic make-up. Nonetheless, this particular bodily configuration and site of experience which I am, did not exist prior to my own conception. As the singular plural existents that we are on Cavarero's own view, we each appear in existence for the first time through gestation, that is, through birth broadly construed. So there *is* an important sense in which we appear by birth *ex nihilo*.

The substantial point of difference between Cavarero and Arendt remains that for Arendt it is of no account for our natality what happens before we leave the womb, namely that we undergo gestation within maternal bodies. For Cavarero, in contrast, an account of human existence must take this into account, otherwise we forget our primary debts to our mothers and the priority of our relations with our mothers vis-à-vis all our other relations. And then we lose sight of the positive value of maternity, which is one strand of the positive value and meaning that we need to rediscover in being female.

This emphasis on maternity also creates problems, however. For Cavarero, because we are born of our mothers—of women—we are born sexed (*sessuata*) (e.g. 1997: 19). For Cavarero, these two things, birth of mothers and being born sexed, necessarily go together: being born presupposes sexual reproduction and therefore that the human kind is sexually differentiated. However, as I've noted, it is no longer the case—if it ever was—that we are born only of mothers; increasingly trans fathers are bearing children too. Further, although our primary intra-uterine relations are with our birth-mothers (or birth-fathers), these are not necessarily the same people with whom we have our closest or most direct post-natal relationships. We may be adopted or, in other ways, cared for primarily by individuals other than those who bore us. Cavarero is silent about such possibilities, and by this silence she occludes the fact that men and fathers can and do play roles in reproduction, birth, and childcare. It is symptomatic that Cavarero quotes Lispector on fifteen million *daughters*, suggesting that life descends only along a single female–maternal line. Of course, Cavarero wants to shake up residual assumptions that patrilineage is normal and that the father is the one who essentially begets a new person while the mother merely incubates them.[19] But in her counter-reaction, Cavarero bends the stick too far the opposite way and establishes symbolic equations amongst females, women, gestation, birth, and childcare which reinforce the norm for childcare to be women's work.

Let's move on. Cavarero argues in *Relating Narratives* ([2000] 2002) that birth is central to each person's unique identity as the particular individual they are. This identity is completely relational, she argues: it is by birth that I come into the evolving web of relationships over time which makes me who I am. Here Cavarero is primarily concerned with *ipse*-identity—unique individuality and character—rather than *idem*-identity—sameness of the self over time.[20] For her, relationships play their role in shaping one's identity by way of the roles that story and narrative simultaneously play here. To explain, let's take one of Cavarero's key examples of how birth, relationships, and stories are key to one's *ipse*-identity: Oedipus.

According to Cavarero, Oedipus can answer the riddle of the Sphinx because of his knowledge of Man. This is Man in general, and Oedipus's knowledge is philosophical in kind, Cavarero claims: it concerns essences, universals, and kinds. Yet Oedipus does not know who he is as an individual. Because he believes that he is the birth-son of Polybus and Merope of Corinth, Oedipus is ignorant that he has actually, unintentionally, fulfilled the prophecy that he would kill his (birth-)father Laius and marry his (birth-)mother Jocasta. After being warned by the prophet Teiresias that he is a murderer and his marriage incestuous, Oedipus begins to unravel the mystery of who he is. And to know who he is, he needs to know the story of his birth:

> Oedipus does not know who he is because he is ignorant of his birth. Therefore, only the story of his birth can reveal the story of which he is the protagonist. For Oedipus,... knowing himself means knowing his birth, because that is where his story begins.... The story of one's life always begins where that person's life begins. We are not speaking of Man in his disembodied and universal substance, but rather of a particular man, a unique being who bears the name of Oedipus.   (2000: 11)

Only by learning that he was actually born to Laius and Jocasta, then, can Oedipus know himself by knowing the complete story of his life and actions as they descend from his birth, under the parricidal and incestuous meanings that they have only because of their relations to his birth.

Cavarero's picture, then, is this. I am born, and born to a particular mother (e.g. Jocasta in Oedipus's case). From this starting-point, I come to act in determinate ways in relation to the others around me (e.g. Oedipus flees from those whom he believes to be his birth-parents, trying to protect them). Others take up, respond to, and interpret my actions from their specific standpoints, as my actions come to bear on them (e.g. Laius gets into a fatal argument with Oedipus when they meet while travelling). These responses prompt further actions from me (Oedipus kills Laius), generating further entanglements with others (Jocasta is thereby widowed and available to marry Oedipus), and so on. The series of actions and entanglements over time constitutes my life; and my life is a *story* insofar as these actions and events form a temporal series of parts that are interconnected in meaningful ways. Their meaningfulness is to reveal who I am: thus, my unique identity unifies my life and binds its events into a story. It is not that my actions express and so reveal an 'inner' identity 'behind' them. My identity is located 'outside' me, as embodied in the succession of my actions under the meanings they have for others and in the entanglements they generate with others. For my actions are always-already interventions into the shared world— what these actions are is what they appear to be; what they mean is what they present themselves as meaning to the several others whom they affect. Thus, 'a unique being is such in the relation, and the context, of a plurality of others,... likewise unique themselves, [who] are distinguished reciprocally'

(2000: 43). And 'the ontological status of a *who* is always relational and contextual' (90).

One consequence is that it is only in hindsight that I can discern, from the sequence of events and relationships composing my life, how they hang together and so who I am. As I am exposed to the world, my character stands revealed through the sequence of actions and events which expose it, and it is only fully revealed in and through this sequence. Any attempted capsule statement of my essence, extracted from the life-story that embodies my identity, will contain mere generalities and platitudes. Moreover, as the meanings of my actions are relational, different people with whom I am in different relations are able to see different sides of, and know about different meanings in, my actions and their entanglements. So to know myself, I must learn from others; I cannot know myself through my individual resources. Hence Oedipus needs to question various parties to the different events and stages of his life so as to piece together who he is. The result is a narrative: his story told in words. To tell someone's story, then, is to narrate it,[21] and a narrative is realistic—rather than fictitious—just when it tells and makes explicit the meanings of the story of someone's real life.[22]

For Cavarero, I am the unique person I am by virtue of my birth because it marks the beginning of the unique temporal series of actions and entanglements in which I will become revealed. Yet at and by birth I am also unique in other respects, to which Cavarero points at times without fully clarifying how they intersect with her focus on actions-and-story. (i) I am unique because I am born into a unique situation—including a unique set of relationships, with my mother amongst others (2000: 43). No-one else can ever come into quite the same relational situation as me: for example, even if a younger sibling is born soon after me to my parents, they arrive by birth into a sibling relationship to me which I did not have to them when I was born (for they were not yet there). My unique set of natal relationships is part of (ii) the unique set of circumstances into which I am born: circumstances of place, time, historical and geographical location, linguistic community, ethnicity, culture and religion, and more besides. Further, (iii) I am also unique in that I am the locus of a particular stream of embodied first-person experience which no-one else has, a stream that begins to unfold with my birth (38). And (iv) the particular body as and with which I am born is unique in its physical, including biological and genetic, make-up (111). Factors (i)–(iv) are irreducible to one another and all pick out ways in which we are each unique just *by* birth, over and above whatever further aspects of uniqueness we may acquire in the longer term as our lives unfold *from* our births.

Let me sum up some core ideas regarding birth which emerge from Cavarero's work. (1) Our existence begins when we are born, for this is when we enter the world that is shared with a plurality of others, to whom we are exposed: as we appear to others, so we are. (2) Our unique selves are therefore relational through-and-through, in ways connected with action, story, and narrative. (3) We are each born to our mothers, corporeally, so that again our existence is relational from the very first. (4) To be born is to come into a line of descent and to take shape as a concrete and finite configuration—a living body—in a way that depends on broader anonymous life-processes. (5) By birth we each come to exist as unique, embodied, first-person individuals located in unique situations and sets of relationships.

Whereas Cavarero sometimes approaches birth in a narrow sense, in ways that run right through her work, I believe that it is with birth in the broad sense that begins at conception that we begin to enter the world— which we do gradually, in stages. With that proviso, I accept Cavarero's insights into our primary and ongoing relationality and our uniqueness by birth. I also accept, through Cavarero, Arendt's insights that we each arrive radically new at birth, such that to be born is to begin existing and to come into the world as one shared with others who are singular plural. However, whereas Cavarero interprets our post-natal relationality primarily in terms of actions and entanglements—our selves are relational because we are exposed to others practically—I will argue that we are constitutively relational because our first and subsequent relationships shape the interior psychical structures that frame the whole way we experience. And where Cavarero sees an unfolding, out of someone's birth, of the series of their actions and entanglements, I will see a succession of situations of each of which we make sense in already-sedimented ways that we've inherited and received from others. In these regards, I will shift our account of natality further away from the Arendtian legacy in Cavarero and specifically from Arendt's focus on action—her version of the idea of spontaneous freedom. Instead, I put more emphasis on our dependency on one another, our situatedness and givenness, our status as inheritors and receivers, and, overall, the weight of the past relative to the openness of the future.[23]

V. A Culture of Death and Violence

Irigaray's and Cavarero's wide-ranging critiques of Western culture form the negative counterpart of their positive conceptions of birth and natality. Irigaray's critique is directed against the West as a culture of violence and war, Cavarero's against its preoccupation with death and mortality. In turn, Grace Jantzen brings these two critical directions together.

As we've seen, for Irigaray, our troubled relations with our maternal origins have led to a patriarchal and matricidal culture, originating in classical Greece. For Irigaray, this culture is pervaded by, and preoccupied with, death and violence, as part of its reaction against the maternal body. In the essay 'A Chance for Life', Irigaray portrays contemporary culture as a culture of generalized violence and destruction. No longer 'contained within the limits of a declared conflict', our whole society has become one vast 'war machine', in which 'death machines are traded around with vast capital expenditure', but where 'death and destruction are not merely the outcome of war. They are found in the physical and mental assaults we have to cope with permanently every day'. Many of our social institutions and practices conduct a constant micro-assault on our bodies and senses—for example, in the background levels of noise and light that come with urban life (1993b: 185–6). How does this attraction to death and violence arise in reaction against our maternal origins? Irigaray argues that because of our unresolved relation with these origins, we generally have unconscious wishes to return into the mother's womb—to return to pre-individuated uterine life, thus to destroy ourselves qua distinct individuals, to dissolve our boundaries. To protect ourselves from this ultimately self-destructive, self-immolating urge, we project it outwards as violence towards other objects and people.[24]

We may be doubtful about this rather speculative line of interpretation, despite its basis in Irigaray's reconstruction of our troubled relations with our maternal origins. But there are alternative ways of making the same sort of feminist cultural critique, notably Cavarero's. Ever since Plato, Cavarero holds, the West has sidelined birth and raised mortality into the defining feature of human existence; and it is above all through Plato's influence that Western culture has become centred upon death.

In Plato's *Symposium*, the priestess Diotima judges the physical generation of new life by women and men to be inferior to the spiritual generation of wisdom and virtue amongst men. People aspire to gain immortality by propagating themselves physically; but the only true path to immortality is to elevate one's soul above the material realm by rising to contemplate the

Forms (Plato 1991: 209a3–4, b8).[25] And in the *Apology*, Socrates advises his followers that there are no good grounds for fearing or trying to avoid death. It is much more important to avoid doing wrong and to cultivate virtue. For in death only the physical body dies, but not the immortal soul, which on (bodily) death will attain to either a blessed sleep or a further state proportionate to its previous level of virtue (2001: 40c–41c). For the virtuous, 'those there [in the afterlife] are happier than those here not only in other things but also in that they are immortal henceforth for the rest of time' (41c). To die having lived well is to become immortal.

In the *Republic*, Socrates elaborates by passing on Er's account of his experience of the after-life (the so-called 'Myth of Er'). Er spent twelve days apparently dead, actually having been granted the chance to witness the after-life so that he can educate others (1993: 10.614b–621d). Er learns that after our bodies die, our souls (*psukhe*)—that is, we ourselves, for we truly are our souls—descend underground for punishment if we acted badly in life. Or, if we were virtuous or have already been punished enough, we enter a region in which we have a chance to choose our next life from a range offered to us, after which we drink a draught of forgetfulness and then proceed into our chosen new bodies. Crucially, how well we choose with respect to our next lives—what kinds of character and body, and indeed species, we are drawn to—depends on the level of virtue and wisdom we acquired in our last life. Thus the most virtuous are set to fare best between incarnations and in their next lives.

In Plato's thought, then, a focus on mortality intersects with a hierarchical division between soul and body. The soul descends, at birth, into material embodiment, where the material realm is imperfect and defective by comparison to the non-material realm of the Forms. Material things are subject to change and loss, so that their being is always compromised by non-being; only the Forms, ideal metaphysical principles, truly are. To be born, then, is to come into an inherently defective condition. Reciprocally, to die is to escape from this inferior condition into one that is in principle better, as long as one has led a life oriented to the good. Ethics becomes preparation for death, in part because virtue requires wisdom, progress along the intellectual ascent towards contemplation of the Forms—whereby we learn to look beyond material life while remaining embedded in it.

These Platonic views have had unprecedented influence because they were synthesized with and incorporated into Christianity, above all by Augustine. Even if most of us today reject Plato's beliefs in the Forms and the immaterial soul, those beliefs have nonetheless shaped prevailing assumptions about birth and death over the centuries, and we are heirs to those assumptions. Moreover, Cavarero argues, Plato's views distil a broader turn towards death and immortality which occurred in classical Greece and embodied a reaction against maternal bodily power. Along with the power to carry, bear, and breast-feed babies, women also have the power to choose *not* to carry, bear, or breast-feed babies, by deciding to terminate a pregnancy, abstain from reproduction, or commit infanticide or child-murder—as does Medea, whom Cavarero locates within a proliferation of feared maternal–female figures of ancient Greek myth: Medusa, her sister Gorgons, the Harpies, the Sphinx. As this proliferation indicates, women's maternal powers of life and death are frightening to those who lack them. In a displacement, the maternal body's fearfulness becomes transposed onto that of death. After all, what the maternal body threatens us with is death: the power that can give life can also take it. Yet death *in general* is not under women's control, but threatens and will come to everyone alike: death is an equalizer. Thus, by orienting ourselves around death rather than birth, we look away from the power of the maternal body to a still higher power that is sex-neutral and gives women no advantage (1990: 68–9).

However, the more we focus our attention on death and so define ourselves as essentially mortals, the more fearful death becomes. Further strategies, then, start to be needed to reduce death's fearfulness—such as Plato's strategy, namely postulating the immortality of the soul. Maternal power is thereby reduced further, because being born is now re-interpreted as being merely the fall of an already existing soul into material encasement, where the immaterial soul is essentially beyond the mother's bodily reach. The mother's power is diminished, then, along with that of the entire material realm: for although material things are subject to finitude, change, and mortality, we can escape these defects insofar as we belong to the spiritual domain. In sum, for Cavarero, philosophy has since its inception in ancient Greece affiliated itself with death; this affiliation is foundational for the Western symbolic order; and it is motivated by a patriarchal reaction against maternal bodily power.[26]

Grace Jantzen unites Irigaray's and Cavarero's cultural critiques in a trilogy of books which begins with *Foundations of Violence* (2005).[27] For Jantzen, again, birth and natality have been neglected in favour of death and mortality within the West, defined as 'the cultural trajectory from Homer through christendom and the enlightenment to secular modernity and "postmodern" thought' (2005: 358). The West's preoccupation with death is crystallized in the statement 'all men are mortal'. It is not that the statement is false, but rather that 'this *one* fact of human existence [i.e. mortality], and not other characteristics, comes disproportionately to define what it is to be human' (58). When 'All men are mortal; Socrates is a man; Socrates is mortal' is taken as the archetypal syllogism, this is because of the background assumption that mortality defines the human condition.

According to Jantzen, this fascination with death—'necrophilia'—took hold in ancient Greece and has pervaded Western culture since. Necrophilia, for Jantzen, unfolds in stages:

(i) We glorify death and celebrate as heroes those who die in war—from Achilles through to the soldiers commemorated by the Cenotaph.

(ii) Fear of death—'necrophobia'—takes hold. For when we glorify and foreground death, its role in human existence becomes magnified— we come to see it everywhere—and this proportionately heightens our fear of death. Ironically, it is within the (necrophiliac) culture that valorizes death that death also becomes a paramount object of fear (necrophobia).

(iii) Necrophobia motivates us to find ways to escape from death into immortality, and to downgrade mortal and secular life in favour of an eternal realm free of change, death, and loss. Hence Platonic–Christian metaphysics, no less than the recent ambition to make humankind immortal by technological means.[28]

(iv) In a further twist, necrophobia leads to the twentieth-century trend to hide from death and push it out of sight and mind—the era of 'forbidden death' (Ariès 1974: Ch. 4). The death of loved ones has been pushed out of the home into hospitals or hospices; cemeteries have been moved to the edges of towns and cities; self-restraint and silence have replaced prolonged displays of grief and mourning; life is prolonged and death treated as a problem for medicine and science, a phenomenon potentially under human control or, at least, that can be delayed and deferred. To be sure, these advances in medicine, nutri- tion, and hygiene, and the extension of the healthy human life-span are welcome developments, but it is not so obvious that the accom- panying tendencies to deny and avoid death are welcome. After all, we will all die and lose loved ones to death sooner or later; mortality is a reality with which we must all come to terms of some sort.

Anyway, we might think that this trend towards 'forbidden death' tells against feminist claims about Western culture's preoccupation with death and mortality. Perhaps it is no longer so preoccupied, and feminist critics are tilting at a windmill that has stopped turning anyway. Jantzen argues, though, that the forbidden-death era is a further manifestation of necrophobia: we have made ourselves so afraid of death that we start to refuse to confront it. The old strategies for assuaging the fear of death by appealing to an eternal, supernatural realm became unviable over the nineteenth century, along with the metaphysical underpinnings of traditional Christian belief. As a result, we needed a new strategy: denial and disavowal.

We disavow death, then, because we fear it, and we fear it because we've set our sights on it. Jantzen therefore speaks of a *suppressed*, disavowed necrophilia which is characteristic of modernity and which (v), in another twist, manifests itself in 'the violent and death-dealing structures of modernity... [f]rom militarization, death camps and genocide to exploit-ation, commodification, and the accumulation of wealth' (2005: 5). That is, instead of confronting and acknowledging our necrophilia, we act it out. The disavowal of death thereby becomes wedded to a violent militarism which inflicts death more widely than ever. Here the series from (i) to (v) closes into a circle, as our militarized culture leads back to a direct glorification of death in, for instance, Hollywood action movies full of explosions, violence, ultra-high-tech weaponry, and so forth.

Jantzen, then, brings together and systematizes Irigaray's and Cavarero's ideas about the culture of death and violence. And she concurs with Cavar-ero that necrophilia first takes hold as a displacement of our fears of maternal bodily power. This displacement is revealed, Jantzen argues, by the persistent association of women and death: for instance, in the ancient Greek myth of Pandora's box, in which death was amongst the evils that Pandora unleashed upon humanity; in Genesis, where Eve brings death into the world through her sin; or in the recurring idea that by bearing children, women bring them into the mortal condition, giving life and with it death. Hence the 'womb-tomb' motif in, for one, Shakespeare's *Romeo and Juliet*: 'The earth that's nature's mother is her tomb; What is her burying grave, that is her womb' (Shakespeare [1597] 1984: 115).[29]

For Jantzen, violence reigns when there is an underlying necrophilia (explicit or suppressed), and so her proposed solution is that we renounce necrophilia and make the transition to a culture that focuses on birth and natality instead. However, perhaps if we did more to acknowledge that we are mortal then we would also have to face the fact that death and bereavement are bad and, with this, that violence and war too are prima facie bad. This is the possibility I will explore later in this book. In partial disagreement with Irigaray, Cavarero, and Jantzen, then, I will suggest that, rather than reversing the tradition so as to orientate ourselves towards birth and not death, we should devote attention to both of these two 'ends' of life, the twin poles of our finitude.

VI. Feminist Thought about Birth: Preliminary Conclusions

Jantzen's work has a positive as well as a critical side. She locates the hope for, and possibility of, positive change in natality. For Jantzen, to be natal is not merely to have physically entered the world by being born. Natality also 'carries significance', namely (1) that 'to be born is to be embodied, enfleshed' (Jantzen 2005: 37). Rather than consisting of an essentially immaterial soul temporarily housed in a mortal body, each person, as natal, is essentially a living body. This calls for (2) a this-worldly ethics, Jantzen holds, since the flourishing of an essentially embodied human being requires that their bodily needs be met. (3) Being embodied, 'all natals are *gendered*...for embodied natals gender is inescapable and of great importance' (37; my emphasis). (4) To be natal is to be relational.

> It is possible to die alone, but it is not possible to be born alone: there must be at least one other person present, and she, in turn, was born of someone else. To be natal means to be part of a web of relationships, both diachronic and synchronic: it means, negatively, that atomistic individualism is not possible for natals. (37)

Further, (5) we depend on others for the care we need to survive, as infants and beyond. For us to flourish, therefore, the webs of relationships on which we depend must be maintained. Hence, the dominant emphases on individual independence and self-sufficiency in modern and political thought have been misguided. (6) Natality, Jantzen says, following Arendt, 'allows for hope':

> [W]ith each new infant, new possibilities are born, new freedom and creativity, the potential that this child will help make the world better. Freedom, creativity, and the potential for a fresh start are central to every human life and are ours in virtue of the fact that we are natals. (38)

Combining Jantzen's claims with those of Irigaray and Cavarero, a composite picture of natality emerges. On this picture, we all begin life by being born; we are 'of woman born'; we are born as bodily beings who are sexually differentiated; we are each born, unique, into a common world that is shared with a plurality of others; we are born dependent on others and within networks of relationships with others which are constitutive of, not accidental to, who we each are. Furthermore, our having been born shapes how we exist right through our lives: perhaps because we wrestle all our lives long with the legacy of our early difficulties differentiating ourselves from our mothers; perhaps because birth marks the beginning of the sequence of actions and entanglements which makes up a person's unique life-story. Either way, as the point when our lives begin, birth is central to the temporal structure of those lives: however far away we may move from our natal situations, it is from and on the basis of those first situations that we get to these new places.

In this chapter I've sought to show how a distinctive body of feminist thought about being born emerges from the work of Irigaray, Cavarero, and Jantzen. But they do not fully explore all the suggestions that they make, some of which are left sufficiently open ended or equivocal that they can be elaborated in various ways. And some of their claims are problematic, particularly around the relations amongst sex and gender, birth-giving, and mothering. So we need to pursue the inquiry into being born further, and go beyond these authors' work while learning from them. I shall begin to do this in Chapter 2.

Notes

1. For Irigaray, the gestating body is always maternal. Cavarero and Jantzen agree. Despite the problems with this position, for accuracy of exposition I largely retain the language of the maternal body in this chapter.
2. On these oppositions, see also Cixous ([1975] 1986) and Lloyd (1984).
3. On this point, Irigaray diverges from Beauvoir, who thinks that any distinctive female identity, however supposedly positive, would perpetuate women's undesirable status as Other.
4. On the idea that Western culture is matricidal, see also Jacobs (2009) and Stone (2011: Ch. 2).
5. Athena says: 'I am always for the male with all my heart, and strongly on my father's side' (Aeschylus 1953: 161, lines 737–8).

6. For kindred accounts of how the conventionally masculine self becomes set against all things maternal, see Chodorow (1978), Di Stefano (1991), Dinnerstein (1976), Flax (1983) and Fox Keller ([1978] 1983).

7. This saying, sometimes ascribed to Augustine, is in fact found in Freud, who himself attributes it only to an unspecified 'church father' (Freud [1901–5] 1953: 31).

8. For example, Nietzsche devalues female physical pregnancy compared to male 'spiritual' or cultural pregnancy. See Ainley (1988) and Oliver (1995: e.g. 105).

9. Arguably, Irigaray is uncharitable to Merleau-Ponty—see Olkowski and Weiss (2006)—but I only want to illustrate her interpretive strategy regarding birth.

10. Irigaray's rather irenic picture here contrasts with David Haig's influential view (1993) that pregnancy is inherently conflictual, as the foetus demands levels of nourishment so high as to endanger the mother's health unless her body establishes counter-measures (see also Sadedin 2014). McDonagh (1996: 81–2) criticizes Haig's view as stereotypically masculinist and conflict-centred, but arguably Irigaray's picture is no less stereotypically feminine. Moreover, Sarah Hrdy (2000) puts Haig's work to feminist use; for Hrdy, pre-natal biological conflicts between mother and foetus continue post-natally in that infants' dependency needs are liable to exhaust their mothers, hence the need for and widespread reality of co-operative child-care and 'allomothering' by older siblings, grandmothers, neighbours, etc. All this aside, we can still learn from Irigaray about the importance of birth in our lives without having to accept her specific vision of the placental economy.

11. As Nancy Chodorow has likewise argued from within Anglo-American psychoanalytic feminism (e.g. Chodorow 1999b: viii).

12. Bernal's claims have been challenged (see, e.g. Lefkowitz 1996), but his work has contributed to a general acceptance that those cultures significantly influenced the ancient Greeks.

13. Here Irigaray assumes that sexual relations are always heterosexual. How far she succumbs to the same heterosexism in her work generally is debated; see Stone (2006).

14. Arendt is inspired by the Gospels' '"glad tidings"—"a child is borne unto us"' (1958: 247)—and by her reading of Augustine (see Arendt 1966). But it is an open question how far Arendt's concept of natality in *The Human Condition* retains any religious dimension: see Biss (2012) and Dolan (2004).

15. Natality as being born, as newness by birth, and as power of *initium*, are three vectors that Schott classifies in terms of natality as natural category, category for the human condition, and political category (2010b: 52).

16. See, amongst others, Birmingham (2006), Biss (2012), Bowen-Moore (1989), Champlin (2013), Dolan (2004), Durst (2003), Guenther (2006: Ch. 2), O'Byrne (2010: Ch. 4), Schott (2010b: 52–7) and Söderbäck (2018). For a range of feminist views on Arendt's thought more broadly, see Honig (1995).

17. Freud remarks: 'There is much more continuity between intra-uterine life and earliest infancy than the impressive caesura of the act of birth would have us believe' ([1926] 1959: 137).

18. As I mentioned earlier, Schües's view here is that in the womb we are only being-*towards*-being-there, whereas after (narrow) birth we are-there properly, having intentional experience of things *as* specific things picked out against the background of the world as total field of significance. Likewise, for Warren: 'The infant at birth enters the human social world, . . . where . . . it becomes involved in social relationships with others, of kinds that can only be *dimly foreshadowed* before birth' (1989: 56; my emphasis). The reality, though, is that late-stage foetuses already have experience and are becoming inducted into the shared world. Svenaeus (2017), too, argues that adults begin to enfold the foetus within social life at least from the quickening onwards and nowadays usually following a first ultrasound scan.

19. On the history of such views, see Tuana (1993: Ch. 6).

20. On the *idem/ipse*, 'what'/'who' distinction, see Ricoeur ([1990] 1995); for Ricoeur, the 'who' pertains to the ethical agent ([1985] 1990: 246), the self that is constant to itself in maintaining consistency of character. For another version of the distinction, see Schechtman (2000: 68–9), who distinguishes the 're-identification' question (what makes a self the same over time?) from the 'characterization' question (what makes actions, experiences, etc., mine?). Cavarero actually says that she is re-uniting *ipse* and *idem* identity, on the grounds that it is my temporally extended life-story that makes me the same person over time. Nonetheless, it is really *ipse* identity that concerns her, hence she repeatedly says that her interest is in 'who', not 'what', we are.

21. Cavarero's is just one way of distinguishing narrative from story. On another version, 'story' is the events of a tale—*what* happened—whereas 'narrative' is *how* these events are told (e.g. Stapleton and Wilson 2017). And whereas for some theorists narratives *construct* stories, Cavarero regards non-fictional narratives as realistic ('truth-tracking', in Matthews and Kennett's terms; 2012). This helps to distinguish Cavarero's account of the narrative self from others such as Dennett's. For Dennett, it is just insofar as I can tell a narrative that integrates various episodes, actions, and experiences by referring them to a single 'centre of narrative gravity' (Dennett 1991: 417), the supposed protagonist of the events, that I have a self: my self is narratively constructed. For Cavarero, in contrast, narrations of my story disclose who I really am: my real character as embodied in successive actions over time. Thus, for her, the self is narrat*able* rather than narratival.

22. In making these claims, Cavarero is modifying claims about action, story, and identity made by Arendt. Unlike Arendt, Cavarero takes it that action occurs not only in the political sphere but also throughout our everyday lives. Even the newborn's first cry is an action, her first unique response to the situation in

which she finds herself. Cavarero also disagrees with Arendt's view that the complete meaning of someone's life is only established when they die: 'the essence of who somebody is...can come into being only when life departs, leaving behind nothing but a story' (Arendt 1958: 193). Cavarero objects that this view conflicts with Arendt's declared re-orientation towards natality and against mortality. Relatedly, Cavarero also professes to depart from Arendt when Arendt takes it that the meaning of who I am is *totally* exterior to me. Instead, Cavarero suggests that I have an immediate sense of myself, a pre-reflexive self-familiarity which falls short of self-knowledge (2000: Ch. 3). This sense of myself comes about through the automatic functioning of memory, which is at work in the durational continuity of experience. But this immediate sense of myself, which is bound up with my awareness of having a past, is entirely empty and promissory. I want to fill it in with a concrete sense of who I am, and this impels me to learn about my story from others. Thus I desire to fill in my 'promissory' self-unity *during* my life by hearing my story told by others: 'within the narrative scene, where each desire engenders the reciprocity of storytelling, death is constitutively excluded from the tale' (2000: 86). I still think that Cavarero foregrounds exteriority more than interiority, partly because her view of interiority is quite thin. There is scope for a richer account than Cavarero gives of how of our relationships with others get right into our interior lives and psyches. I develop such an account in later chapters.

23. Of course, Arendt does not neglect these phenomena, but neither—in my view—does she give them their full weight. For example, on her insufficient recognition of how much is given to us by birth, see Birmingham (2005) and Guenther (2006: Ch. 2).

24. Irigaray relies on Freud's speculative picture of the death and life drives. For Freud, we have inherent death drives which compel us to try to return to a zero-degree of excitation and, ultimately, to nothingness, the absence of experience—an inorganic state (Freud [1920] 1955). For Freud, we survive what would otherwise be the lethal effects of this impulse by projecting it outwards in the shape of violence to others. Irigaray translates Freud's death-drives into the wish to return into the womb. For Freud, however, violence is inevitable, given its roots in our nature (Freud [1933] 1960: 210). Irigaray, in contrast, thinks that the 'death drives' (in her version of them) could be bound and kept in check, and their force reduced, if we could come to accept life outside the maternal womb; see Whitford (1991).

25. That said, many feminists highlight strands in the *Symposium* that complicate this hierarchical framework; see, for just two examples, Irigaray (1993a: 20–33) and Nye (2015).

26. I disagree with Cavarero's claim that philosophy has its inception in ancient Greece. There are also Indian, Asian, African, and indigenous traditions of philosophy, and ancient Greek philosophy and culture already incorporated African—specifically, Egyptian—influences, as I observed earlier. Notwithstanding,

Cavarero's critique, like Irigaray's, is telling about certain dominant strands of Western culture.

27. On Jantzen's debt to Irigarayan 'French feminism', see Carrette and Joy (in Jantzen 2010: x–xi). *Foundations of Violence* is on death and violence in the classical civilizations; the second volume is on Judaism and Christianity (2008), the third on the Quaker alternative (2010). Carrette and Joy completed these last two volumes after Jantzen's death.

28. Philosophically, this ambition is associated with Nick Bostrum (e.g. 2005), who aspires for us to use technology to extend the human 'health-span' as far as possible.

29. On women's association with death, see Beauvoir (1972: e.g. 179–80), Clack (2002: 3–4) and Heinämää (2010: esp. 73–5).

2

History, Inheritance, and Vulnerability

I have two aims in this chapter. The first is to address some questions regarding existing feminist thought about being born. (1) For Irigaray, Cavarero, and Jantzen we are all born of women, our mothers. I'll argue that this claim needs to be qualified given, amongst other factors, the diversity of actual and possible arrangements for child-bearing and child-caring, and the fact that increasing numbers of trans men—that is, fathers—are bearing children. (2) *Has* Western culture really privileged death over birth as Irigaray, Cavarero, and Jantzen claim? I'll argue that it has, and unjustifiably so, taking existentialism as a case in point. (3) Does being born, as Robin May Schott argues, have negative aspects which feminist philosophers have neglected, construing birth unduly positively? I'll agree with Schott that being born does have its negative side, in part through its links with vulnerability.

My second aim is to make the transition from discussing existing feminist work to exploring natality in its own right. In dialogue with Camus and Beauvoir, I'll suggest that to be born is to *receive* and *inherit* the meaningful fabric of our lives and involvements from the others around and before us. Reception precedes creation, although we always modify what we inherit just in taking it forward. I also discuss *vulnerability*. I distinguish between vulnerability *in* being born—coming into existence in more or less advantageous locations in the world—and *by virtue of* being born—as infants who are helpless and so depend on adult care-givers. Several other connections with natality arise in relation to both of these dimensions of vulnerability.

I. Sex, Gender, and Birth

A tangle of problems around sex, gender, and birth arises out of Irigaray's, Cavarero's and Jantzen's work. We are all born. But are we all born to mothers? So Irigaray takes it. As we saw in Chapter 1 of this volume, she maintains that we all have maternal origins which we should remember,

Being born: Birth and Philosophy. Alison Stone, Oxford University Press (2019). © Alison Stone.
DOI: 10.1093/oso/9780198845782.001.0001

and that exiting the maternal body presages the post-natal process of becoming psychologically differentiated from one's mother. Thus, Irigaray assumes that one is born of and has one's primary relationship with one and the same person, one's birth- and care-giving mother. Cavarero takes it that, having been born, infants are initially helpless and therefore paradigmatically vulnerable: 'as a creature totally consigned to relationship, a child is the vulnerable being par excellence and constitutes the primary paradigm of any discourse on vulnerability', she writes ([2007] 2009: 30). But she assumes that infants are vulnerable to being harmed or, alternatively, cared for by their *mothers*; thus, her exemplar of an adult who harms instead of caring is a female and maternal figure, Medea.

However, sometimes one's birth-mother is a different person from one's post-natal, social mother, say if one's birth-mother died in childbirth, or in cases of surrogacy and adoption—or one may have no social mother, say if one has two (homosexual) fathers and was gestated by a surrogate. The roles of gestational and genetic mother can come apart too, if a woman conceives using a donated egg. And the roles of social and legal mother can differ, for instance if a child has a permanent foster mother who has not legally adopted her. In lesbian families, a child has two mothers—either of whom may or may not be the gestational or genetic mother.[1] Moreover, a mother in any of these senses is not necessarily a child's main care-giver; in the past and today, there are numerous ways of distributing the care of children. Childcare can come from, amongst others, wet-nurses, nannies, paid nursery staff, older siblings, grandmothers, and 'other-mothers'— 'women who assist bloodmothers by sharing mothering responsibilities' (Hill Collins 1990: Ch. 8). Childcare can also come from men, including fathers—who, again, may be fathers in any of several senses (social, legal, genetic).

Thus, compacted in the figure of 'the mother' is a plurality of functions that can come apart—ovulation, gestation, birth-giving, breast-feeding, child-caring. And children can be cared for by people who stand in very varied relations to them. Yet in historical and social fact, it usually has been and continues to be women, often birth-mothers, who are the key carers for children, their own and other people's. The dilemma, then, is that we need to acknowledge this emotional and material work, 'hard labour', that women so often invest in child-caring, without suggesting that only women or mothers can properly do this care-giving work.[2] I therefore speak sometimes about children's main care-givers and sometimes their mothers, in an attempt to honour both sides of this dilemma.

For Adrienne Rich, we are all 'of woman born' (1976). Many feminist authors concur, especially those writing about birth and natality.[3] This reflects, again, the understandable desire to acknowledge women's past and present child-bearing labours. Nonetheless, in fact we are not *all* of woman born: increasing numbers of trans men are becoming pregnant and giving birth. Globally, thousands of people are involved and the numbers may rise considerably if trans identities become more accepted, including by the medical profession.[4] The conservative writer Shane Morris (2016) claims that these fathers really remain 'biological women' (he means biological females) although they identify as men. But trans men's gender identity affects how they live and experience their bodies—namely, as masculine—because our bodies are not merely biological entities but are lived, and so imbued with varying affective meanings.[5] Accordingly, for example, trans fathers sometimes chest-feed rather than breast-feed their infants: the same lactating body parts that mothers live as breasts, (trans) fathers live as chests.

This said, the vast majority of babies have been and still are born to women. Even so, being 'of woman born' is only a general, not a universal condition. Should we therefore speak of gestating rather than maternal bodies so as to accommodate trans fathers (as does, for example, Söderbäck 2018), as well as cases where people's genetic, gestational, and/or social mothers are different individuals? Or should we speak of maternal bodies to acknowledge that the vast majority of gestating people have been, and still are, women? There is no easy solution here, especially because meanings and imaginings around the maternal body are deeply sedimented and entrenched in our culture and minds, and this inherited fabric of beliefs and images cannot simply be set aside. I try to honour both sides of the dilemma by speaking sometimes of mothers and sometimes of gestators, while sometimes avoiding the choice by talking neutrally of 'the womb'.

A further question is whether Cavarero and Jantzen are right that to be born is to be born sexed, female or male. In fact, a minority of people is born intersexed. To acknowledge this, Elizabeth Grosz speaks of 'at least two' sexes into which we are born (e.g. 2005: 166). An alternative view is that we are sexed as a result of social and cultural construction, not nature. Butler speaks of babies being 'girled' or 'boyed' at birth (1993: 7–8). As Georgia Warnke reconstructs Butler's reasoning, it is only because of an entrenched socio-cultural valorization of heterosexual reproduction that we pick out certain biological properties—wombs, penises, etc.—as naturally clustering together to constitute individuals as sexed (2001). Given other social-political interests, different properties would become salient for us, based on which we might categorize individuals differently, say as blue-, brown- or green-eyed. Certainly, for anyone to be born, there must be people with the biological properties that enable sexed reproduction to occur. But those who can reproduce do not thereby necessarily fall under the categories *male* and *female*, unless we give reproduction a privileged role in the classification of human beings. To do that, for Warnke, Butler, and others, is a political move rather than one mandated by nature: political because it embodies the assumption that heterosexuality and reproduction are normal and desirable.

We may not be wholly convinced that sex is a cultural artefact, but Warnke's argument at least shows that it is neither obvious nor self-evident that just by virtue of being born we are born sexed. We are born embodied, but it remains open whether our bodies are born naturally sexed or whether gender and sex are social constructions that begin to be imposed on us from birth. Since this remains open, in this book I shall remain neutral between naturalist and constructionist views.[6]

II. The Historical Bias towards Death

For Cavarero and Jantzen, death has been foregrounded and birth neglected in the history of Western culture. 'All men are mortal', not 'all human beings are natal', has been the leading idea. It might be objected that Christianity actually celebrates birth—of the baby Jesus—and the victory of rebirth over death—in the Resurrection. Yet in the way that the Resurrection has often been understood, it promises us that, although our bodies will die, as souls we can hope to live on. Jesus's triumph over death was a triumph of immortal spirit over perishable matter. In this scheme, birth is devalued as part of the material realm, from which death offers us release and—ironically—passage into *im*mortality.

This metaphysical scheme underwrites the Christian attitudes towards death that Philippe Ariès traces running through European culture from c. 650 to 1650 AD. Death was ever-present in people's lives, familiar, 'tamed', and accepted. It was 'tamed' in that it was understood in religious terms as a transition in which one was not 'annihilated but *put to sleep*' until the Second Coming (Ariès 1974: 29–31, 104). Death had a meaningful place within the cosmos, as a key threshold where the spiritual and material planes came into contact. And as death and what it offers were known about, life assumed the purpose of preparing for the afterlife: 'attitudes towards life were very much shaped by beliefs about death' (Bovey 2015).

This metaphysical–religious world view fell apart with modernity. Death was thereby 'untamed' and re-emerged in its unalloyed reality and fearfulness. Hence the preoccupation with death, dying, and disease in the early modern world, which 'led to such strange artistic forms as the dance of death, memento mori poems and luridly meditative paintings showing a living poet such as John Donne in his shrouds' (Lennartz 2013: 241). And hence, later, the trend to disavow death, medically manage and postpone it, and banish it from social life. As Jantzen suggests, it makes sense to conceal death once it is focused upon, found frightening, *and* once the Christian-metaphysical horizon for taming its terrors has fallen apart. Thus, the very tendency to conceal death today testifies to the fact that our underlying sights remain focused on it—not on birth.

The same can be seen from the extensive twentieth-century counter-reaction to the 'forbidden-death' era: the wide-ranging counter-culture that insists on confronting mortality and opposes the mainstream cultural aversion to death, dying, and the dead. This counter-culture includes existentialism—Heidegger, Camus, and Beauvoir all take death to be fundamental in structuring human existence—and also ranges across the array of forms of popular and artistic fascination with death, the afterlife, spirits, and the undead, which for Christopher Partridge are part of 'occulture': 'a vast spectrum of beliefs sourced by Eastern spirituality,...Spiritualism, Theosophy, [and]...a general interest in the paranormal' (2006: 4).[7] Approaching this multifaceted counter-culture from Jantzen's perspective, we can see that it is because we tacitly assume that human beings are mortal above all else that we assume that confronting our condition authentically means looking death and its manifestations in the face.

In existentialism, then, death remains privileged over birth, albeit in different ways from the older Christian–metaphysical ones. A case in point is Camus's classic existentialist novel, *The Outsider (L'Étranger)*. Its opening words are stark: 'Today mother died. Or maybe yesterday, I don't know. I got a telegram from the home. "Mother deceased. Funeral tomorrow. Deep sympathy". That means nothing. It could have been yesterday' (Camus [1942] 1982: 9; translation amended). These words come from the protagonist, Meursault, who is a *pied-noir*—a descendant of white settlers—in colonial Algeria. Events continue as he remains unemotional at his mother's wake and funeral, and does not cry; he embarks on a new sexual relationship, with Marie, the next day; he forms a growing friendship with his neighbour, Raymond, rumoured to be a pimp; and Part One culminates when, with no clear motivation, Meursault shoots and kills an unnamed

Arab who has been following him and Raymond around, apparently threateningly, because Raymond had been violent to his former girlfriend, the Arab's sister. In Part Two Meursault awaits his trial in prison, attends the trial and hears the cases for his prosecution and defence, is convicted and sentenced to death, and awaits his execution, rebuffing attempts by the prison chaplain to bring him round to Christianity. During the trial Meursault is treated as a monster, a man devoid of all normal emotions. His failure to be upset and cry at his mother's funeral is taken as key evidence of his brutal state of mind and his heartless character. And his 'association with Raymond, his "irregular" affair with Marie, his laughing at a . . . film after his mother's death and his acceptance of coffee and a cigarette at her deathbed are all pivotal factors in his . . . conviction' (Reynolds 2005: 17).

The plot thus unfolds between three deaths: of Meursault's mother, at the very start; of the Arab whom Meursault shoots, ending Part One; and Meursault's own death, imminent when Part Two ends (even *Meur*-sault's name evokes the phrase 'Il meurt': 'he dies'). The mother's death sets the tone and symbolizes the same message that Camus spells out in non-fictional terms in *The Myth of Sisyphus* ([1942] 1975), a companion essay to *L'Étranger*: the world in itself, as it is mind-independently, is meaningless. We moderns no longer inhabit the living, intrinsically meaningful cosmos of the medievals, for whom the world was a living mother, an organic and life-directing whole (Merchant 1980). We moderns live—more honestly, for Camus—in a dead world of causally interacting matter. In effect, the telegram reporting Meursault's mother's death announces that this is the meaningless universe in which Meursault is operating.

We find the world's meaninglessness hard to bear, according to Camus. If life, including one's own life, has no intrinsic meaning or value, why not commit suicide? The answer, Camus says, is that we desire that there be meaning and value; we look for them in the world; and not finding them there we create them, thereby giving our lives value (at least for us):

> The world in itself is not reasonable, that is all that can be said. But what is absurd is the confrontation of the irrational and the wild longing for clarity whose call echoes in the human heart . . . The absurd is . . . that divorce between the mind that desires and the world that disappoints, my nostalgia for unity, this fragmented universe and the contradiction that binds them together.   (1975: 26, 50).

Meursault provokes discomfort in people around him because he refuses to project such meaning and value upon the world. From Meursault's perspective, life has no intrinsic value; so why not kill the Arab who has been hovering around him and Raymond? And why not fire further bullets into the dead body, since this act has no inherent meaning of desecrating a corpse? It would mean that only if Meursault chose so to view it, but he doesn't: a dead body is just a lump of matter. There are no intrinsic grounds to do one thing rather than another, so why shouldn't Raymond beat his girlfriend? And why shouldn't Meursault simply pursue his own pleasures? At the novel's end, having resisted conversion by the chaplain, Meursault reaches new insight into his guiding outlook: 'I opened myself up', he writes, 'for the first time to the benign indifference of the world. And finding it so similar to me,...I felt that I had been happy, and I still was' (1982: 117; translation amended).

Camus celebrates Meursault as a heroic figure who is willing to die for the truth that the world has no meaning other than that which we give it by our creative choices, choices that Camus calls acts of 'revolt' against the absurd. In his 1955 afterword, he writes:

> A long time ago, I summed up *The Outsider* in a sentence... 'In our society any man who doesn't cry at his mother's funeral is liable to be condemned to death'. I simply meant that the hero of the book is condemned because he doesn't play the game. In this sense, he is an outsider to the society in which he lives.   (1982: 118)

To be sure, Meursault chooses no values, but his heroism for Camus is that by this refusal he exposes the people around him to the truth that the values they live by are their own creations, such that they do not have to create these particular values but could do things differently. Thus, Meursault discloses to those around him a disturbing contingency in their arrangements. If, for Camus, there is heroic honesty in freely creating values in the face of the absurd, as long as we do not deceive ourselves that these values are anything but our creations, there is also heroic honesty in Meursault's acknowledgement that no values are out there obtaining independently of our choices.

When we 'revolt' and create value, we resist death: we combat the inherent 'deadness' of the outer world, and give ourselves reasons to remain alive and desire life and not death. This is the life-affirming side of Camus's thought. Even so, death remains central to his vision, albeit in a decidedly modern way. He does not see death as having a definite place within a meaningful, spiritual universe or as giving life a fixed meaning as preparation for the afterlife. Rather, death foregrounds human life's absurdity, the absence of meaning in the mind-independent world, and our responsibility for making meaning by our own agency. Even so, this is old wine in new bottles: a new reconfiguration of a much older set of connections amongst death, meaning, and value which makes death—not birth—central to human existence. That birth is of no significance in this vision is conveyed, again, by *L'Étranger*'s opening lines. The mother who gave Meursault birth has died, and he is unaffected. His birth means nothing to him.

It is revealing about the taken-for-granted racism of French colonial culture in the 1930s that Camus can treat Meursault as a hero even though he kills an Arab—who remains unnamed throughout the novel, treated not as a unique individual but as just one amongst countless, interchangeable others of his race. (Kamel Daoud, in his post-colonial novel *Meursault, contre-enquête*, combats this by naming Meursault's victim Musa; see Daoud [2013] 2015). Throughout *L'Étranger* Arabs figure as mysterious, malevolent, background presences, alien to the white world. There have been cogent criticisms, as well as qualified defences, of Camus's stance on colonialism and race in *L'Étranger*.[8] I specifically want to highlight the link between Meursault's (and/or Camus's) unreflective racism and Meursault's apparent indifference towards his birth.

As a working-class *pied-noir*, Meursault is estranged from both Algeria's native Arab population—by race and descent—and its colonial elite—by wealth and culture. He is rootless, hence the shiftlessness of his day-to-day life. This gives Meursault insight into the contingency of human values, but it leaves him with no sense of communal belonging or shared mores. He feels that he inherits nothing, receives no handed-down cultural legacy. This is bound up with his detachment from his birth, for generally to be born is to come into a cultural location and a set of relationships from which we receive many values long before we form any powers to question them. Then again, after all, Meursault does inherit from his white working-class location his very sense of dislocation and not-belonging amongst the native Algerians around him. Thus, when Meursault kills 'Musa', the murder expresses Meursault's sense of not being a native as the Arabs are, of being a foreigner who cannot share their ways and finds them threateningly unfamiliar. Meursault's actions are motivated by his natal inheritance, then—both by the taken-for-granted racism of settler culture, and by the sense of dislocation and rootlessness which leads him mistakenly to feel that he inherits nothing by birth (even though this very sense of rootlessness is something he inherits by his birth as both a white settler and working class). But because Camus foregrounds death and not birth philosophically, he praises Meursault for his purported heroic *detachment* from the values practised around him, rather than noticing how Meursault is *faithful* to the colonial milieu into which he was born.

In *The Myth of Sisyphus*, Camus treats meaning-creation as an individual affair, but in *The Rebel* ([1951] 1953), he adopts the more collectivist view that my creation of value can only be successful and sustained if others join me—and I join them—and we create shared values together. Beauvoir argues similarly in *Pyrrhus and Cinéas* ([1944] 2004). I freely create values, she holds—they are not given—but my projects risk being brought to nothing by my death. Either these projects will be left unfinished or, if I had completed them (say, having finished writing a book), I will no longer be there to invest this achievement with value and meaning. The book that meant so much to me will end up a mere dusty tome languishing untouched on a shelf. The photographs of the child I loved will become mere fading pictures of an unknown, forgotten human specimen. Beauvoir's solution is for me to share my projects and values with others who can then take up and continue them both during my life and after my death.[9] So Beauvoir, like Camus, sees in death a threat to the meaningfulness of human existence, but a threat that motivates us to overcome it through collective meaning-creation.

Yet this exclusive concentration on death—for Beauvoir in *An Ethics of Ambiguity*, 'every living moment is a sliding towards death' ([1947] 1964: 127)—is not inevitable. The problem that exercises Beauvoir in *Pyrrhus and Cinéas* can be viewed from the opposite, natal direction. In pursuing a certain project, I do not take it up just out of nowhere—as if I found myself in a blank space where indefinitely many possibilities are open to me and I must pick one in a kind of random plump. I am always-already pursuing particular projects, upholding certain meanings, which I have taken on from the others around me who have influenced me. For instance, I (AS) have always read voraciously, something I took over from my mother, long before I realized that it was from her that I had taken it. In pursuing particular projects, we are always, however unknowingly, carrying forward meanings embraced by others before us. Further, since they had acquired their projects and meanings from others who came before them, we are always carrying forward webs of meaning that have come down to us along chains of predecessors.[10] My death, then, threatens not meanings that I as a single individual have invented but webs of meaning I have inherited from others. If I find the prospect of the loss of this web of meanings threatening, this is, at least in part, because of my attachment to what I have inherited and to the others before and around me whose meanings I want to see kept alive.

Had Beauvoir considered birth, then, things would have looked different to her, and the same goes for Camus. For him, the world around us is inherently meaningless, and each of us has the daunting task of creating meaning from scratch. But as in fact we always-already inhabit webs of meanings inherited from others before us, the world—as one that is shared, that we inhabit together and not in isolation—is not meaningless after all. In our everyday lives, the world that we live in is suffused with shared meanings through and through. To be born is to come into the world in places within networks of relationships from which we receive and inherit values and meanings. If mortality is connected with meaning-creation for Camus and Beauvoir, natality is connected with meaning-*reception*.

I have argued that there has been a historical bias towards death and not birth, and that existentialism illustrates this bias in one of its more recent incarnations. It might be objected that this focus on death alone, not birth, is not an arbitrary bias but justified. But if this focus is said to be justified just because we are mortal and need to come to terms with death, this is question-begging, presuming that we have no equivalent need to come to terms with having been born and its ramifications. However, three further arguments purporting to justify a concentration on death are made by Françoise Dastur ([1994] 1996).

First, Dastur suggests that death is at the origin of culture: it is distinctive of human beings compared to animals that we live with the dead—memorializing, mourning, burying them; narrating our ancestors' history and mythology; and so on. Thus 'every culture is in a broad sense culture of the dead' (1996: 9). This is also true in that we all carry on the unfinished projects of those who came before us (67–8). Second, the preoccupation with death has run through Western culture ever since the Epic of Gilgamesh, for Dastur, because the awareness and fear of death are fundamental to human life qua finite. Consequently, the 'conquering of death is the aim not only of metaphysics . . . , but also of religion . . . ; of science . . . and . . . of the whole of human culture' (1–2). Third, Dastur holds, the fear of death troubles us more deeply than the mystery of birth, understood as the insoluble question of why there is something rather than nothing. 'The question of the origin of things is indeed a source of disquietude for our understanding, but the question of their end constitutes the torment of our entire being' (36).

All three arguments for focusing on death and not birth may be contested. First, human beings have always handled birth in culturally variable ways and given birth cultural meanings, just as they have with death (Held 1989). And while the living do carry forward the projects of previous generations, and in this sense always exist together with the dead, this is also bound up with our natality, whereby we are born into and receive the heritage of those who have preceded us. Both birth and death underpin intergenerational transmission.

Second, human life is finite in two directions—beginning at birth and ending in death—so that if we are indeed inescapably aware of being finite, this need not orientate us exclusively towards death.[11] To be sure, we do not relate to birth and death symmetrically. We fear death, or at least many people do, as we do not fear having been born. (By fear of death here I mean fear of non-existence, of being dead, rather than fears of being injured, sick, hurt, and dying—much as we may fear those too.) For several reasons, fearing one's death makes sense as fearing one's birth does not. (i) One's death lies ahead, in the future, whereas one's birth is in the past. But in fear's intentional structure as an emotion, what we fear is the possibility of bad events occurring in the future, whether imminently or in the longer term. So, fear of one's birth makes no emotional sense. Moreover (ii) my death will deprive me of existence and its good aspects, whereas my birth initiated me into existence (Nagel [1970] 1979), and the time before my birth did not yet deprive me of anything as I did not then exist. Here again, fear of one's birth makes no sense.[12] But, although we do not fear having been born, birth may still figure into our existence and orientate our lives in its own set of ways, differently from death. And birth's particular ways of orientating us may also be important and pervasive.

Third, if being born is not fearful, it is at least disquieting, as Dastur herself admits; it may trouble us deeply. When I think of the long swathes of time that elapsed before I was there, I can feel disturbed and perplexed. How could I ever not have been there? When I try to grasp this past time, I surreptitiously presuppose that I was already there perceiving it. And the transition from not having been there to being there seems so absolute that it is incomprehensible how I can have crossed it—how, having previously not existed, I could ever have come to exist. The anxieties aroused by these perplexities are not the same as fear of death, but they remain real and (I'll argue later) play a more pervasive role in our existence than has been acknowledged.

While death has been foregrounded and not birth, then, it is not obvious that this exclusive focus on death is rationally justified. My account of being born in the rest of this book will, I hope, further substantiate the thought that birth as well as death is important for human existence, so that both 'ends' of human life deserve attention.

III. Reception and Inheritance

Secreted within Camus's and Beauvoir's death-focused views, we begin to see some ways in which being born also structures human existence. We *receive* and inherit horizons of meaning and value by birth, through the networks of relationships and the locations in society into which birth places us. Death threatens these relationships and the meanings and values that express them: thus, death threatens us, together, at least as much as it threatens me, individually. In addition, to be born is for much of my horizon of meaning and value to be *given* to me by others who are there in the world before and alongside me, rather than my creating this horizon single-handed.

Christina Schües for this reason describes birth as 'generative'. To be born is to come *from* other people—from my mother and the chain of her foremothers, but also others who make up the relational network around me. And to be born is to come from some*where*—from the history of relationships and culture to which these people have belonged (2016: 339).[13] Cutting across these vectors along which we inherit our horizon from the past, to be born is also to come into the world alongside a given set of others, my contemporaries, all of whom have been generated within roughly the same twenty-five years.[14] The net result is that, although we are meaning-making beings, none of us makes the meanings of our lives alone or independently of others. Being born, we are placed from the start into already-existing horizons of meaning which we directly begin to imbibe and inhabit prior to any possibility of reshaping, recreating, or revising them.

As Derrida says, then: 'That we are heirs does not mean that we have or that we receive this or that, some inheritance that enriches us one day with this or that, but that the being of what we are is first of all inheritance, whether we like it or know it or not' (1994: 54). What we inherit constitutes us, rather than being added accidentally to a pre-existing individual who can exercise free choice with respect to it, take or leave and chop and change it. But this need not mean that by virtue of being born we are doomed to perpetuate the past unchanged. I may try to do so, yet even then I will inevitably end up modifying the meaning of the practices, ideas, or values which

I wish to perpetuate, just by holding them intact while other circumstances change. Having taken on my mother's project of reading voraciously, I (AS) try to keep this project alive today in the same shape it had for her—reading physical books from the library. In doing so, I increasingly set my version of reading against that encouraged in the world around me, in which reading is more and more carried out virtually. My mother, though, had no such preference for physical as opposed to virtual reading, as she lived almost wholly before the advent of the internet. To carry forward what we receive by birth, then, is inescapably to modify it; we cannot reproduce or perpetuate the past unaltered.

Moreover, taking what Derrida calls a 'reactionary' attitude to one's past—trying to keep it going unchanged—is only one possible way of doing the inheriting that one cannot but do anyway. One might instead want or set out to change one's inheritance. One might become unhappy to have been born into privilege and to have inherited ideas and assumptions which are bound up with it, thereby becoming critical of one's inheritance and wishing to revise it. Or one might be unhappy to have been born into circumstances that are oppressive, disadvantageous, harsh, or difficult and to have acquired an inheritance that is indexed to those circumstances. Along these and other routes one can become motivated to change one's inheritance, whether radically or subtly, minutely or extensively. Yet if we do so we are still, necessarily, carrying our inheritance forward as well. Just as one cannot carry forward a heritage without modifying it, reciprocally one cannot turn against and re-make a heritage without still perpetuating it to some degree, if only by inhabiting it as that which one seeks to re-make.

In all this, it is important to remember that we do not all inhabit our inheritances easily or comfortably, or inherit one single culture. We can be uneasily positioned in and between two or more inherited horizons, as are US Latina women who, according to Maria Lugones, Gloria Anzaldúa, Mariana Ortega, and others, not infrequently feel that they are 'world-travellers', negotiating between different, conflicting cultures and rarely feeling peacefully at home in one single way of life.[15] On the one hand, the 'world-travelling' situation of US Latina women illuminates the heterogeneity of all cultures. Even those who feel like comfortable members of a single culture actually inherit many uneven, variable strands of meaning, the more so because all cultures overlap with others and none are self-contained. To that extent we all 'travel' amongst inherited worlds. On the other hand, the situation of US Latina women is specific: because it is marked by the history of conflicts of power between US and Latin American cultures, US Latina women find themselves navigating between worlds that are opposed and not merely different, and that differ as (entire) worlds rather than as diverse strands of a single, if uneven and internally variegated, world. Sometimes, then, the differences within and between cultures are muted, subtle, and easily overlooked, but at other times they rise to become stark and conflictual.

There are also circumstances in which what one inherits by birth is a state of complete dispossession and alienation. As Orlando Patterson argues (1983), those born into slavery in the US suffered 'natal alienation', since slaves' only legally recognized kin ties were to their owners, and their natal ties of bodily kinship with other slaves were unrecognized and routinely violated. Thus, slaves were alienated from networks of kinship and descent along which cultural meanings, values, and goods could be transmitted to them; to be born a slave was to inherit only this alienated status. Yet the very idea of 'inheriting' may seem out-of-place here. Can one meaningfully be said to 'inherit' if what is inherited is the absence of an inheritance?

Saidiya Hartman suggests that the notion of inheritance still applies in such cases in *Lose Your Mother*, her exploration of the 'afterlives' of slavery. She writes of the 'tribe of the Middle Passage', 'the tribe of those stolen from their natal land, stripped of their "country marks", and severed from their kin ... The slave was as an orphan ... The only sure inheritance passed from one generation to the next was this loss, and it defined the tribe' (2007: 103). What slaves inherited was the state and status of having lost their natal ties, and people today who are descended from slaves continue to inherit and wrestle with the effects and ramifications of that earlier state of loss. Even when what is inherited is loss, then, this is still an inheritance. As this shows, inheritance is not always seamless and straightforward: it can be fractured and complicated, marked by deep losses and scars. And, again, these losses can motivate us to question our inheritances, look for ways to take them forward differently, and so pass on to others more positive and enabling inheritances than we received ourselves.

IV. Natality and Vulnerability

We have started to see some ways in which being born is not necessarily a wholly positive condition. By birth, we may inherit meanings, practices, and values that we come to wish to reject or modify, or that present us with difficulties and conflicts; or we may be born into conditions of radical dispossession. Robin May Schott remarks on the negative side of natality in critical response to Jantzen, objecting that Jantzen tends to polarize birth and death and heap all positive value onto the former (Schott 2010a: 8). Schott responds that death and mortality have positive dimensions, while birth and natality have negative ones. Whereas Jantzen treats natality and mortality as opposites, for Schott understanding human existence requires a unified frame of reference that spans birth *and* death and locates human existence between these two poles.

Regarding death's positive aspect, Schott argues that our mortality—the fact that we will die and our awareness of this, however tacit—is a necessary condition of our lives, relationships, and activities having meaning for us (2010a: 3–6). She draws on Beauvoir's novel *All Men are Mortal* and restates its conclusion thus.[16] If I had infinite time before me, I could make no real commitment to any one project or relationship rather than another, for I would know that I can return to any or all of the others in the future. Rather than valuing X and not Y and thereby making this valuation into an important part of who I am, I would only be able to dally indifferently with every option in turn. On this kind of existentialist position, without my actively chosen commitment and investment, nothing that I do or am has meaning. Hence if I were immortal, and so could make no real commitments, my existence would be empty.

I have some doubts about this view. Much of what is meaningful for us and that we value is handed down to us by others who have preceded us, prior to any choices on our part. When we make choices and commitments, we do so having already internalized and taken on a whole horizon of meaning and value without choosing it, and this horizon motivates and animates whatever choices we do make. Nonetheless, the awareness that we will die intensifies the value to us of the things that we already value. Knowing that we will not enjoy these things for ever but will lose them at death encourages us to appreciate and savour them now, and makes us more vividly aware of what we value in them. Or as Andrew Marvell put it: 'Had we but world enough and time,/ This coyness, Lady, were no crime.... But at my back I always hear/ Time's winged chariot hurrying near...Thy beauty shall no more be found;/ Nor, in thy marble vault, shall sound/ My echoing song...Now, therefore,...let us sport us while we may' ([1681] 1972: 51). Unless Marvell already wanted to 'sport' with his mistress, though, there would be nothing for the passage of time and the approach of death to make more urgent. Death does not create value altogether, but it can enhance our appreciation of it.[17]

To this extent Schott is right that mortality can play a positive role in our lives. Even so, mortality can only play this positive role because it has a more fundamentally negative significance. It is only because death will—negatively—deprive me forever of what I value and care about that the awareness of death can bring home to me that I must appreciate these things now, while I can. It is in our reaction against the negative significance of death that our appreciation of the meaning and value of our lives can positively be heightened, as we gain a richer sense of what we were always-already caught up in valuing anyway. But those valuings in which we were already engaged were ones we inherited from and through birth. Birth, then, remains linked with the positive phenomena of meaning and value more directly than death is.

Schott forwards a network of further concepts to characterize human existence as it elapses between the two ends of birth and death. These concepts are *change*; *separateness* or *difference* (between different human individuals), and thus also *plurality*; and *vulnerability*. All have connections with natality, Schott contends, but they also entail that natality is not solely positive, in at least three ways:

1. The passage from one's mother's womb into the common world is tumultuous, dramatic, and difficult.[18]

2. To be born, for Schott, is to enter a condition of plurality (as for Arendt and Cavarero) in which, concomitantly, separations and dis-agreements, even violent conflicts, are always possible. Therefore, Schott argues, violence is not rightly located exclusively on the side of death and mortality, for risks of violence flow out of the plurality that is part of our natal condition.

3. Being born entails vulnerability. Schott reminds us that sometimes babies are born unwelcome and unwanted or into conditions of poverty, abuse, illness, and misery. That is, to be born is—negatively—to be vulnerable to coming into miserable, unfortunate and oppressive locations in the world (Schott 2010a: 10–11). The kinds of vulnerability at work here are several, as I will now explore.

Schott makes these claims about vulnerability against the background of an explosion of feminist writing on vulnerability, arising from several sources, including Butler's work (2004, 2009).[19] Within this literature, different dimensions along which we are vulnerable have been identified and analysed, and different categorizations of vulnerability set out. I want to revisit some of these distinctions so as to identify how certain aspects of our vulnerability are connected with birth. In this regard I shall distinguish between vulnerability in being born and vulnerability by virtue of being born. Thereafter, in Sec. V, I'll return to how far birth has negative or positive significance for our existence.

As Butler's work has heavily influenced this field of feminist discussion, let's begin with her. Butler maintains that vulnerability is part of our ontological or existential condition. It is not only specific groups—women, say, or ageing or disabled people—who are vulnerable and need protection from others who are less vulnerable. Rather, we are all vulnerable and this is an ineradicable feature of human existence. For Butler, our existential vulnerability has at least three facets.

(1) We are vulnerable because we are embodied and therefore have material needs—for example for food, drink, warmth, shelter, rest—that can go unmet (Butler 2004: 26). Our bodies can be injured or wounded (*vulnus*) or suffer pain; we can suffer from bodily illnesses and impairments; and, through illness, injury, or our needs being unmet, we can die.

(2) We are vulnerable because as inhabitants of a shared world we are permanently exposed to the actions, potentially harmful, of the others with whom we are in relations (26). These include the people we know intimately, on which personal level 'we are emotionally and psychologically vulnerable to others in myriad ways: to loss and grief; to neglect, abuse and lack of care; to rejection, ostracism, and humiliation' (as Mackenzie, Rogers, and Dodds put it; 2006: 1). At the other end of the spectrum, the actions of indefinitely many other barely known, unknown, and anonymous others can, despite their relative distance, still impact on us.

(3) Our relations with others are always structured in definite ways socially and politically, and we are vulnerable to the effects of the unequal distributions of power which these social structures can and often do enshrine (Butler 2004: 26–7). We are thereby vulnerable to exploitation, oppression, manipulation, enslavement, the colonization of our native lands, and many other forms of social inequality.

The above are not necessarily the only three sources of existential vulnerability: change and chance, plausibly, are amongst the others. But let's stick with the sources to which Butler attends: embodiment, relationality, and power. Now, talk of vulnerability may seem merely to put a new spin on older notions that harm and suffering are bad and should be minimized. However, there are several new aspects of and reasons for the feminist turn to vulnerability. Historically, the prevailing view—in Hobbes, for instance—has been that it is undesirable to be vulnerable, and that political arrangements ought to reduce our vulnerability. It is presupposed here that the ideal human condition is one of *in*vulnerability, sovereign control over one's own life, actions, and body. Feminist theorists have criticized this presupposition, seeing it as part of the broader over-valorization of autonomy in political thought.[20] In contrast, Butler and others regard human beings as inherently needy, fragile, exposed to others, and needing their care. Neediness and fragility are not regrettable deviations from the ideal human condition but just are the human condition. The ethical goal, therefore, is not to eradicate vulnerability—which would be impossible anyway—but to acknowledge its pervasiveness, and so become better able to respond to others' vulnerability with care.

Some vulnerability theorists, however, have questioned the focus on universal, existential kinds of vulnerability which everyone shares (see, e.g. Oliver 2018: ch. 5). Some groups are *specially* vulnerable to particular types of harm, and it is these areas of special vulnerability that matter ethically, to which we particularly need to respond (the phrase 'special vulnerability' is from Scully 2014). The young, the old, and people with disabilities and ill-health conditions are cases in point. Infants and young children, for instance, are especially vulnerable to being abused or neglected by their parents or care-givers because of their helplessness and dependence on these adult figures. If we treat everyone as being just as vulnerable as everyone else, then we risk overlooking the particular needs for care of some groups of people and spreading our care more evenly than the ethical situation warrants.

Special vulnerabilities do not always arise entirely out of inherent features of the individuals that have them. We can distinguish 'inherent' and 'situational' sources of vulnerability (Mackenzie, Rogers and Dodds 2014b). Here 'situational' essentially means 'social': social factors can produce vulnerabilities in particular groups and individuals and can also exacerbate inherent vulnerabilities. In the US, for instance, black people (like people of African descent everywhere) are inherently more vulnerable than white people to certain genetically inherited illnesses such as sickle-cell anaemia. But situationally—that is, socially—black Americans are also more vulnerable than whites to many illnesses including HIV, stroke, diabetes, and many cancers. The social factors involved are multiple: compared with whites, black Americans tend to have worse-quality health care, lower incomes and lower levels of education, and face worse conditions at work and in their home neighbourhoods (CDC 2005).

Given the many axes of inequality in the world, then, many groups of people are rendered specially vulnerable in certain respects (for instance, women are more vulnerable than men to being raped). There is no simple divide between vulnerable and non-vulnerable people but an uneven, mottled distribution of various areas of greater and lesser vulnerability. Also, relatively few vulnerabilities are entirely inherent.[21] Even with those that are largely inherent, such as those of infancy, social components usually play a part too. Inherently, infants are especially vulnerable to abuse and neglect, but this is regularly exacerbated by customs, norms, and laws that entitle adults to use violence against children.

To the extent that the distribution of vulnerabilities is social, it arises out of our ontological vulnerability to the effects of social and political relations. That vulnerability makes it possible for us to be affected by social divisions such that we become more vulnerable to others in certain domains, depending what social groups we belong to (e.g. gender inequality renders women especially vulnerable to rape). Given the resulting uneven distribution of areas of vulnerability amongst different groups, Butler advocates working towards as equal an overall distribution of vulnerability as possible. 'Normatively construed', she says, 'there ought to be a more inclusive and egalitarian way of recognizing precariousness, and... this should take the form of concrete social policy regarding issues such as shelter, work, food, medical care, and legal status' (Butler 2009: 13; as here, Butler sometimes uses 'precariousness' to mean 'inherent vulnerability').[22] The proposed strategy has two fronts: to reduce as far as possible socially produced disparities in vulnerability, and to recognize dimensions of inherent vulnerability and respond to them with appropriate care.

We may now turn to vulnerability's connections with being born. First, the special vulnerability of infants and children arises out of their having been born in the shape it has within the human species: namely, that we are born almost wholly helpless, with very undeveloped bodily and mental powers, into a lengthy period of dependence on adult care. Babies and infants' helplessness makes them vulnerable to their bodily needs going unmet or being misunderstood; to injury; to illnesses that may not be easily diagnosed; to feelings of suffering and frustration; and to waves of intense impulse, need, and sensation of which they can make little sense and which they have little power to regulate. Babies' and infants' correspondingly near-total dependence on adult care renders them vulnerable to failures, mistakes, indifference, inattention and malice on the part of their care-givers. These vulnerabilities stem from two basic sources of human vulnerability: embodiment and relationality. We are vulnerable to others harming us right through our lives, corporeally and emotionally; but in infants and children this vulnerability is particularly visible and acute (Cavarero 2009: 30).

Our openness to the effects of relationships with others, including harmful effects, is thus especially pronounced when we are infants. This is not only because of our dependency and helplessness but also because we are so unformed as infants. Consequently, our first relationships mark us very heavily: their impact forms us, as no later relationships can ever do as straightforwardly, because when we enter into the latter we have undergone at least some formation already. Being as formative as they are, our first relationships establish propensities in us to form particular kinds of further relationships with others: if my first care-giver was ambivalent about me, I may well become disposed to keep forming relationships with others who are similarly ambivalent about me (see Karen 1994). Thus, our vulnerability as infants to the impact of our relationships with others carries forwards into our degrees of vulnerability to being harmed by others, and in what respects, later in life. Because we are unformed as infants, we are specially vulnerable at this time to harm—the harms to which we are exposed form, affect, and imprint us, and get right inside us—and in turn we become vulnerable to suffering the same harms again in adulthood, as we repeat with successive others our earliest, most formative patterns of relationship.

Infants are also specially vulnerable to the impact of social power relations, which from the very start are conveyed to them through their caregivers' behaviour along with countless other features of their surroundings: what languages are spoken around them, what sort of houses they live in, what toys they are given (e.g. dolls or cars), and so on. Butler interprets this kind of infantile vulnerability as follows. Infants from the outset need and desire to be recognized, affirmed as members of the world they find themselves in. But social frameworks always limit what kinds of people and activities can be recognized or found intelligible and what falls outside the bounds of conceivability. So, infants adapt, making themselves become intelligible in the available ways—say, as a boy or girl, whatever that is taken to involve. Furthermore, infants have no capacity yet to criticize, or distance themselves from, the social norms in force around them (Butler 1997: 7–8; 2004: 27). Consequently, infants assimilate and learn to comply with social norms before they ever come to criticize them: the reception of norms precedes any possibility of their criticism.

Again, then, our vulnerability to the effects of social power relations is most pronounced in our infancy and childhood, for we cannot yet criticize these relations and we desire to be recognized under whatever terms society affords. And again, this special vulnerability arises because we are born, in the shape this takes for human beings, where we begin life highly unformed and malleable by the world around us. We remain vulnerable to social power throughout our lives, but less acutely than in infancy and childhood. For by now we have acquired greater capacities for taking critical distance from our surroundings, and we already bear within ourselves a level of formation by prior power relations, carried forwards from childhood, which has its own resilience. The power relations that imprinted us earliest tend to be those to which we are most 'stubbornly attached', in Butler's phrase (1997: Ch. 1). Our adult levels of vulnerability to different forms of social power are thus patterned on what we were exposed to during our period of childhood vulnerability.

Infants and children are vulnerable in the preceding ways as a consequence of—by virtue of—being born. The patterns of adult vulnerability which these childhood vulnerabilities bequeath to us are thus also indirect consequences of our being born. Both can be distinguished from our vulnerability just *in* being born. To be born is, necessarily, to come into the world in some particular location within it—in a given country and community, family and line of ancestry; into a given economic status; as a member of one racial category or another (in societies that use such categories); and so on. We are not born abstract individuals who then, additionally, occupy social, cultural, geographical locations; rather, we are born as located individuals. This is an intrinsic part of what it is to be born—to come not, somehow, into the world *in toto* but into a definite body, place, set of relationships, and situation in society, culture, and history. But the locations we are born into are not equal. Some locations are more advantageous or disadvantageous than others, under various uneven, mottled distributions. These inequalities are largely social artefacts, although they can also have inherent dimensions, as when someone is born with a body whose genetic make-up raises her breast cancer risk compared to the general population. The second link between birth and vulnerability, then, is that to be born is to be vulnerable to arriving in the world in a more-or-less disadvantaged place within it. If we reduced social inequalities, then our vulnerability in being born would be correspondingly lessened.

One might object that our vulnerability to inequality of locations has no special connection with birth other than that birth is the first of indefinitely many occasions when an inequality in which we are located affects us. But because our natal circumstances and relationships stamp us especially heavily, the beginning carries particular weight for our whole lives. Its effects are enduring. This is not to deny that people can be born very disadvantaged yet still manage to forge a good life. A fictional instance is Peter Carey's character Jack Maggs (1997), born in one of the most ill-starred of all early nineteenth-century London addresses, Pepper Alley Stairs. Maggs soon becomes a skilled thief but is caught, convicted, and deported to New South Wales—where, however, he becomes rich through a successful career making bricks. Maggs has transcended his inauspicious beginning in geographic and economic terms; yet his past remains with him and continues to trouble him—in memory, nightmares, and when he is under hypnosis. Moreover, Maggs's story illustrates how our very possibilities for transcending our natal locations are constrained by those same locations and their effects and ramifications. Maggs could only succeed in Australia, leaving his past behind, because he was deported there, which in turn happened only because he had had to take up thieving for lack of any other viable livelihood around Pepper Alley Stairs. Maggs's birthplace shapes the very pathway along which he becomes able to make a partial escape from its disadvantages. In short, the effects of our natal locations are never readily left behind.

Not all the ways in which we are existentially vulnerable stem directly from our being born. We are vulnerable because we are embodied and open to relationships with others and to social power arrangements, all enduring features of our existence right through the life-span. So, it would be oversimplifying to claim that human vulnerability derives in a linear way from natality. Even so, our three sources of existential vulnerability each have connections with birth. (I) Our vulnerabilities in respect of (1) embodiment, (2) relationality and (3) power are writ large in infancy and childhood—that is, because we are born. Further, the effects on us of specific relationships and power arrangements when we are children—effects that go as deep as they do because of our natal vulnerability—shape where, how, and how much we are vulnerable to the effects of particular kinds of personal and social relations later in life. (II) We are vulnerable to being born in disadvantageous locations (3) socially and in terms of (1) what bodies we are born with and (2) what relationships we are born into. And these locations exert lifelong effects on us, not only because birth is the temporal starting-point from which our lives unfold along determinate pathways but also because of our childhood openness to formation. Here again, our vulnerability in being born affects how we remain vulnerable across our lives, while these two sorts of vulnerability—(I) and (II)—intersect. Birth does not cause vulnerability in any linear way, but natal vulnerability nonetheless shapes, along several criss-crossing routes, how our later-life vulnerabilities manifest themselves. Overall, the connections between birth and vulnerability are sufficiently rich and multi-faceted that we can only fully appreciate the extent and nature of our vulnerability by considering it together with birth.[23]

V. Vulnerability and Negativity

Schott saw birth's connection with vulnerability as one of its negative aspects. But *is* vulnerability a negative condition? Perhaps; on the face of it, to be *vuln*erable is to be woundable, hurtable, harmable, and liable to suffer, even to the point of death (consequently, some authors connect vulnerability with mortality: e.g. Nussbaum 2006: 132, Rogers 2014: 75). Some theorists therefore object to what they see as the unduly negative tenor of the recent attention to vulnerability. For example, Bonnie Honig objects that, in foregrounding our shared human vulnerability, Butler espouses a 'mortalist humanism' (Honig 2013: 17), and neglects what 'natalists' attend to: pleasure, appetite, abundance—our potentials for bodily flourishing, enrichment, expansion in power, enjoyment. That is, perhaps the focus on vulnerability is just a new guise of the longstanding preoccupation with mortality. And perhaps this highlights the riskiness and insecurity of our existence to the neglect of our positive capacities for flourishing and expansion in vitality.

However, some vulnerability theorists argue that although historically vulnerability has mainly been construed negatively, as by Hobbes, in fact vulnerability is normal, unavoidable, and not in itself bad. Rather, it is ambiguous: one can be wounded by others *or* receive care from them (Cavarero 2009). To be vulnerable is to be open to being *either* harmed *or* benefited (Gilson 2013: 15).[24] We are intrinsically and fundamentally open to others and to the outer world so that we can be, and continually are, either harmed or benefited by them. We cannot be as open as we are to being harmed without also being open to positive and beneficial effects. Our bodily needs can go unmet, but equally they can be met and our bodies can be enriched, pleased, and delighted. Besides being able to be injured, our bodies can be healed, strengthened, and their powers expanded, and they can prosper and gain in vitality. Others may neglect, reject, or abandon us; but they can also care for and attend to us, love us and foster our well-being.

Social arrangements may promote and cement inequality, but they can also promote equality and ensure the conditions of people's flourishing. Indeed, this Janus-faced situation is what gives vulnerability its normative force, Erinn Gilson argues (2013: 15). If someone is vulnerable to a given harm, others have grounds to respond to that person with care only because that person can also be benefited and protected from harm—whereas if the harm were inevitable, nothing could be done.

Jackie Leach Scully objects that we do not ordinarily say that people are 'vulnerable' to being healthy or well off. In everyday language, to be vulnerable is to be liable to suffer from things that are bad (2006: 205). But perhaps that is merely an embedded legacy of the traditional view that vulnerability is undesirable and invulnerability ideal. Erinn Gilson therefore urges us to change *vulnerability*'s meaning so that it is ambiguous rather than largely negative. On the other hand, perhaps the traditional bias towards self-sufficiency is embedded in the very fact that our openness to being harmed or benefited by others is characterized as vulnerability, where given its history this term emphasizes our openness to harm. Moreover, plausibly the weight of history and past usage is such that *vulnerability* has, and is liable to retain, the negative valence that Scully points out. Perhaps, then, the ambiguous, Janus-faced condition that Gilson and others call 'vulnerability' would be better described under a more neutral category, as when Butler suggests that vulnerability is really a basic openness to others (2009: 33–4).

Schematically, then, we may: (a) foreground vulnerability as a primarily negative condition of harmability; (b) take vulnerability to be primarily negative but therefore caution against focussing on it (as does, e.g. Honig); (c) re-interpret vulnerability as an ambiguous condition (e.g. Gilson); (d) take our condition to be ambiguous but call it something other than vulnerability ('openness', perhaps). Or—my preference—we may (e) take our condition to be ambiguous; call its negative side vulnerability; agree that it is worth emphasizing vulnerability because of its normative force; but qualify that vulnerability is just one side of our broader ambiguous condition.

Regarding vulnerability's normative force, I agree with Gilson and Butler that our vulnerability to unequal social power relations obliges us to reduce these inequalities, while people's existential vulnerabilities oblige us to respond to them with care. Further obligations arise out of our vulnerability, as children, to being formed by power relations and attendant frameworks of meaning before we acquire any capacities to question them. For these frameworks often make sense of the inequalities with which they are bound up by justifying them (e.g. rationalizing women's vulnerability to rape through ideas that men are naturally predatory).[25] As we internalize such frameworks, our capacities to respond to others' vulnerability become correspondingly diminished. For example, if we internalize a belief that when people are homeless it is their own fault, the result of their own poor choices, then this diminishes our capacity to respond with care to homeless people we meet on the street (see Gilson 2011: 311, 317–18). Thus, our obligation of care gives us a further obligation to develop our capacities to take critical distance from existing frameworks of meaning: to learn when and how to be unfaithful to these frameworks, despite having inherited and become attached to them.

For Schott, birth's connection with vulnerability is one of its negative aspects. But this negative aspect is embedded in a broader ambiguity of being born. Being born not only renders us vulnerable to harms but also enables us, positively, to enjoy the goods of existence. This positive potential in being born is just as essential to it as the negative one. To be born is to be liable to come into the world in disadvantageous or beneficial locations—or, more often, locations with a mix of both. To begin life as an infant who is highly receptive to the world, culture and other people is to be open, not only to being harmed, but also to being benefited, enriched, and empowered by them. So, when Schott says that by birth we become vulnerable to harms without also saying that birth gives us access to benefits, she paints birth in an unduly pessimistic light. I note this partly because it is one manifestation of a broader pessimistic tendency in some current thinking around birth. Another manifestation is David Benatar's much-discussed book *Better Never To Have Been*, to which I now briefly turn because of its pertinence to how far being born is something negative or positive.[26]

Benatar's core argument is that it is always wrong to bring a new person into life by procreating because we thereby harm that person, causing them to suffer pains (or injuries, harms, etc.) that they would not otherwise have suffered, having not otherwise existed at all. But, Benatar argues, one cannot rightly reply that we equally benefit the person given life by enabling them to experience pleasures and enjoy benefits (rewarding relationships and activities, etc.) that they could not have enjoyed had they remained non-existent. For had the person never come to exist, they would not have been deprived of these things: to be deprived of anything one must first exist (Benatar 2006: 30). Thus, for Benatar there is an asymmetry between the pleasures and pains incumbent on existence, such that coming into existence is always harmful to a person who does so.

Along with some other critics, I am not convinced about this asymmetry. Let's for now assume that what is good and bad about existence and non-existence can be adequately captured under the simplifying rubric of pleasures and pains.[27] Benatar then argues for the asymmetry as follows. When we compare: result (ai) of procreation, the presence of pain for the person born, which is bad, with result (bi) of non-procreation, the absence of pain for the person who would otherwise have been born, which is good; and compare result (aii) of procreation, the presence of pleasure for the one born, which is good, with result (bii) of non-procreation, the absence of pleasure for the one who would otherwise have been born, which is not bad (or is neither good nor bad); then we find that the balance favours non-procreation (2006: 38–41). But as Elizabeth Harman objects:

> If we are willing to grant that the absence of something that would have been bad for someone, is good for him (…even in a world where he doesn't exist), then it seems that the absence of something that would have been good for him, [must also be] bad for him [and not merely neutral] (…even in a world where he doesn't exist).   (Harman 2009: 785)

We might also think that pleasures weigh more heavily on the positive scale than mere absences of pain. In that case, to quote Brian McLean this time:

> [E]xistence has an advantage over non-existence, at least provided that existence…contain[s] enough pleasures. Presumably we would have to look at how much pain and pleasure is in X's life, and under what distribution, to get an overall judgment on whether it was better for X to have been born…. [F]or many…lives, it would be [better] to have been born than not to have been born. This is, I think, the intuitive view: we think that it's better for us to have existed if the good in our lives outweighs the bad.   (2015: 86–7)

To be sure, in some human lives suffering unfortunately outweighs flourishing. But given the flaws in Benatar's reasoning this generates moral grounds not to avoid anyone ever being born but, rather, to respond with appropriate care to our inherent differences in vulnerability and to endeavour to bring in egalitarian social arrangements that redistribute (situational) vulnerabilities as evenly as possible. That is: being born does make us vulnerable to harms as well as open to being benefited, so that, for each of us, it is possible that the harms may outweigh the benefits. This creates a moral case for trying to ensure instead that the benefits outweigh the harms, moving towards the goal of making as many lives as possible into ones that are better lived than not lived.

As we saw earlier, Schott argues that we should not idealize or romanticize natality but acknowledge its negative aspects. I agree. However, the negative aspect on which I have focused—vulnerability—goes hand-in-hand with a positive aspect of birth. To be born is to come into the world and thereby become susceptible to various harms, but concomitantly to become able to enter into enriching, empowering, and rewarding relationships and endeavours of many kinds. Conversely, I have suggested, our mortality has such positive value as it does only because the awareness that our lives will end can enhance our appreciation of the value things already have for us. And we already value these things because we have inherited particular horizons of meaning and value from the relationships, cultures, and societies into which we were born. For these reasons, there is significantly more positive value in being born, and in our natal condition, than there is in death and mortality.

Notes

1. For two accounts of queer, especially lesbian, mothering, see Moraga (1997) and Park (2014).
2. Gatrell (2004) describes parenting as 'hard labour' and documents how much of it continues to be done by women.
3. For example, for Mary Rawlinson, 'everyone is born of a woman' (2016: 147). This, and with it everyone's broader dependence on the 'generativity of others', is one of two real universals, for Rawlinson (the other being that everyone must eat). Likewise, for Schües, our universal experience is to be born of a woman (2016: 404): '*all* human beings have been born of a woman' (445; my emphasis).
4. See Beresford (2017), Hempel (2016), and Obedin-Maliver and Makadon (2016). The best-known trans father is perhaps Thomas Beatie (see Beatie 2009). There have almost certainly been individuals throughout history who, while gestating and bearing children, identified as men. For instance, the Egyptian ruler Hapshethut (*c.* 1479–1458 BC), who had a daughter, presented herself as a man; see Brant (1997). For one study providing evidence of the existence of trans men in different historical periods, see Skidmore (2017).
5. Some trans theorists have found the phenomenological conception of the lived body helpful because, in Gayle Salamon's words, it 'offers an expansive conception of the body in which it is more than merely its materiality, emphasizing the importance of how one feels in and senses with and inhabits one's body. The

phenomenological claim... allows an understanding of the body as defined and constituted by what I feel and not simply what others see' (Salamon 2014; see also Salamon 2010: esp. Ch. 2, and, on phenomenology and trans thought more broadly, Rubin 1998).

6. However, perhaps the projects of thinking about birth philosophically and acknowledging birth's importance culturally give us interests in classifying human beings in terms of their birth-related and therefore reproductive capacities, i.e. by sex. If so, then recognizing natality would seem to be politically problematic from Butler's perspective, as it would entrench heterosexual privilege. I'll return to this issue in Chapter 7, and will argue that, although there is a real problem here, ultimately we can recognize natality in a non-heteronormative way.

7. On the centrality of death in Beauvoir's philosophical and literary work, see Marks (1972, 1986).

8. For the criticisms, see O'Brien (1981) and Said (2004: 204–24), and, for the qualified defences, Foley (2008: 15–16) and Kulkani (1997).

9. For Beauvoir, we must keep re-investing our creations with meaning to stop them falling back into being meaningless givens. But when we die, we can no longer continue this movement: 'I need them [others] because once I have surpassed my own goals, my actions will fall back upon themselves, inert and useless, if they have not been carried off toward a new future by new projects' (2004: 135). 'A man alone in the world would be paralyzed by the manifest vision of the vanity of all his goals. He would undoubtedly not be able to stand living. But man is not alone in the world.... As soon as a child has finished a drawing or a page of writing, he runs to show them to his parents.... From then on there is a real boat, a real horse there' (115–16). I thank Rafe MacGregor for alerting me to the structure of Beauvoir's argument here.

10. Contra Beauvoir: 'There exists no ready-made attachment between the world and me.... A country is not mine if I only grew there like a plant. What is built up...without me, is not mine' (2004: 92). Heinämää, however, argues that Beauvoir does recognize inheritance in *Ethics of Ambiguity* (2010: 137; see Beauvoir 1964: 77).

11. Of course we are finite in other ways too: for example, our cognitive and practical capacities are limited and we cannot be everywhere or exist at all times at once.

12. It may be argued that fear of death does not 'make sense' either but rather is simply instinctual (and so immune to rational arguments against fearing death such as Epicurus's). However, Nagel's deprivation account provides grounds to see the fear of death as rational.

13. Guenther likewise speaks of our 'being-*from*-others' by virtue of being born (2008), supplementing Heidegger's account of our being-*with*-others, and simultaneously expanding the import of his category of 'inheritance' or 'heritage'

(*Erbe*) (as when Heidegger refers to the possibilities that each Dasein has 'inherited' (*ererbten*), e.g. 1962: 435/384).

14. Schües sets out her picture, in part, as an extension of Husserl's 1930s work (Schües 2016: esp. Ch. IV). Here Husserl recognized that sense-constitution necessarily extends beyond the individual subject which, moreover, cannot include death or birth in its experience as they are at its limits. But birth and death are involved in the constitution of meaning *between* generations, into which each subject comes as an inheritor. As Johanna Oksala puts the point, reflecting on Anthony Steinbock's kindred version of generative phenomenology: 'Generative world constitution extends beyond and after the individual subject in a continuity of generations' (Oksala 2004: 20). Here birth and death count as not merely empirical events in the world but essential conditions of the constitution *of* the world of meaning. Specifically, birth and death are conditions of the diachronic and synchronic relationships through which we share, make, and pass on meanings and thus constitute this world (Schües 2016: 421).

15. See inter alia, Lugones (1989), Anzaldúa (1987), and Ortega (2001).

16. I interpret Beauvoir's novel differently; see Chapter 6.

17. Freud agrees: The 'transience of what is beautiful involves [no] loss in its worth. On the contrary, an increase! Transience value is scarcity value in time. Limitation in the possibility of an enjoyment raises the value of the enjoyment' ([1916] (1942): 305). However, for Freud, transience adds to both enjoyment or appreciation of value and value itself; I am claiming only the former.

18. Indeed, Otto Rank sees this exit as traumatic, as does Freud albeit differently; see Chapter 5.

19. Amongst them are Cavarero (2009), Drichel (2013a, b), Fineman (2008), Gilson (2011, 2013), Lloyd (2015), Mackenzie, Rogers, and Dodds (2014a, 2014b), Murphy (2011), Oliver (2018), Petherbridge (2016), Scully (2014) and Shildrick (2002).

20. See, e.g., Shildrick (2002: 71), Gilson (2011: 309–10), and Drichel (2013a: 5).

21. As Scully argues, in broad agreement with social theories of disability (e.g. Shakespeare 2006), social processes contribute to making impairments or ability differences into disabilities. For instance, currently having impaired vision (and wearing glasses) is not treated as a disability, unlike using a wheelchair or prosthetic leg.

22. Whereas Butler calls socially produced vulnerability 'precarity' (see Lloyd 2015).

23. I thank Veronica Vasterling for pushing me to clarify the relations between natality and vulnerability.

24. Shildrick (2002: esp. 85–6), Murphy (2011) and Petherbridge (2016) also aim to reconceive vulnerability as something more positive or 'ambivalent'.

25. Linda Alcoff points out a reason why our shared ways of making sense of forms of oppression tend to be justificatory: 'If...most people prefer to think of

themselves as moral or at least excusable in their actions, then in unjust societies those in dominant and privileged positions must be able to construct representations of themselves and others to support a fantasyland of moral approbation' (2007: 49).

26. Benatar's anti-natalism belongs within a broader set of anti-natalist political campaigns and activities; see, e.g. Gander (2017).

27. I also pass over the puzzle of how something can be good or bad for someone non-existent (to which of course Benatar offers answers).

3

Dependency, Relationality, Power, and Situatedness

In this chapter I look at four features of human existence: *dependency, relationality*, embeddedness in *social power*, and *situatedness*. I argue that all these features are connected with our being born: they either flow down from birth into the rest of our lives or they take the shape they do within our lives because we are born.

I. Dependency

In this section I explore how our dependency is connected with our being born, in the particular form that being born takes in the human species. I take up the idea that human beings are 'secondary nestlings', articulated by Stephen Jay Gould amongst others (1977: Ch. 8). On this basis I give an account of what I call our natal dependency, which I then connect with several further aspects of human dependency. In discussing the latter, I build on recent work in ethics which recognizes how deeply human beings are dependent on care, something long neglected in moral and political thought (Kittay 1999, MacIntyre 1999).

To be dependent is to be reliant on care or help from others to meet one's needs, develop, or function. Human infants are paradigm cases of dependent beings. Indeed, the helplessness of human babies is so pronounced that they have been called 'exterogestate' foetuses (Montagu [1971] 1986: 54–7). A weeks-old baby cannot sit or hold up her own head unaided, crawl or walk, stand, eat solid food, or hold objects, and has almost no voluntary control over her bodily movements. At a year old, most babies have gained some mastery of these things, but they still lack many basic abilities, including the abilities to speak and regulate their bowel and bladder movements. Babies depend on their care-givers—often their parents, especially their mothers—for all they cannot yet do themselves; for sleep regulation,

Being born: Birth and Philosophy. Alison Stone, Oxford University Press (2019). © Alison Stone.
DOI: 10.1093/oso/9780198845782.001.0001

food provision, cleaning, comfort when injured, care when sick, and more. Generally, children continue to depend heavily on care-givers in these and other ways until they are at least 4 or 5 years old and usually long after that. Consider, by contrast, puppies: they generally crawl by 2 weeks (equivalent to 3 months for humans), walk by 3 weeks (5 human months), gain some bladder and bowel control by 4 weeks (6 to 7 human months), and wean onto solid food by 8 weeks (13 human months), at which point they can be permanently separated from their mothers and siblings.

In addition, young humans remain dependent on older people for care and education right through childhood and juvenility (i.e. from 7 until puberty), often across adolescence, and sometimes into young adulthood. This reflects the high level of cognitive, emotional, and imaginative development that human beings have to reach: extended dependency is the trade-off for high levels of eventual skill. Putting all this together, compared to other animal species there is an especially large gap between humans' initial immaturity and their eventual powers, an especially long developmental journey to be made.

Regarding initial immaturity, zoologists and ethologists distinguish *precocial* species—whose offspring very soon after birth begin to move and fend for themselves—from *altricial* species—whose young at first are helpless and dependent on parental care. Altricial species include marsupials, songbirds, and some mammals, humans amongst them. Altriciality and precociality are matters of degree: dogs and humans alike count as altricial, but humans remain so for considerably longer, as we've seen. Within viviparous species, how far the young are altricial or precocial depends very largely on how developed foetuses' brains are at birth: the more developed the brain at birth, the more precocial the species. (In contrast, within oviparous species the key factor is how large and nutrient-rich an egg the mother-bird can produce.) Altriciality has the advantage that the brain can ultimately enlarge and develop further outside the womb than it could within uterine constraints, allowing for greater intelligence—but at the cost of greater vulnerability during the early helpless period.

Humanity's closest relatives—primates such as chimpanzees, orang-utans, and bonobos—are precocial. Indeed, most species that, like humans, produce few offspring, and have long uterine gestation periods, are precocial. So why are humans altricial? A widely accepted explanation is that humans are 'secondary nestlings', as zoologist Adolf Portmann initially phrased it ([1942] 1969: 65)—*secondarily* altricial. Having been precocial earlier in their evolutionary history, hominids evolved to become altricial because of the obstetric dilemma. As early hominids became bipedal, their pelvises and birth canals narrowed, at the same time as the human brain was expanding. The combined result was that, to pass along and out of the birth canal, human babies had to be born much earlier in their development, at 9 months, than would be needed for them to be born as precocial as our nearest primate neighbours (which would be at 18 to 21 months by Portmann's reckoning; 1969: 58). The result is a baby that, for its first year, is essentially a foetus outside the womb.[1]

Being only secondarily altricial, however, young humans share many features with young (precocial) primates. Both develop complex mental skills by learning them, at length, from first their parents or primary caregivers then, in later childhood, the wider social or kin group. It's often said that humans spend longer undergoing this learning than other primates: 'physically humans are slower developing,...and spend longer periods of their life history in infantile and child phases of life' (Crews 2003: 86). However, this should be set against the fact that humans have a longer average life-span than their closest primate relatives—70 or more years against 50 for chimpanzees. Even so, some hold that in humans the 'formative period and dependency on parents last longer proportionally' (Haag 1963: 76). Yet by one measurement, the proportion of life spent in immaturity actually lasts longer in chimpanzees: 10 years compared to 12 for humans (Haviland et al. 2017: 92). That measurement takes human immaturity to end at puberty, though. But in many societies human dependency and learning continue to some degree right up to young adulthood or beyond. Many social institutions and practices rest on high levels of skill, learning, and specialization, which extend the period of (formal or informal) education that is needed before people can fully enter into social life. And the cultural richness of human societies also calls for an extended learning period reaching past puberty, because each generation has much to inherit. To this extent, human dependency does last longer than that of other primates, not only absolutely but also as a proportion of the life-span.[2]

Now, arguably, our secondary altriciality is crucial to our status as meaning-making beings for whom culture is second nature. Because our brains are so undeveloped at birth, we encounter the world outside the maternal womb while most of our practical and mental capacities are still nascent (Portmann 1969: 79, 81). This opens up an increased margin in which our mental development can become shaped by the surrounding world. Human infants are therefore especially 'plastic' in the face of the world around them, especially open to and malleable by their circumstances.[3]

On this basis, the philosophical anthropologist Arnold Gehlen maintains that humans are specially open-ended, 'undetermined', and so 'world-open' beings ([1940] 1988: 24).[4] But in the specific way that Gehlen articulates this view, we are world-open (*weltoffen*), not primarily in the sense of being receptive to the already-existing cultures in which we are situated, but rather in being freely motivated to *create* culture. Gehlen thus prioritizes action (*handeln*) rather than reception (1988: 16). For him the infant is a *self-developing agent*, propelled to develop himself to overcome the peculiar vulnerability to injury and death which stems from his unformed, indefinite, unspecialized bodily and mental structure (27–8). Moreover, Gehlen claims that, because human babies are effectively born 'early' (following Portmann), they develop relatively freely from maternal influence. While the baby's cognitive and motor capacities are still incipient, he encounters the world directly—without mediation through the maternal body—which motivates him to make sense of things using his own resources (36–7). In sum, Gehlen downplays our dependence both on our mothers and on the already-existing cultures into which we are born.

Having said this, Gehlen also remarks that:

> If we agree with Portmann's description of the human being as a 'secondary nestling', then we must further say that not only maternal care, but also communicative contact with other humans, and indeed, even the indefinite open stimulation from . . . surroundings, all become 'obligatory functions of the entire ontogenesis'.   (37)

This suggests that, after all, human infants are primarily open to *receiving* care and culture. Being helpless, infants depend on their care-givers very heavily and, as all their bodily needs and impulses are at stake in this dependency, their attachment to these care-givers becomes immensely affectively charged. Because infants are also largely helpless cognitively, they become heavily guided by their care-givers in making sense of the world. For example, when an infant starts to speak, she speaks the language her care-givers speak, *because* they speak it, so that she can communicate with and understand them and because that language is there, in use around her, providing the given horizon for sense-making. Thus, because human infants are altricial *and* learn advanced mental skills from their care-givers (as do our precocial primate relatives), human infants become not only especially cultural but also especially relational beings who are deeply attached to others and who acquire skills and cultural horizons which are through-and-through infused with relational significance.

To sum up, young humans are particularly dependent on older care-givers in at least four ways because they are born, under the particular shape that being born has in the human species (involving altriciality, etc.). (1) Babies and infants start off helpless and acutely dependent on adult care for nearly everything. (2) Young humans remain dependent on adult supervision, guidance, and education for a lengthy period. (3) Because of their pronounced initial immaturity, human infants are specially open to culture: they are 'world-receptive'. (4) And, from all of (1)–(3), human infants attach themselves intensely to their care-givers, and these relation-ships guide and pervade their initial acquisition of culture. These four features make up our *natal dependency*, the aspects of our dependency on others which flow directly out of our being born.

It begins to look surprising that *in*dependence and autonomy, not dependence or relationality, have been the central values in modern moral and political thought. Indeed, autonomy has 'come to be the only value we moderns can take to be of ultimate significance', Christopher Yeomans remarks (2017: 243). *Autonomy* and *independence* are not synonyms, but they have often been run closely together. Thus, on one standard view, someone can act, reason, or choose autonomously only when she can do so independently of influence or coercion from others and independently of the sort of uncontrollable compulsion by her own desires that occurs in addiction or mental illness. Take Kant, for whom 'Enlightenment is man's exit from his self-incurred tutelage' ([1784] 1991: 54): the individual becomes enlightened by directing, for himself, the use of his reason, by thinking and judging for himself—standing back from existing arrange-ments and reaching his own independent assessment of their merits. Under various versions, it is only by standing back from the influence of other people, authorities, and social norms that one can act, choose, or judge in accordance with one's true self, or reason, or the moral law.

Many feminist philosophers have challenged this entrenched focus on independence and autonomy, particularly feminist care ethicists writing in the wake of Gilligan (1982), Noddings (1984), and Ruddick (1989). Amongst them, Eva Kittay urges a thorough-going re-orientation of ethics and political thought starting from the facts of dependence (1999, 2011). She points out that human beings are dependent on the care of others in their youth, old age, when they are ill or injured, and when they have impairments or disabilities. In addition, those who care for others—mothers of babies, for instance—are often so occupied with care-giving that they need others to care for their needs in turn. Kittay thus envisions society in terms of nested chains of dependency. Moreover, she argues, dependency is prior to interdependence, for those who are independent enough to care for others are still dependent in other respects, whereas some of those who are dependent—including infants and some people with disabilities—cannot care for others reciprocally. The starting fact is not interdependence but dependence.

Nonetheless, a widespread assumption in moral and political thinking has been that independence is the default human condition from which the dependencies of the young, old, injured, ill, and disabled deviate more-or-less temporarily. Independence has been deemed desirable, with those who lack it being judged to be either defective, suffering, or not leading the ideal human life. As US Senator Daniel Moynihan stated in 1973, 'being dependent...is an incomplete state in life; normal in the child, abnormal in the adult' (quoted in Fraser and Gordon 1994: 309). These anti-dependency assumptions manifest themselves, for example, when disabled people are stigmatized for needing care, say when 'special needs' is used as an insult; and in the stigmatization of 'welfare dependency', spearheaded by the US, but since taken up in Britain in widespread hostility to people who claim welfare benefits (however legitimately).

Yet considering the extent of our dependency due to youth, old age, illness, and so on, dependency emerges as the normal human condition from which we only sometimes, temporarily and partially, rise to greater levels of independence. If dependency is the norm rather than the deviation, it makes no sense to idealize the independent life. Or, at least, if we idealize it, we will effectively be unjustly privileging and overvaluing the lives of a select minority—able-bodied adult heads of household in the prime of life. Conversely, if we recognized dependency as our normal condition, we would be better placed and motivated to meet one another's needs as dependent beings, and to value and support one another in giving care.

To press Kittay's point about how normal dependency is, even a healthy, non-disabled, well-off, child-free adult who would conventionally qualify as 'independent' is actually deeply dependent in numerous ways.[5] First, they depend on language to communicate with others and organize their experience, and language is necessarily a shared, not an individual, possession. Second, we are materially dependent on others. I am now typing on a computer assembled by other people, from components built by other people again; if the computer breaks down, I'll need others to mend it.

Through society's infrastructure and division of labour, we each depend on countless unknown, anonymous others. A third axis of dependency obtains in our personal and intimate relationships, which are generally vital to our emotional well-being. Fourth, we depend on others in the most mundane and routine of our everyday interactions, as the Danish phenomenologist Løgstrup highlights. Boarding a bus and paying for my ticket, I trust the driver to accept my payment, give me a ticket, then drive the bus on its assigned route, pausing at each stop including mine. 'It is a characteristic of human life that we normally encounter one another with natural trust', Løgstrup comments ([1956] 1997: 8, 17). Social norms spell out how not to violate others' trust in any given case—as a bus passenger, by requesting my ticket politely, paying for it, taking a seat in an orderly and timely way. These norms vary, but in different ways they specify how to maintain the basic relations of trust on which everyday social intercourse relies (56–7).

We begin to see how extensive our dependency is. To be sure, not all these aspects of dependency derive directly from our being born: it is not obviously *because* we are born that language is a communal possession or that we depend on other people's labour. Nonetheless, the above four aspects of our dependency are connected with our natality. We first acquire language while we are natally dependent, a dependence that makes us particularly open to language, culture, and symbolism so that they come to shape the whole way we experience. Emotionally, we depend as deeply as we do on personal and intimate relationships with particular others because we have been relational beings from the outset, deeply attached to our first care-givers; this establishes the emotional pathways along which we form subsequent attachments. Our mundane everyday trust in one another, too, is something we learn in infancy—or not, if neglect or abuse impede us from doing so.

Does our dependence on others' material labour have any links with being born? This form of dependence arises, Marx and Engels argue in *The German Ideology*, just because we are embodied beings with physical needs (Marx 2000: 181–2)—not specifically because we are born. However, the ways we labour together are shaped by culture, communication, and the whole order of meaning. As Engels eventually conceded to his interlocutors, not only does production affect culture but also, reciprocally, culture affects production (Engels [1894] 2000). For example, modern modes of production presuppose scientific knowledge, which is part of culture in the broad sense. And divisions of labour tend to be gendered—for instance, most care workers are women, and these jobs are taken to require 'feminine' traits—so that here, too, cultural norms and expectations shape how we depend on one another's labour. Thus, our ways of organizing our material dependence on others are shaped by horizons of meaning in which we participate, through inheritance and reception, from birth.

Overall, only some of our dependency is direct natal dependency, yet the several aspects of our ongoing adult dependency still connect with natality along the routes I've outlined. As a result, the ways in which we depend on others would not be as they are if we were not the natal beings we are. And natality and dependency are also linked in another way: once we acknowledge that we are all born, then we are pushed towards acknowledging the extent of our dependency. To acknowledge natality is to remember that we have all begun life as acutely dependent infants who only became more independent gradually and—given the continuities between childhood and adulthood—partially. None of this means that we need to abandon the values of independence and autonomy altogether. But independence occurs, when it occurs, against the broader background of our generalized dependency on one another. Dependency remains the more ultimate condition.

II. Relational Selves

In this section I argue that our selves are constituted by our relationships with others, beginning with our first care-givers.[6] Through these relationships, each of us acquires a concrete personality structure which provides the template on which we approach subsequent relationships, through which the structure becomes modified but rarely, if ever, abandoned. Thus, our earliest relationships are the most formative ones. In two main ways, this is because we are born. (1) As we are born, our lives have beginnings. Consequently, certain relationships come first for us in time, and so they shape us as subsequent relationships can only ever *re*shape us. (2) Being born, we are natally dependent, so that our first relationships affect us when we are least formed and most receptive, while our dependency also leads us to attach to our first care-givers with special intensity. Being born thus shapes our relationality, both through its place at the temporal start of our lives and by way of our natal dependency and its consequences.

Many feminist philosophers maintain that our selves are relational. Susan Brison writes:

> It is a truism to say that selves exist in relation to other selves. What is more controversial is the view, defended by many feminist philosophers,

that selves exist *only* in relation to other selves, that is, that they are fundamentally relational entities. On this view, persons or selves...are what
Annette Baier has called 'second persons'. On her account, '[a] person...is
best seen as someone who was long enough dependent on other persons to
acquire the essential arts of personhood. Persons are essentially second
persons who grow up with other persons' [quoting Baier (1985: 84)].... In
Western philosophical traditions, [however, the]...primary preoccupations
concerning personal identity were: (1) what makes someone the same unique
individual over time...and (2) what distinguishes human beings from non-
human animals...Little attention was paid to the question of how we *become*
persons.   (2017: 218)

Broadly, then, many feminists agree that relationships, above all our first
relationships, constitute our selves.[7] They agree that traditional metaphysical accounts of selves misleadingly abstract them from the embodiment,
intimate relationships, and social identities which are actually central to
them (James 2000, Christman 2009: 4). Beyond this, feminists give different
accounts of how relationships constitute the self.[8] Here I offer an account
that draws on the psychoanalytic tradition. I do so because psychoanalysis
foregrounds our first relationships and our bodily and emotional nature,
treats the self concretely rather than abstractly, and offers a well-elaborated
model of how our first relationships with our care-givers form our selves.

Freud came to hold that each person's ego (*Ich*) is 'a precipitate of
abandoned object-cathexes' ([1923] 1961a: 29). As children, we make
intense erotic and loving investments ('cathexes') in others, which we
relinquish as we learn that these others are forbidden or unavailable to us.
To compensate and make the relinquishment tolerable, we 'identify' with the
others we are giving up. We 'identify' in the sense that we take these figures
as we imagine them into ourselves, to comprise facets of our personalities—
specifically, sets of dispositions which when sustained over time constitute
personality traits. How we imagine these others is crucial here. Freud
thought that little boys come to identify with their fathers imagined as
authoritarian and threatening figures—figures who may be quite far
removed from the boys' actual empirical fathers, and may instead be modelled on powerful father-figures depicted in culture.[9] Or it may simply be
that we identify with particular aspects of people's behaviour which we find
significant or salient; for instance, I (AS) have taken on my mother's
tendency to over-use the word 'actually'. Thus we 'identify' with or 'internalize' others just in acquiring dispositions to do the things that these others

habitually do—deal out judgement and punishment, monitor and chastize ourselves closely for transgressions, over-use 'actually'. Or, at least, we internalize the things that we experience or imagine these others to do, particularly in their relation to us.

In the gradual process by which we successively identify with various others, it need not always be that we do this because these others are prohibited from us, which was what Freud focused on. We may instead identify with others as compensation when we realize that they are different individuals from us with minds of our own, who will not do what we want or love us as exclusively or deeply as we wish. Thus, as we encounter difficulties and obstacles in our relationships, we respond by internalizing aspects of the people concerned so as to keep them close to us—so close that they become part of who we are. Through these identificatory processes one does not acquire a mere aggregate of traits in which none carries more weight than any other. Rather, we acquire sets of connected traits standing in organized relations to one another. For example, as Freud saw it, the boy internalizes his imagined father and this forms the core of his super-ego, the prohibitive, prescriptive, and punitive mental agency that from now on sits in judgement on the boy's other thoughts and wishes—and on his ego, which now takes shape as the part of his mind subject to judgement by the super-ego. That is, the boy's personality becomes internally differentiated into super-ego and ego (and id, into which any wishes that are judged unacceptable get repressed). Setting this particular topology of Freud's aside, more broadly, as I internalize others this constitutes particular sets of dispositions in me which stand in definite relations to one another, so that I simultaneously acquire a structured personality.[10]

Much of what we internalize of others is their perceived-cum-imagined bodily features, expressions, and patterns of behaviour: say, one's father's tone of voice and accent, his gestural tics and idiosyncrasies. This is not just because others are embodied but also because, as infants, the way we relate to others is highly bodily. To infants, pre-semantic body language is vital, and infants' relationships are imbued with all the force of their bodily needs, impulses, and desires. Moreover, we can acknowledge the importance of identifications without ruling out a role for innate factors in shaping our personalities. Arguably, we are each born with a given instinctual make-up that feeds into our perceptions of, and feelings about, our care-givers and so affects the versions of them with which we come to identify. A baby inclined to impatience and frustration might experience her father as frustrating and incorporate a correspondingly restrictive and frustrating super-ego, whereas for a more sanguine baby, things would proceed differently.

Our selves in the sense of our concrete personalities are relational, then, in that the interwoven sets of dispositions of which these selves are built result from identifications with, and internalized relationships with, others: internally, 'I' am always a 'we'. The point does not apply only to the initial period of personality formation. As long as a given disposition remains active in me, it continues to embody the corresponding identification. If someone remains a harsh self-judger right through his life, he does so in a continuing identification with the father he once found harsh and judgemental; across changing circumstances, the old identification remains alive and well.

However, we might ask: Mustn't I already have a self to be able to identify with others—to have the self-directed agency to make identifications, and to have a level of self-awareness which I amplify and enrich by feeding identifications into it? If so, then the self at its most basic is not relational after all; rather, its relationality presupposes and depends on a prior non-relational self. Support for that last claim might be drawn from Daniel Stern's *The Interpersonal World of the Infant* (1985/1998). Synthesizing a wealth of infancy research, Stern maintains that infants develop a sense of self in stages, each restructuring the preceding sense into a more complex successor. In the first stage, during the baby's first two months of life, she forms a 'sense of an emergent self': a rudimentary sense of 'physical cohesion' (1998: 11). In the next stage, lasting until around six months, the 'core self' is formed: an 'organizing subjective perspective'. Next come the 'subjective self', 'verbal self', and (in Stern's 1998 edition) the 'narrative self'. For now, let's stick with the core self. This precipitates as the baby forms some sense of her motor agency; of the continuity of her experience in short-term memory; of her affects as being her own; and once she can begin to co-ordinate her diverse sensory experiences, for instance correlating higher and lower pitches with higher and lower points in space. These vectors converge so that the baby now begins to grasp her experiences as being her own—tacitly taking it, for instance, that in having hunger pangs *she* is the one having them. The baby's sense of having a single, persisting self to which its experiences belong thus arises in proportion as it can correlate and co-ordinate its many kinds of experience by implicitly attributing them to a single locus. Obviously, the baby has no concept of self yet, but in practically co-ordinating her experiences she tacitly refers them to a single locus that she will later grasp under the explicit concept of the self. In acquiring this sense of herself the baby has not gained some extra component of her experience additional to all the others. Rather, there has been a global change in *how* she now experiences, that is, in a way that tacitly refers all her experiences to a single site.[11] This also means that the baby's germinating sense of herself coincides with her sense of the unity of her body as the site of all her sensory experiences.[12]

Stern talks of the 6-month-old baby having both a self *and* a sense of self. By implication, the sense of having a self, or that all one's experiences are one's own, is constitutive of selfhood: one has a self just insofar as one takes oneself to do so. Before reaching this stage, the baby has a stream of experience but with no sense, not even a tacit and practical one, of its being hers. Nonetheless, she begins from the very first to work towards forming that sense.

In the first (1985) edition of his book, however, Stern took insufficient account of the 'primary relationality' in which the baby lives (Benjamin 1988). For Jessica Benjamin, the young baby's world centres on reciprocal face-to-face interaction and imitative behaviour with the mother (or some other primary care-giver), whose presence provides the all-surrounding context in which the baby's sense of self develops. By six months, then, the baby indeed has a sense of herself, but as intrinsically located within a field of bodily connectedness with the other. Implied along with the self to which my experiences refer is the other with whom that self is ever-present. Stern revised his account in light of relational views such as Benjamin's. In his book's second edition (1998), he argues that the core self is a core self-*with-another*. Acutely dependent as babies are, near-constantly accompanied by their care-givers, all the experiences they are learning to co-ordinate occur in, and so are imbued with, the quality of these others' regulating presence. To feel hunger is to feel hunger in the other's presence; to gain some capacity to move one's arm is to do so in response to, and imitation of, the other.

According to Benjamin and Stern, at around 8 months the baby begins to recognize that *two* minds are involved in its relational interactions, and that the mother's self is not the same as its own self. Once more, this occurs on the level of how the baby experiences at a bodily and practical level—in her growing capacities to make gestures, movements, and responses on her own initiative relatively independently of, although still in the regulating context of, what the mother is doing at the time. The infant then begins to recognize, with fear and displeasure, that there are two selves at work in its relational environment. This sparks the baby's difficult development towards understanding and accepting difference. It is at this developmental point that the infant can begin to make identifications with and internalize aspects of beloved others (primarily the mother, if she is the main care-giver). For identification can help the infant to accept difference: by identifying with aspects of her mother, the infant can make their difference more tolerable, more of a difference-within-connectedness than out-and-out separateness. And having adopted this response vis-à-vis her mother, the infant can extend it to others to deal with difficulties in other relationships when they arise.

Identification, then, does presuppose at least a dawning sense of the difference between self and other. To that extent, one must already have some sense of self to be able to make identifications. However, the infant's earlier, pre-identificatory sense of self is already a sense of self-as-intrinsically-with-the-other (a core self-with-another, for Stern). So, the infant's very earliest sense of its self is still relational; the self is relational all the way down. Furthermore, this sheds light on why identification becomes helpful to the infant: just when others threaten to emerge as being different, the infant identifies with others and so preserves, as best she can, her prior relationality and feeling of being with those others. In sum, through successive identifications, the child gains a complex personality structure into which others are intrinsically built. That structure is the child's self in its thick form as an organized personality, as distinct from its initial, relatively thin, core self.

One might wonder whether personality formation in childhood really has the life-long impact that I am claiming it does. Our childhood relationships certainly matter enormously to us at the time, but perhaps their importance gives way later to new relationships—with friends, lovers, partners, peers, children of our own. I agree with psychoanalytic theorists, though, that our earliest relationships provide the template for our subsequent ones. We continually engage in transference (*Übertragung*), carrying forward into new contexts the expectations, dispositions, and patterns of response which we acquired in previous relationships. Indeed, the psychoanalytic feminist Nancy Chodorow argues that *all* experience is shaped by transference, as one reproduces in the present various facets of one's past, all of which one experienced together with particular others: memories, feelings, habitual responses, and so on. Transference, and with it past relationships, give our experience the affective richness and depth without which it would not be experience as we know it at all (Chodorow 1999b: 23). Through the pervasiveness of transference in our lives, then, our first relationships can remain very important as the sources of our ingrained ways of being, even when our explicit focus has moved on to new relationships.

Although we approach others in light of our pasts, those others can of course always act contrary to our embedded expectations. Over time this can lead us to revise our dispositions and the identifications they embody—not deliberately, but in an unconscious work of mental processing and self-reformation. In view of how a new friend of mine acts, I may start to remember different aspects of my parents, so that what I identify with in them changes, and I begin to act and feel differently. Along such routes, our personality structures can undergo modification over time, or occasionally dramatic transformation—although even then, the transformations are wrought upon traits and structures that already exist. One's resulting personality is a composite of older, ingrained structures and newer modifications. But however many modifications we make, there is no point at which our initial relationships and their effects are wholly erased. At least something of them always persists under however many over-writings, partly in that I have only undergone just these successive modifications because I started from the initial relationships that I did.

Our earliest relationships, thus, carry so much weight because they *form* our selves, whereas subsequent relationships can only ever *re-form* selves that are already formed. Subsequent experiences affect what is already established, whereas our first relationships establish it in the first place. First relationships therefore have a formative power that no later relationships can equal. This is partly because our first relationships come first in time; partly because we experience them just when our minds and bodies are still undeveloped and plastic due to our natal immaturity; and partly because we attach to these relationships so intensely because of our natal dependency. Indeed, it is because of our acute natal dependency that our first caregivers have to be near-constantly with and around us, such that our first sense of ourselves is as selves-with-these-others. In all these ways, our natality means that our earliest relationships have special and unrivalled power to mould our emerging selves.

It might be objected that I am foregrounding our personal, intimate, and familial relationships to the neglect of other ways in which our selves are relational, such as those highlighted by Hegel, Marx, and Heidegger—to name just three philosophers who regard the self as relational, if not in those very words.[13] For Hegel, each civilization and national community has an 'objective spirit': 'the common spirit of a social group, embodied in its customs, laws and institutions, and permeating the character and consciousness of the individuals belonging to the group' (Inwood 1992: 275). A community's spirit animates, unites, and manifests itself through all of its art, literature, religion, government, customs, norms, and institutions. Together, these educate and cultivate the individuals living in that community so that they thoroughly adhere to its way of life. For Marx, in critical reaction against Hegel, what above all shapes any community's way of life are the social relations that organize its material production of the means of its members' subsistence:

> The social relations in which individuals produce, the social relations of production...in their totality form what we call social relations, society, and specifically a society at a definite historical stage of development, a society with a distinctive, differentiating character.
>
> (Marx [1849/1891] 2017: 25)

For his part, Heidegger understands our sociality in terms of our everyday practical dealings with the items of equipment that figure into our projects (e.g., hammers). These items and projects always belong within inter-referring networks—'referential totalities' (Heidegger 1962: 121/88). (For example, the hammer is for connecting the parts of a rabbit run, to be located in the garden, for giving the rabbits outdoor time.) In all these mundane goings-on, the co-existence of others in the world alongside me is presupposed: say, those who made the parts of the run and the hammer, or who help me to assemble the hutch. It is also presupposed that these others are of a different order to items of equipment such as hammers: I relate to others differently in kind than I do to hammers, hutches, and the like. To exist in the world as we do—engaging in projects using equipment—is necessarily to be with-others; our sharing the world with them is constitutive of, not accidental to, our being.

Hegel, Marx and Heidegger all offer insights here, but those insights can be enriched by taking account of the formative impact of our early relationships. Whether we belong to a shared community spirit or set of social production relations or world of practical involvements, we *come* to belong to and participate in them from birth onwards. We do not spring into existence as full-fledged adults but enter into shared ways of life through a temporal and developmental process. Through this process we receive and inherit from others, and learn to participate with others in, a pre-existing communal spirit, or set of production relations, or network of shared involvements—or something of all these.[14]

On the one hand, then, our first relationships mediate the social and cultural world to us. On the other hand, they do this because these relationships themselves are already shaped by and occur in that social and cultural world. My mother transmitted English to me as my mother tongue because she had already been brought up to speak English and used it for everyday conversation. This further means that when we internalize the behaviours and expressions of our first care-givers into our traits and personalities, we are taking on behaviours and expressions pervaded with cultural and social meaning and value. When I took on my mother's habits of speech intonation, I unknowingly took on a restrained, measured, precisely articulated vocal style that in the UK is recognizably middle-class ('BBC English'). As we acquire relational selves, then, we are also assuming locations in specific cultures and imbibing horizons of meaning which are culturally laden.

III. Power

In this section I explore how, as beings who are born, we inhabit power relations from the very start of our existence. I define power relations in this way: members of group A have power over or relative to members of group B when those in A are more able than those in B (i) to steer the course of their own actions, desires, and lives; (ii) to affect how the other group's members act, desire, and live; and (iii) to shape arrangements that embody and prolong this state of affairs.[15] Such power relations may be socially constructed or arise inherently. Because we inhabit such relations immediately from birth, I shall argue, the presence of power relations in our lives is normal rather than aberrant, and these relations constitute our selves, traits, and abilities.[16] Also, any powers to criticize particular power relations which people may acquire are themselves shaped by and embody power relations, possibly the same ones that are under criticism.

I am guided in these thoughts by Christine Battersby. For her, if we treat as normal rather than aberrant the position of the female subject as someone who can give birth, or is assumed to be able to do so, then we see that it is normal and not anomalous for the self to be located within power relations:

> [Because of] the ontological dependence of the foetus on the mother, and the fact that (in our culture at least) the woman is socialized as the primary carer for any children...the 'female' subject-position is normalized as linked to a set of relationships in which power-dependencies and inequalities are basic. For the human female, inequalities in power relationships cannot...be treated as atypical, abstracted or put to one side.   (1998: 8)

For Battersby, this is part and parcel of 'natality—the conceptual link between the paradigm "woman" and the body that births' (7). Thus, for Battersby, a philosophy of natality concerns what it is to be a self that can give birth. But Battersby's point about the normal and pervasive presence of power relations also applies to the self as born. To be born is to come into relationships with both one's care-givers and the surrounding culture in which 'power-dependencies are basic'.[17] Let me elaborate.

By birth, children come into relations in which their parents or other care-givers have powers over them due to children's initial helplessness, immaturity, and prolonged dependency. The powers here include those to feed children, regulate their lives, educate them, veto certain activities and encourage others, decide what cultures they are inducted into, and so on. Although children have some reciprocal powers, for example to affect their care-givers emotionally, on the whole the power relations here are asymmetrical, the more so the younger the child is. This is especially so because children begin life with very little capacity to question or reject their parents' decisions in their regard (as distinct from bursting out with short-lived defiance).

In addition, our earliest relationships entrain us into the many power relations existing in the surrounding culture and society, relations that get reflected and transmitted to us largely beyond the intentions or even awareness of anyone involved. In acquiring a given language, for instance, we imbibe and come to take for granted whatever power relations that language embodies, such as the gendered power relations that are conveyed in French by the rule that if a group of people, however large, includes even one male then it is called ils, not elles. In seeing our mothers exhibit more restrained and reserved bodily habits and gestures than our fathers,[18] and possibly internalizing similar habits if we are female, we become caught up in the corresponding power differential. Divisions of economic and global power are embodied in where a child lives, what level of material comfort she enjoys, what neighbourhood and type of house she lives in, and myriad other factors. Children are born into and become familiar with and enculturated in all these aspects of power long before they gain any capacity to reflect upon or criticize them.[19]

Thus because, being born, we begin life immature and highly receptive to the world, the power relations of the surrounding socio-cultural world—as well as the powers our care-givers have over us—stamp us particularly heavily during our period of natal dependency, partly because we cannot yet question or criticize these power relations. In practice, the society-wide and intimate forms of power operate together, for it is through our relation-ships with our particular care-givers, and with the people and circumstances immediately around us, that the cultural world comes to imprint us and assume authority in our lives along with the care-givers who mediate its influence. It is, say, by observing the interactions between my parents or the people in my neighbourhood that I take in the society-wide power relations that these interactions embody.[20]

Beginning life under the sway of our care-givers and the surrounding culture is a necessary, inherent concomitant of our being born dependent and deeply open to formation by the world around us. But the extent to which, through culture, we come under the sway of power relations of gender, class, race, etc. obviously depends on whether our societies embody these hierarchies—their existence is not a natural necessity but a matter of political choice. That said, it has sometimes been argued that the powers of parents or care-givers over children are also a product of political choice and social construction, rather than arising inherently from children's dependent condition. Certainly, by law and custom, parental power over children can be expanded, as with, say, the Roman *paterfamilias* who wielded rights of life and death over his children. That power can also be limited, as in the more typical modern configuration whereby parental powers gradually reduce over time as children gain in autonomy. But to view parental power as entirely socially constructed neglects the fact that we begin life as dependent and immature as we do: this view misleadingly treats children as being, all along, more-or-less autonomous agents, overlooking the fact that powers of autonomy are necessarily developed over (a lengthy period of) time.[21]

Because we start off natally dependent and immature, then, we come under the sway of personal and inter-group power relations in a context where we cannot yet criticize them. One might object that this kind of permeability by power is peculiar to children, and so is not normal but a deviation from the ideal human condition of adulthood, in which we are independent of power relations and come under their sway only as far as we choose to do so. But, alternatively, we can reconsider the nature of adult independence in light of the fact that all adults used to be children. When we were children, power came right into our selves. For instance, it shaped what bodily and mental powers we formed. Because children start off very undeveloped, nearly all their powers are ones that they have yet to develop and that they acquire in social and relational settings. Of course, many children endogenously develop powers to control their bodily movements, walk, run, talk, etc. But how they walk, talk, etc. as the outcome of this development—under what gait, posture, style; in what language, with what accent and pattern of intonation—is shaped by what is practised by the people around them. Our most mundane habits and capacities thus come to reflect power relations, so that whenever we enact these habits and capacities we reproduce those relations. In addition, I've argued, our personalities are built up through identifications with the people around us, and as these people act in ways that embody social power relations, those relations become ingrained in our traits and the structures of our selves. One might still say that in becoming adults we learn to distance ourselves from all that we have imbibed, to re-assess it on a rational basis, and make autonomous decisions about how far to accept it. But I find it more realistic to say that, while we often do become relatively autonomous as adults, our capacities to exercise autonomy and to question, reject, or revisit our culture and relationships are shaped by our relationships and the power arrangements that they embody in the first place.

That much is argued by many feminist theorists of relational autonomy (see, above all, Mackenzie and Stoljar 2000). These theorists accept that to be autonomous is to be 'self-defining and self-governing... [and to be able to] make decisions and act on the basis of...values or commitments that are authentically "one's own"' (Mackenzie 2017: 515), for instance because one has rationally endorsed those values or judged that they express or align with one's true self, the character and traits one endorses in oneself. But, as Diana Meyers points out, this capacity for autonomy actually consists in a complex bundle of capacities that are not only cognitive but also emotional, imaginative, and critical. To make an autonomous decision in some situation, one needs to be able to interpret one's actions, imagine various alternative actions and scenarios, and attend to and reflect critically on one's emotional reactions to these possibilities (Meyers 1987: 151). The result is that one can have autonomy to varying degrees, depending on which of these sub-capacities one has developed and to what extent. And, for Meyers and other relational autonomy theorists, social conditions, including personal relationships, can foster or hinder the development and exercise of these several capacities—so that autonomy is only ever possible given 'extensive interpersonal, social, and institutional scaffolding' (516). The right kinds of socialization are needed both to establish the capacities that contribute to autonomy in the first place, and to sustain them and enable their development and sedimentation over time.

Imagine a parent who provides her child with a reliable, soothing bedtime routine. Carrying out the routine brings the child comfort and security, which helps her fall asleep. This makes it possible that, when the parent is away or the child is older, she can feel secure enough to get to sleep by repeating the routine or remembering it, with the feelings of comfort this brings. This counts as autonomous behaviour to a degree, because the child is regulating her own actions in light of feelings (of comfort) and experiences (of remembered comfort) that are 'her own'. But they are only 'her own' insofar as she has internalized the figure of her parent as someone with her, who regulates her, and who by so doing confers reliability and safety. As the child regulates her own sleep habits in a way that embodies this parent-figure, this confers comfort in turn. And in having internalized this parent-figure and continuing to act on this internalized figure, the child has at an implicit level endorsed it as part of herself, such that acting on it expresses who she is.

To be sure, autonomy theorists generally have higher-level, more critically self-reflective capacities in mind. But my point is that our capacities for critical, self-conscious reflection on actions and values emerge out of lower-level, more emotionally rooted dispositions of self-regulation and self-care.[22] Only once we already have those latter dispositions can we make the further move to render them more reflective. Thus, adult autonomy develops out of lower-level childhood behaviours that at least foreshadow autonomy, or rather that, given Meyers's picture, realize autonomy to a lesser degree than some relevant adult behaviours—but still to a degree. And those childhood behaviours develop in the relational setting that is all-pervasive in childhood. Along such low-level, mundane pathways as parents helping their children to sleep, our relationships with others can foster or impede us in developing capacities for autonomy.[23]

That relational setting of childhood, though, is one shaped by power relations. Thus, when we develop powers of autonomy within this setting, we do so in ways that reflect these power relations as well. In my example, the child's developing capacity for autonomous self-regulation arises as the internalization of her parent's prior power to regulate her sleep habits. More broadly, we must internalize a wealth of cultural norms, meanings, and values before we can ever become able to engage in criticism of the culture around us. Just as the reception of meaning precedes its creation, the internalization of power relations precedes the possibility of their criticism.

As natal beings, then, we are deeply shaped by power relations. Yet there are also features of our natal condition which generate reasons to be critical of many of the power relations that shape us. As we saw in the last chapter, we are vulnerable in being born to coming into the world in disadvantaged locations, and that vulnerability is heightened the greater are the inequalities of the world we come into. We are also vulnerable, by virtue of being born, to suffering especially harmful and damaging effects from the power relations that affect us during our early lives. It would be desirable for these kinds of natal vulnerability to be both reduced and distributed more evenly than they presently are. Yet precisely because power relations shape us as natal beings, it can be hard for us to think critically about these relations and even to develop the capacities to be critical of them. This is the more so because, as natal beings, we inherit frameworks of meaning which tend to be bound up with and justify the power arrangements with which they co-exist—to make sense of those arrangements in ways that paint them as legitimate. As we imbibe these frameworks, they limit our capacities to be critical of the power arrangements in force and, in turn, to respond to others' vulnerabilities and dependencies when doing so would take us beyond the terms of existing arrangements.

Even so, the fact that power relations have this influence on us does not mean that no one can ever criticize the particular power relations by which they have been shaped.[24] Possibilities for criticism emerge along several routes. (i) The systems of power relations that shape any given individual are various and uneven, so that one can come to criticize one system—say, gendered power—in light of values, norms, or ideals one has imbibed under another system—say, as the beneficiary of divisions in economic power. (ii) Because any set of power relations shapes the powers of thought and action of those subjected to it, one can come to exercise and develop those powers in ways that bear critically on the very conditions out of which they arose. And because of (i) and (ii), (iii) any set of power relations over time becomes the subject of multiple challenges, questionings, and reworkings by those involved in it, yielding a multifaceted and unstable legacy inherited by all those who come under the same set of power relations subsequently. In taking on this legacy, one takes on an already internally fissured and shifting set of power relations within which multiple vantage points are available. As a result, whatever we take forward, we will always be positioned more-or-less critically towards at least some of the legacy of what has gone before us.

IV. Situatedness: A First Sketch

When we are born we come into the world situated in particular relationships with those who care for us and in particular places within sets of power relations. But so far I have presupposed rather than examined what being *situated* is. Let's now begin to explore situatedness and its connections with being born.

Situatedness is discussed in two main bodies of philosophical writing. The first consists of work by Sartre, Heidegger, other existentialists and phenomenologists, and those who interpret and develop their ideas. Here the central idea is that 'the self is from the start "dipped into" a shared realm of objective meanings, that every building, stone, word, and emotional expression is pre-understood by subjects situated in the respectively shared context' (Kögler 2007: 369). Kate Withy helpfully clarifies with reference to Heidegger. For Withy, I am situated insofar as, whatever I am in the midst of doing, and wherever and whenever I am doing it, I always make sense of things in and from a particular context. In any given case, that context is drawn from such combined factors as my geographical location, the point I've reached in my life from out of my prior life-history, a certain culture and tradition, and my gender, personality, and values (2014: 63–5). Additionally, what is around me at this point to be made sense *of*—what 'corner of the world' I am in—is part of my situation (64). I am situated, then, (i) as to what is around me to make sense of and (ii) in how I can and do make sense of it as this is affected by my life-history, values, personality, etc. And so, I am situated specifically as someone who makes sense of things: whose mode of existence is fundamentally one of understanding in a broad, not narrowly intellectual or cognitive sense. My situation is the background against and out of which I do my sense-making.

The second set of discussions of situatedness is found in feminist philosophy, including feminist epistemology: many influential theorists such as Sandra Harding (1991) and Donna Haraway (1991) have argued that what we can and cannot know is shaped by our social locations with respect to gender—and other social categories such as race, as critical race theorists such as Charles Mills (2007) have pointed out. When we engage in knowing about some subject-matter, we do not and cannot set our social backgrounds aside. Rather, we always see from a perspective, from here and not there, and from any 'here' certain things are visible and others invisible, and what is visible shows itself under a certain light. Arguably, for example, being born and brought up as a man makes it harder—albeit not impossible—to understand some aspects of gendered power. As Linda Alcoff explains, one's location with respect to gender, race, or other power relations enables one to know some things and not others, conferring a mix of epistemic advantages and disadvantages regarding particular subject-matters (Alcoff 2007: 42). But also, Alcoff argues, those in privileged groups can have positive interests in seeing the world wrongly, for example, as being more meritocratic than it is: privilege is liable to motivate the active pursuit and maintenance of ignorance as a practice (47–8).

Linking these politically oriented discussions with more phenomenological ones, Alcoff draws out the implication that we inescapably operate within horizons of meaning which shape how we act as well as what we know, where these horizons are shaped by and express our social locations:

> One's racial and gender identity is fundamental to one's social and familial interactions. It contributes to one's perspective on events...and it determines in large part one's status within the community...Thus, our 'visible' and acknowledged identity affects our relations in the world, which in turn affects our interior life, that is, our lived experience or subjectivity. If social identities such as race and gender are fundamental in this way to one's experiences, then it only makes sense to say that they are fundamental to the self.   (Alcoff 2006: 92)[25]

Feminist and existentialist views of situation converge to a considerable extent. On both views, we are situated in that we navigate through life within horizons of meaning which we have imbibed over time from our contexts, contexts that also account for our being in those corners of the world of which we are presently making sense from within these horizons. For readers of Heidegger such as Withy, the contextual factors in question include geographical location, life-history, culture and tradition, gendered body, and personality and values; whereas feminist authors emphasize more social divisions of gender and race—as well as class, sexuality, and the global international order as it has been shaped by colonialism (and arguably remains neo-colonial),[26] where this list could be elongated. We need not choose between the more and less politically focused accounts, but can learn from both. Feminists and existentialists further agree that it is as bodily beings that we are situated. Whatever corner of the world I am in and am making sense of, I am in it as a body; and however I make sense of it, I do so as a body—say by perceiving what's around me with my senses, inspecting its elements from different angles, and reacting to it emotionally in ways that have felt, somatic components. Even when my context calls me to engage in some very abstract and demanding kind of intellectual understanding, in the end it is still as a body that I so engage, using the powers and habits I have cultivated in my body, nervous system, and brain over time.[27]

Now, this might suggest that I am situated just as a living, perceiving, sense-making body, and that my situatedness has no special connection with my birth. However, as we've seen from the above views of situatedness, what situation I am in on any given occasion—both in terms of where I am and how I am making sense of it—is always one I have *come* to be in, over time. For I have always reached the situation I am now in from another one that preceded it. To give a banal example, I am jotting these words down on paper while sitting in the bath, having come into the bath from the living room where I had been working on the sofa. In this way, I am in my current situation (note-making, in the bath) because of my (trivial) response to my previous situation—to want a change of scene in the hope it will ease the writing of this paragraph. Each situation materializes for me out of the one before it, and so on right back to my very first situation, the one into which I came by birth. Even though I had no definite framework at that time for making sense of what was going on, I still did make sense of it, (apparently) by crying loudly and at length—taking 'sense-making', here, in its broadest sense. For nascent, visceral, inarticulate responses are still ways of sense-making, and they provide the starting-point on which successive more advanced levels of understanding will be built. Moreover, another way in which one starts immediately to make sense of having left one's mother's womb is just by registering the change—feeling the bombardment of myriad sensations and of strong visual impressions, feeling the influx of air into the lungs, etc.—and, perhaps, by feeling overwhelmed or even traumatized by the magnitude of the transition one has undergone, or distressed to find oneself outside what was hitherto one's home.[28]

Situation is connected with birth, then, because each situation that I am in ultimately flows down from my initial natal situation. This connection is essential and not accidental to what it is to be situated, for sense-making is situated just in being done *from* somewhere—from one's point of view, values, life-history, and so on. To be situated is thus to make sense in a way that arises out of one's past, which goes back to one's birth. If we were not born, then, we would not be situated in the way we are. Reciprocally, the concept of situatedness sheds light on what it is to be born, namely, to come into the world not just as such—were that somehow possible—but *somewhere* and *somewhen* within it. I (AS) was born in 1972 on the planet earth, certainly—but not just everywhere on the earth, rather in a particular hospital in Billericay, Essex, England, Europe, etc. Earlier I agreed with Arendt and Cavarero that to be born is to come into the world amongst a plurality of others. But that formulation needs to be expanded. To be born is to come into a *particular set of relationships* with specific others and a *particular situation* in the world—here and not there, where every 'here' is where certain traditions and practices of meaning-making are already in force. I also agreed with Arendt that to be born is to *begin* existing. But necessarily one can only begin existing at some definite point in time, such as 1972.

Given the links between birth and situatedness, we can begin to think further about the factors that contribute to people's situations by considering the factors that typically make up a person's natal situation. For our subsequent situations unfold from our original natal ones, which in turn are as they are because of the factors that compose them. A first factor in any individual's natal situation is the place where they are born, geographically, which immediately brings matters of culture and politics with it. (For instance, most people are born into nation-states and so acquire citizenship by birth, but increasing numbers of people are born in refugee camps and so are at risk of being stateless by birth.) A second factor is the time when one is born, such as 1972, a time that carries with it a given location within history (where the use of a given calendar for placing one's birth in time reflects cultural and historical factors in itself: e.g., I was—supposedly—born 1972 years after Jesus was). A third factor is the given culture or set of cultures practiced by the people amongst whom is born (Christianity, for instance). A fourth factor is that by birth one comes into a particular point on each axis along which power is unequally distributed—gender, race, class, etc. Moreover, one's natal situation within power does not result from simple summation of these points; rather, they *intersect* in one's particular case to yield one's overall placement in power, where each of its aspects affects the others.[29] A fifth factor is the unique constellation of relationships into which one comes by birth—not only (i) with one's parents or first care-givers, but also, through them, (ii) with the various others with whom those care-givers stand in further relationships as to family, work, friendship, community, etc., and (iii) into lines both of biological descent and socially recognized kinship. Those two can diverge, for instance if one's genetic, gestational, social, or legal parents differ. To unpack some of what is involved here, we need to turn briefly to the phenomenon of generations.

To belong to a line of descent is to be located in a temporal series of generationally linked individuals, reproduction and birth marking each link in the chain. To be born is to come into a position of descent 'downstream' from the generation before one, which is descended from that before it, and so on. The succession of generations in this biological sense is connected with stages in human life, from infancy through juvenility to reproductive maturity, menopause, then old age. To age, whether or not one has children, is to move 'upstream' relative to first one new generation and then another and another (depending how long one lives). But biological generations can 'flow' at different speeds in different families or within a single family, as well as in different cultures and regions of the world. Take the Kent family, which was at the centre of the once-famous Road Hill murder case in England (given semi-fictional reconstruction by Summerscale 2008: see, esp., xvii). Samuel Kent had thirteen children, ten by his first wife and three by his second; six of the former ten died in infancy. The eldest of them to survive to adulthood, Mary Ann, was 26 when Francis Saville was born to Kent's second wife Mary who was then aged 37; and Mary Ann was 28 when, aged 39, Mary had her youngest child Eveline. Mary Ann was thus far closer in generation to her stepmother than her half-siblings. Such family patterns were common in nineteenth-century Britain, and they illustrate that patterns of generational descent are by no means uniform.

Moreover, cultural factors enter in several ways into what an individual's line of descent is taken to be in the first place. One respect concerns how time is conceived: for instance, if time is understood broadly in terms of a linear progression, as in Western modernity, then each new generation will be envisaged to be further along the line than its predecessor.[30] Culture also enters by way of conceptions of parentage or kinship. In patrilineal systems, the father counts as the 'true', primary, or decisive parent and progenitor so that children inherit names, property, and ancestry along the father's line. We might therefore distinguish the biological succession of generations from the conceptions of time and kinship relations under which we make sense of it legally, symbolically, and practically (Guenther 2012: 11). Reproduction and the biological succession of generations may in themselves press us towards recognizing them under conceptions of kinship, but social and legal institutions can prevent us from recognizing at least some of these incipient ties. Systems of patrilineal descent deny significance to people's maternal lineage and bonds, as Irigaray remarks:

> Under the rule of patriarchy the girl is separated from her mother and from her family in general. She is transplanted into the genealogy of her husband; she must live with him, carry his name, bear his children, etc.
>
> (Irigaray 1993c: 2)

More drastically, societies can refuse to recognize *all* of the incipient kin ties amongst certain groups of people, as when black slaves in the US were counted only as members of their owners' households while their biological and reproductive relationships with one another were deemed null.[31] Slaves were therefore in the state of 'natal alienation' analysed by Orlando Patterson: they were alienated from the incipient kin relations arising out of their own lived activities and experiences of reproduction, birth-giving, and being born.

A final aspect of generational membership arises where biological succession intersects with historical change, leading to the formation of generations in another sense, treated by Karl Mannheim in 'The Problem of Generations' ([1927/28] 1952)—cultural generations, such as the 60s' generation, the baby-boomers, Generation X, the millennials, etc. Actually, Mannheim speaks not of 'cultural generations' (the phrase preferred by Pilcher 1994) or 'cultural cohorts' (Glenn 1977), but simply of 'generations'. Nonetheless, as the substance of his claims makes clear, it is generations in cultural–historical terms which concern him. On Mannheim's view, people belong to a single (cultural) generation if, (i) due to being born within the same few years (ii) in the same cultural and geographical region, they are (iii) exposed to the same range of historical events and experiences—say, the Second World War—(iv) during the crucial formative years of adolescence and young adulthood. This may seem to contradict my claim that childhood is the most formative period, but it need not, as Mannheim's concern is specifically with what period is most formative of our cultural generational membership; childhood can still be the period that most deeply forms our basic selves. Adolescence and young adulthood are most formative for cultural generational membership, though, because this is when individuals first start to participate in social life in their own right, relatively independently of familial guidance and mediation (so that, for example, people usually attach themselves most passionately to the popular music they hear in adolescence and young adulthood).

The existence of cultural generations is made possible by the succession of biological generations—and evidently too, although Mannheim does not make it explicit, by the transition from childhood to adulthood. But biological succession is not sufficient to distinguish or constitute cultural generations, for members of different (or the same) biological generations can be cultural contemporaries (or non-contemporaries). History, as well as biological succession, is necessary for cultural generations to arise, when historical events make their mark on what would otherwise have been mere biological cohorts.[32]

V. Birth, Dependency, and Culture: Summing Up So Far

Since this chapter has covered a lot of terrain, let me sum up. In the nature of human birth, we begin life highly dependent on care, and we undergo an extended period of dependency and cultural learning. In several further respects—language, labour, personal life, trust—we remain dependent on others throughout our lives, and these dependencies have continuities with our early natal dependencies. Also in the nature of human birth, we begin life very immature and unformed and so highly permeable by, and receptive to, culture. As such, we begin to receive and inherit a set of cultural horizons from the very first, well before we have any ability to stand back critically from them.

Given our initial dependency and receptivity, as well as our highly bodily mode of existence in infancy, we attach intensely to our first care-givers and become profoundly affected by them, absorbing many cultural influences through their influence. In these regards, and because these are our first relationships—for being born, we begin, hence certain events come first for us—the effects of these early relationships upon us are uniquely formative. They constitute our emerging selves, both as selves-with-others and in terms of our concrete personality structures. Our personalities are not thereby set in stone: subsequent relationships continuously re-form our already formed selves across our lives. Yet our earlier relationships provide the templates on which the later ones have their effects.

Partly through the impact of our first relationships, and partly due to our natal receptivity, we take on from the start the power relations of the world into which we have arrived. We generally become able to criticize these relations to some degree later on, and we have grounds to do so. But we acquire these critical capacities along routes made possible by the same socio-cultural horizons that have shaped us.

Finally, being born, we begin life situated within the world with respect to many variables. Amongst them are culture; gender, race, class and other social divisions; geography; history; body; and placement in a specific set of personal and wider relationships, including kin networks and generational differences. We almost immediately begin to draw upon some of these variables to make sense of how things are in the places where we find ourselves. In this way we are situated both as regards what we have to make sense of, and as regards the inherited avenues along which we make sense of it. As we make sense of and respond to where we are, we come to move over time through successive situations, each flowing down from our initial natal situation. In this way, however far one's life travels from where one started at birth, it is still from that natal starting-point that one's journey has unfolded.

Notes

1. 'Secondary nestlings' is an old phrase, but the idea of humans' secondary altriciality remains widely accepted amongst ethologists and human anthropologists (e.g. Gómez-Robles et al. 2015; Gould 1977: Ch. 8; Walrath 2006: 61). However, Dunsworth et al. (2012) challenge the view that the obstetric dilemma explains secondary altriciality, appealing instead to the mother's metabolic—rather than pelvic—capacities. Even so, Dunsworth makes this challenge against a background where explanatory appeal to the obstetric dilemma remains standard (see, e.g. Hrdy 2000: 165).

2. Thanks to Clare Palmer and Bron Szerzynski for pushing me to clarify this.

3. One team of researchers reports that 'cerebral cortical anatomy is substantially less genetically heritable...in humans [than chimpanzees], indicating greater plasticity and increased environmental influence on neurodevelopment in our species.... A major result of increased plasticity is that [human]...behavior is shaped by the environmental, social, and cultural context more intensively... than in other primate species' (Gómez-Robles et al. 2015: 147–99).

4. Thanks to Lewis Coyne for alerting me to Gehlen's relevance to my argument.

5. Some feminist theorists view dependency more narrowly. For example, for Susan Dodds, we are all vulnerable to some degree at all times, but we are not all dependent; rather, dependency is a specific form of vulnerability. However, Dodds takes this view because she takes people to be dependent only when they rely on the care of *specific individuals*, so that their dependency can be reduced if their needs are instead met by institutions (2014: 183). I instead believe—with Jackie Scully—that we all depend on other members of our communities at all times, be they specific individuals, the anonymous collectivity, or mediating institutions. I also agree with Scully that some dependencies are so normal and taken for granted that they are wrongly overlooked and not counted as the dependencies they are (Scully 2014: 214–17). An instance is the four aspects of dependency I discuss below regarding language, labour, personal relationships, and trust.

6. Admittedly, not all our relationships constitute our selves. Some relationships are more superficial and transitory, others more indirect and distant. I (AS) have limited acquaintance with my neighbours; these relationships affect me at an

emotional level only slightly and superficially. (I may still be heavily dependent on such more distant relationships: my quality of life would deteriorate sharply, say, if my neighbours all moved away and left their houses vacant and in disrepair.) But the relationships that constitute my self are the important ones that I care deeply about. That said, the division between constitutive and non-constitutive relationships is not sharp; it is a matter of degree how far any relationship affects us internally, and any given relationship can change or fluctuate in its importance to us over time.

7. As Brison notes, Baier particularly stresses that each person *becomes* a person through childhood enculturation (Baier 1985: Ch. 5).

8. One such account, Cavarero's story-based one, was discussed in Chapter 1. Brison (2003, 2017), Code (1995), and Griffiths (1995) also offer narrative accounts of the relational self. Alcoff stresses the role of group and cultural identities in constituting our selves (2006: 59–62 and Ch. 4). For other feminist accounts of the self, see Meyers (1997).

9. See Freud ([1913 (1955)], [1924] (1961b)]: 172–9). This very stress on imagination signals a problem in Freud's account of personality formation: I internalize others as they figure in *my* imagination, as 'others-for-me', so to speak. Freud gives little sense of the infant relating to and struggling with others who have their *own* minds, separate from its imaginings. Thus, as Jessica Benjamin complains (1988), Freud lacks an account of genuine intersubjectivity. I address this problem by folding my Freud-derived account of personality formation through identification into Benjamin's account of intersubjectivity.

10. I say 'personality', not 'character', because the latter is ethically oriented, suggesting patterns of virtue and vice acquired through education. However, ideas of personality and character alike are potentially vulnerable to 'situationist' criticisms. According to John Doris (2002), experiments show that much human behaviour does not stem from stable character traits but rather reflects contingent features of the situations in which people choose what to do. For instance, the Princeton 'Good Samaritan' experiment found that subjects who were told they were late for the study were less likely to help a seemingly distressed passer-by than those not so told (Darley and Batson 1973). However, others have argued that character is such a complex and multi-faceted phenomenon that such experimental results do not tell against it (Homiak 2016: 5.2). I agree, and would say the same about personality.

11. Here I'm adopting a formulation from Zahavi (2014).

12. One might wonder whether the mere having of a stream of experience presupposes some still more basic sense of the self whose stream it is. On such lines Dan Zahavi argues that just in its first-personal character, lived experience already incorporates the sense of a 'minimal', pre-social self (2014), which by implication is even more basic than Stern's core self. However, Myriam Kyselo (2016) argues that Zahavi neglects the fact that the 'minimal' self needs to be formed—from

birth, over time—in ways that depend on social interactions. But if the self must be formed, then the initial unfolding of a particular stream of embodied experience cannot already embody a sense of self. Perhaps that stream, instead, calls to be made sense of *through* the formation of a sense of the self that has it—hence the fact that babies embark straightaway on this formation.

13. I thank Stephen Houlgate for asking me to clarify this.

14. Krell (2015a), MacAvoy (1996: esp. 84–5), and Schües (2016: esp. 188) criticize Heidegger for his neglect of childhood and of how we come over time into the world of practical involvements.

15. Needless to say, this is only one of many possible definitions of power relations. It is informed by Patterson (1990: 1); regarding (iii), by Lukes (1974/2005), and, regarding inter-group power relations, by feminist theorists (see Oksala 2017).

16. On power as constitutive, I am indebted to Foucault, for whom power is primarily productive and only ever secondarily restrictive or repressive; qua productive, power operates by shaping our capacities and habits and enabling us to acquire them (see, e.g. Foucault 1982). I don't distinguish power-over from power-to, for on a Foucauldian productive view these are deeply entangled. The power of parents *to* feed their children given foods is equally one of their forms of power-*over* their children. Gendered power relations sometimes involve powers of men *to* Ø to women—e.g. to harass women sexually—which is also a power of men *over* women; but they sometimes involve asymmetrical distributions of men's and women's respective powers-*to*—e.g. to move freely or with more restraint. Filtering out the many combinations of powers-to and powers-over would add little of substance to the discussion.

17. For Cavarero, too, newborns come into 'absolute dependence' on their care-givers, making this the most 'asymmetrical and unbalanced' of human relations ([2014] 2016: 13, 27). For Guenther, we begin life not 'free and equal' but in a state of 'radical asymmetry' between child and care-giver (2006: 45). Söderbäck agrees, but points out that it is not only infants and children who are under the power of their care-givers, but that mothers and other care-givers are also situated within social power relations that pertain specifically to parenting, maternity, and childcare (2018).

18. On the social convention for women's bodily movements to be relatively restrained, see Young ([1980] 2005a).

19. Another set of power relations often at work here is that whereby parents or legal guardians delegate certain child-caring powers to others such as nannies, nursery workers, etc. Generally, power inequalities in terms of class, race, and/or nationality play in here: to give just one instance, parents, especially mothers, sometimes favour nannies from particular ethnic groups because they expect those nannies—based on ethnic stereotypes—to employ some desired child-caring style. See Macdonald (2010).

20. Judith Butler makes essentially the same points (esp. 1997), although not in these terms.

21. Firestone (1970: Ch. 4), for example, supported children's liberation. For a critique of the programme, see Archard (1993: Ch. 5).

22. For example, the attachment theorist Mary Ainsworth (1978) argues that basic capacities for autonomy are already established—or, alternatively, thwarted, and the seeds of lifelong dependency laid instead—in early mother–infant relationships. Ainsworth's work has problems, but it still offers insight into how very early relationships can foster individuals' capacities for autonomy, or not.

23. My example might suggest that I regard relationships as causing our autonomy-capacities to come into being but not as being and remaining constitutive of those capacities in an ongoing way. In fact I do take the latter view—that ongoing supportive scaffolding from relationships is needed to maintain and conserve our autonomy-capacities over time, where without that support those capacities can become undermined, damaged, or fall into disrepair.

24. There are two issues here: 'how-possible'—if criticism depends on power, then how can it ever target that power without collapsing in self-contradiction? And 'whether-permissible'—if criticism only has normative validity within a given field of power/knowledge, then how can it ever target that field without voiding itself of legitimacy? See Han-Pile (2016), who distinguishes, names, and addresses these two issues with regard to Foucault. Relatedly, various feminist theorists have worried that Foucault's view that power is both ubiquitous and productive makes criticism of power either impossible (Hartsock 1990) or illegitimate (Fraser 1989), or both. Even so feminist defences and uses of Foucault are many, including Bartky (1988), Butler (1990), (1997), and Oksala (2005). Assessing some feminist positions for and against Foucault, see Allen (2016: 3.5).

25. Gender and race are identities that we are generally aware of having, if we have them. We are ascribed a race and gender based on our visible properties (Haslanger 2000); these ascriptions shape how others treat us, and we become attached to, and take up these identities for ourselves. There are some other social identities, notably of class, which we can have without necessarily explicitly identifying with them (if we don't, we belong to a 'class-in-itself' rather than a self-conscious 'class-for-itself'; see Lukács [1920] 1971). Whether explicitly adopted or not, our social identities still shape our experience fundamentally, in the ways Alcoff highlights for race and gender.

26. 'Neo-colonial' is Nkruma's (1966) characterization but see, alternatively, Quijano's account of the 'coloniality of power' (2000).

27. See Ciavatta (2017) on some ways in which thought and cognition are higher-level versions of bodily, sensory ways of 'synthesizing' or organizing experience, e.g. into background and foreground, where the higher-level variants continue to

presuppose and rest on the continual operation of the more 'primitive' ones. (Ciavatta is explicating ideas of Merleau-Ponty's.)

28. Evidently, I'm taking it that one's first situation is the one entered upon leaving the gestator's womb. Yet we already start to make sense of things *in utero*, so perhaps the foetus too is situated (the concomitant of its having experience). If so, then our first situation is that of the womb and the womb of a particular individual, herself occupying a definite set of personal, social, and temporal locations. However, there is probably no single point when intra-uterine experience and situatedness begin, but rather a gradual process in which they shade into presence. The intra-uterine situation is thus a situation in a more equivocal, partial, and shadowy way than any post-natal situations. Hence, for simplicity, the first *ex utero* situation can be taken to be each person's first full, proper situation.

29. On intersectionality, see the classic accounts by the Combahee River Collective ([1978] 1983) and Kimberlé Crenshaw (1991).

30. One alternative view of time is that of some pre-colonial African peoples, according to John Mbiti: referring especially to the Wakamba people, he claims that they regard the centre of temporal gravity as the past (*tene*) so that each new generation is counted as being in the most recent part '*of the tene period*' (Mbiti 1971: 28).

31. That said, slave status was inherited in the maternal line, under the British-instituted law *partus sequitur ventrem*—'the offspring follows the womb'. See Harris (1996: 328–43, esp. 330), who points out that this element of matrilineality was not to women's benefit: 'This reversal of the usual common law tradition that the status of the child was determined by the father facilitated the reproduction of the slaveholder's own labor force. [And] ... control over Black women's procreation and sexuality was key to the institution of slavery and was the means through which property was increased' (338).

32. Mannheim further distinguishes passive from active membership of one's generation. Also, on generations, see O'Byrne (2010: Ch. 2), Ricoeur ([1985] 1990: 109–16), Schües (2016: esp. Ch. 4) and, from sociology, Edmunds and Turner (2002) amongst others.

4

The Radical Contingency of Being Born

In this chapter I argue that, for each of us, there is a radical contingency to one's being born into one's particular life as it unfolds from one's birth onwards. One can always ask, 'Why is *this* life the one that I am leading?' and 'Why was I born as this particular individual?' In Section I, I motivate these questions and suggest that they are genuine, not merely confused. Yet these questions admit of no answer because, in each case, it is just an ultimate fact that I was born the individual I am and no-one else.

In Sections II and III, I explore this fact by drawing on Sartre's concept of facticity in *Being and Nothingness* ([1943] 1958). *Facticity* means the given circumstances in which I exist at every temporal point of my life, circumstances that include my body and its state, my place and environment, my past, and my relations with others—personal, familial, social, and symbolic. Ultimately, all these circumstances come down from my birth; thus our facticity is part-and-parcel of our natality. My facticity flows down from my being born the particular individual I am, over which I have no choice. Sartre describes this lack of choice in terms of my *contingency*. I add that insofar as there is no reason or explanation why I am born the specific individual I am, my existence is *groundless*. In Section IV, I examine groundlessness—which is another aspect of our natality—by looking at Sartre's novel *Nausea* ([1938] 1965) alongside Schelling's essay on human freedom ([1809] 2006).

In Section V, I return to the concept of situatedness, now in light of Sartre, for whom facticity and situation are correlative phenomena. For him, *situation* designates my circumstances specifically under their aspect of enabling and serving as the conditions in which I exercise my freedom. I criticize Sartre's account of freedom and, linking back to my discussion of situatedness in Chapter 3 of this volume, and drawing on Heidegger, I redefine situation in terms of circumstances, not that we freely transcend, but of which we make sense in sedimented ways.[1] In making sense of where we are, we both receive and build on prior layers of meaning, and interweave

Being born: Birth and Philosophy. Alison Stone, Oxford University Press (2019). © Alison Stone.
DOI: 10.1093/oso/9780198845782.001.0001

new layers; autonomous choice is merely a subset of our ways of making sense of circumstances.

Overall in this chapter, I aim to show that because we are natal beings, facticity is always part of our lives; that, being born, we always make and find meaning from our particular situations in the world; that there is a radical contingency to whom we each are born as, and so which lives we are leading; and that therefore there is an inescapable element of groundlessness to our lives.

I. Why Am I This Particular Individual?

Considering my life as it has unfolded so far, I may wonder: why is *this* the life I am leading? After all, I am one amongst many people, but I am leading my life, not any of theirs, from the inside. I am concerned about how my life is going; I face choices about its direction. I am directly aware of the weave of my experience as I never am with others' experience. Others, though, lead their lives from the inside too. This may prompt me to wonder why this life is the one I am leading, why this stream of experience is the one of which I am directly aware.

Moreover, we have our streams of personal experience as bodies, and our embodiment is essential to our experience being the way it is. For instance, whenever I perceive things around me, my body is presupposed as the place from which I perceive them; if I did not perceive them from a place it is not clear how I could perceive them at all. Yet my body mostly remains unobtrusive, its role in experience taken for granted rather than explicitly attended to. In addition, it is my body's biological powers and properties that make it possible for me to perceive, feel, remember, and so on, although in everyday experience my body is present for me—tacitly, unobtrusively—not as the sort of object analysed by the biological sciences but just as the background of my experience: the place from which I perceive, the organizing centre of my spatial field, the vehicle of my agency. So, given that the life I am leading is an embodied one, another question occurs: Why is this particular body and none other the one that I have, and am?

These questions lead to another. My life, as an embodied one, has unfolded through a series of events and experiences that run back to a starting-point—my birth, in the broad sense that includes my gestation, during which the particular body that I am took shape and became sentient *in utero.* So, I am leading this life because I have been doing so since I was born. But why was I born me in the first place?

The following explanation might be given. I was born the way I was because of my parents' genetic contributions and the physical environment in my mother's womb (and perhaps, too, the external causal factors affecting that environment and the wider social environment shaping these factors). Had my parents conceived a month earlier, with a different egg and sperm, this would have set in motion the formation of a physically different being; and that would have been a different individual, since we are the experiencing subjects that we are as the particular bodies we are. This answer as to why I am the particular individual I am refers to the specific set of physical materials that came together to constitute my body. But what this appeal to originating materials accounts for is what makes this body the unique individual body that it is and gives it its distinctive make-up, whereas the question that concerns me here is different. For there are many unique individual bodies in the world that are all conscious, having their particular streams of first-person experience. Knowing that the body that I am is the uniquely constituted body it is because of the specific set of originating materials that went into it does not in itself explain why this is the body whose conscious standpoint I inhabit from the inside as I don't with any other body. For each human body likewise has a set of originating materials that have constituted it, but I am not any of those other bodies.[2]

One might doubt that this question—why am I me?—is a genuine question. Rather, one might say, it is simply the case that (like every person) I can be described in two ways: (i) from an external third-person perspective, as one amongst other embodied individuals all with their particular constitutions and properties, physical and mental; and (ii) from my internal, first-person perspective. But the two descriptions pick out one and the same being. There is no metaphysical puzzle here: many things can be described in different, even conflicting ways (freedom fighter/terrorist, cute little dog/yappy nuisance). However, descriptions from first- and third-person perspectives are not on a par with such cases where we describe specific items or events differently depending on our values, angles of vision, levels of knowledge, and so on. The difference between first- and third-person perspectives is a more fundamental difference within reality and our relation to it which has global import.

Thomas Nagel argues that we struggle to combine these two perspectives, the impersonal, objective 'view from nowhere' and the personal, subjective view from within one's own life. We all begin inside our subjective perspectives, but inevitably come to ask questions that propel us to try to transcend our subjectivity towards greater objectivity. Then problems arise about how to reconcile the two perspectives and the knowledge they make available. It becomes tempting to reduce one perspective away, most often by adopting a naturalistic or scientistic approach that treats the subjective perspective as mere illusion.[3] For Nagel, such strategies are unsatisfactory because:

> [T]here are things about the world and life and ourselves that cannot be adequately understood from a maximally objective standpoint... A great deal is essentially connected to a particular point of view,... and the attempt to give a complete account of the world in objective terms detached from these perspectives inevitably leads to false reductions or to outright denial that certain patently real phenomena exist at all.   (1986: 7)

Amongst these phenomena are those I noted above, and which are treated by Kierkegaard and other existentialists: that we live our lives from the inside with engaged concern, each directly acquainted with the weft of our own experience, and so on.[4] So both perspectives stand, irreducible to one another. Yet they disclose, and indeed comprise, very different realities. We seem driven to conclude that reality itself is at bottom ambiguous, as Simone de Beauvoir argues in *The Ethics of Ambiguity* ([1948] 1964).

It is from the subjective perspective that there is a question about why the life I am living is this one and, since I have been leading it since birth, why I was born this particular embodied individual and none other. From the objective perspective we can answer that my body was born with the unique make-up it was because of the originating materials, and other causal factors, that went into it. But that does not answer the question we were asking, which was not why the body I am is constituted as it is but why this is the body that I first-personally am at all. This question arises within the subjective perspective, not the objective one.[5]

One might object to my asking 'Why was I born me?' on different grounds—that, according to my account of being born, I was *not* yet me at birth. For, I argued in Chapter 3, it is only through the relationships into which I came by birth that I began to acquire a self and then a concrete personality, acquisitions that were bound up with my incorporating the cultural horizons obtaining in the situation in the world into which I came at birth. Prior to all this, one might say, I did not yet have a self at all and so I was not yet me. On this view, I explain why I am me by tracing the unique chain of processes by which I incorporated certain social, personal, and cultural relationships and thereby acquired a unique self—that is, became me—unique by virtue of the unique set of relational factors and processes from which this self has coalesced. However, in another sense I was me prior to all these processes taking place: I was already a particular sensing body, something that began to be the case during my gestation. Arguably, I did not have a self back then—selfhood came later, during my first post-natal months. But my question here is why I am me in the prior, more minimal sense of being this particular sensing body.[6]

For their part, religious traditions supply various answers to the question 'Why am I me?' Historically, many strands of Christian doctrine and belief distinguish the immortal soul from the mortal body and hold that I, as soul, am joined with this particular living, sentient body because God has infused my soul into it. At the first Vatican Council of 1869–70, the Catholic Church agreed that the soul of each individual is created by God and attached to a certain embryo at the time of conception (see Hick 1976: 39–40). More broadly according to Christian tradition, each person's soul comes into existence in conjunction with the formation of a given foetus.[7] This infusion of soul into the developing body explains why I am leading the particular life I am: because the body whose life I am leading is the one into which God infused the soul that I essentially am.

We might reject such accounts on the grounds that they presuppose the existence of immortal souls. But that aside, Sartre makes another objection to these accounts specifically as attempted explanations of why I am me: that they only explain why I must be someone or other, not why I am the specific someone that I am (Sartre [1943] 1958: 81/124). Appeal to God might show that the soul that I am had to be attached to *some* developing individual body or other, but not why God attached my soul to this particular individual body. Perhaps God's will or reasons are inscrutable, but then we have really only restated that it is a mystery why I am this specific individual. Otherwise, some further explanatory factor must be invoked. Perhaps God created my soul with certain basic ethical dispositions or orientations and then chose a living body with characteristics suitable for realizing these dispositions. But if these dispositions are quite general and widely shared by many souls, then we still do not know why I had to receive this particular body to realize them. Conversely if my dispositions are particular to me, then the question arises of why God imparted them to this particular soul that I am and no-one else—we have merely pushed the source of mystery back.

An alternative family of explanations for why I am me makes reference to rebirth or reincarnation. Both Eastern and Western variants exist; the latter include Plato's version, which he presents through Er's account of the afterlife in the *Republic* (Plato 1993: 10.614–621). To simplify Er's account: My soul—which I truly am—is immortal; I have been through a whole series of incarnations. After the death of my previous body, I spent a time in the immaterial realm, where I chose a new body in which to become reborn. That choice—and what kind of body I was drawn to choose—reflected the character and level of virtue and wisdom I had acquired over my past life or lives. Overall, each time my soul is reborn it assumes a kind and quality of body through which it reaps the consequences of what it has sown by its conduct in previous lives. Ultimately, then, I was born as the individual I was because of the history of my conduct across successive incarnations.

Appeal to rebirth looks most promising in terms of explaining why we are born the individuals we are. But problems arise when accounts of rebirth involve the postulation of essentially immaterial souls in addition to living bodies, as with Plato's account. For without a body, it is not clear how the soul can possibly have the powers of judgement, choice, and perception which Plato takes it to have when he claims that in the between-lives realm we see various possible lives presented to us between which we choose in accordance with our acquired ethical dispositions. The powers in question are essentially dependent on embodiment: it is *as* living bodies that we judge, choose, perceive, build up a sedimented ethical history, and so on. One response to this problem is to redefine the pre- or non-embodied soul in much thinner terms, as in some Eastern traditions (see Phillips 2009: 110–11, 119–30). But then my soul no longer coincides with me as a particular psychological individual. In that case, the question comes back again of why my soul has been reborn as this particular, embodied, and psychologically distinct individual that I am. The problem of why I am born as this individual therefore persists.

We seem to be left with no explanation for why we are each living the particular lives we are. Indeed, I suggest, this is because there is no explanation to be had. That I am born the individual I am is just a fact—an ultimate fact for which no grounds can be supplied. To wonder 'why am I me?' is to encounter this, the *facticity* of our existence. By invoking facticity, I do not explain why I am me; rather, 'facticity' names the reality that my being me is an ultimate fact behind which we can penetrate no further.

II. The Contingency of Who I Am

Sartre asks: 'Why am I conscious...of *this* Me?' (1958: 82/125; my emphasis). Why is *this* the life I'm in? As we've seen, Sartre notes that one might reply that God attached my soul to this living body, but that that would not explain why this particular living body had to be picked. We might instead appeal to pre-incarnation choices exercised by souls, as in Plato's myth of Er. However, Sartre argues, no such entities as immaterial souls exist: one can only have experience from a particular point-of-view, hence as a body; disembodied personal immortality is impossible. These attempted explanations having failed, Sartre concludes that there is nothing that causes me to be the particular individual I am. For him, this means that it is absolutely *contingent* that I am born inhabiting this and not that bodily point-of-view, in this and not that person's womb, in this and not that place: 'for me birth and the place which it assigns me are contingent things' (490/571).

This kind of contingency can be distinguished from another sort of contingency which is arguably involved in my birth, namely causal contingency. Under the standard use of 'contingent' to describe an event that might or might not have happened, my being born is causally contingent in that I might never have been born: the particular foetus that was me might never have been generated had, say, my biological parents conceived a month earlier. Had they done so, it is not that *my* initial make-up would have been different; rather, a different individual would have been conceived. Thus, each of us could only be born at the time and place, to the parents, from the particular egg and sperm that we were; otherwise the one born would have been someone else.[8] My having been born me, then, was not at all contingent in the sense that I could equally well have been born someone else: I could not. But what is contingent here is the fact that this particular body, the one I happen to be, was conceived at all. Indeed, given that my parents might have conceived a month earlier or not at all, might never have met at all, etc., it might seem to have been very unlikely, only minutely probable, that I was born: 'Any seemingly trivial deviation in the antecedent course of events would have spelled non-existence for us' (Reader 2017: 42). Alternatively, though, one might claim that if we filled in all the links in the relevant causal chain it would emerge that my parents could only have conceived the particular foetus that I am, all other alternatives having been ruled out by countervailing causal factors. On an existentialist-type view, though, there is no such all-encompassing causal chain because human freedom is everywhere at work. In that case, once again, for each of us it is the case that we might never have been conceived. In this sense my birth was causally contingent.[9]

However, the radical contingency of my being born me is different from this. The conception of the particular embodied individual that I happen to be is causally contingent in that it might not have happened. Given different actions, circumstances, and originating materials, a different body would have been conceived instead. And that would have been a different person because, being a different body, it would have been the site of a stream of first-person experience different from the one that I occupy, which is localized to my body. But that this particular embodied perspective *is* the one I occupy and none other is what is contingent in the radical sense—in the sense that my being first-personally this very individual that I am is an inexplicable and ultimate fact, which obtains without there being any explanatory ground of its doing so. Nothing third-personal suffices to explain it, because the first- and third-personal registers differ; and nothing first-personal can explain why I am me because, prior to my beginning to be me, there *is* no first-personal field for me within which some elements can explain others.

My coming by birth to begin to lead this particular subjective life that is mine, then, is *just* a fact. It is contingent under another common use of the adjective 'contingent' to describe events or states of affairs, not insofar as they might or might not happen given different antecedents, but insofar as they come about by *pure* chance or accident, unpredictably—for no reason. These events are radically contingent because they are contingent not on any antecedent X but absolutely so. Such events are also 'absurd', for Sartre; for him, a state of affairs or fact is 'absurd' when it is 'absolute and incomprehensible...A fact of pure contingency—an absurd fact' (491/572). An absurd fact, then, is *groundless*; we cannot understand or explain why it obtains, just because there are no causal factors here to be understood: this fact is a brute, inexplicable given. This is the sense in which it is radically contingent who I am.

Initially, it is a matter of radical contingency whom I am born as. But in being born into and as a body, I am born in a particular spot in the world, in history, and so on. Just as there is no explanation for my coming into the specific body I have, neither is there any explanation for my starting off in the unique set of circumstances that I do. And because my whole life unfolds out of this initially contingent starting-point, a dimension of contingency descends into and through my entire life. Had I started somewhere different—Nairobi, say, not Billericay in Essex—my life would have gone differently throughout. That I make choices does not affect this: given a different starting-point, I would have come to make a whole series of different choices, reacting to different circumstances at each point. So, just as it is radically contingent what individual I am born as and therefore what life I am leading, equally an ever-present dimension of radical contingency runs through whatever concrete course my life takes.

A fictional example may help. In *The Hollow Men* (McCarthy 2016), police surgeon Harry Kent has for years felt hollow and empty, dating back to a disastrous episode during his service as an army doctor in the Afghanistan war. His team co-member and long-term friend James Lahiri went to the toilet just when a local policeman launched a rifle attack on the team, killing two men and injuring several others, inflicting serious injuries on Kent and leaving senior officer Peter Tammas permanently paralysed from the neck down. Emerging from the toilet, James, a doctor like Harry, saves Harry's life. Harry broods constantly on the contingency that it was James who was in the toilet at the key moment, and that this chance event had such immense repercussions, leaving James uninjured and able, with heroic calmness amidst the chaos, to perform the necessary medical procedures to save Harry. Harry feels angry and resentful towards James— why couldn't Harry have been the one having the toilet break, and so able to show his heroism? But this is only the symptom of Harry's broader concern: Why is he condemned to leading the life that he is—unheroic, in need of rescue, ashamed, embittered? Why is this, and not James's, the life that it has fallen to Harry to inhabit? Harry vents his anger to Lammas, who replies: 'Sometimes I worry about you, Harry...Cause you're hollow.... T. S. Eliot.... I think he meant that we are all born hollow' (59). That is, in the end, Harry's 'hollow' feeling embodies his awareness that there is just no explanation to be had for his being in this life and not James's. Harry may be able to narrate how it came about that James and not he went to the toilet when he did. But this could only happen because James and Harry were each leading their different lives already starting at the specific points in time, space, and society that they did. And that, in the end, is a fact that can only be accepted, or resisted, but not explained.

To be born is to come into existence as some particular person without there being any ground for this happening. Who I am is just a fact that I cannot explain but only accept. With this initial sense of our facticity in place, we can now explore our facticity further with the aid of Sartre's account of it.

III. Sartre, Facticity, and Birth

In *Being and Nothingness*, Sartre treats facticity as a fundamental dimension of human existence which flows out of our being born. I therefore turn now to Sartre's work, not primarily so as to engage in Sartre scholarship but rather to use his thought to illuminate birth. Sartre's potential to contribute to feminist thinking about birth has been underappreciated, for his work overall has shortcomings from a feminist perspective.[10] Indeed, his view of birth itself can seem unpromising, as when he writes:

> Someone will say 'I did not ask to be born'. This is...naïve...I am responsible for everything, in fact,...I am ashamed of being born or I am astonished at it or I rejoice over it,...Thus in a certain sense I *choose* to be born.   (1958: 555–6/641)

Lisa Guenther says about this passage:

> While Sartre acknowledges that 'I am not the foundation of my being', he argues that this very fact compels me to *assume* my own foundation, as if I had chosen it for myself....This responsibility is inescapable, since whether I find my existence joyful or hateful, my subjective response remains the final arbiter of its meaning....I am the author of my own existence...Responsibility for my existence derives...from this act of self-production...[and] in this proud assertion of self-authorship, the significance of my birth to a mother is reduced to the status of raw material waiting to bear my stamp.   (2006: 25)

A more charitable interpretation of Sartre is possible, namely that while I can choose how to respond to my birth, I can never choose to have been born in the circumstances that I was. As a result, my freedom of response is always entangled with unchosen circumstances—at the outset of my life and, in consequence, throughout the rest of it. My freedom is always situated, and my life takes shape in an admixture of the chosen and the unchosen.

Others such as Tanja Staehler (2012) prefer Heidegger's conception of thrown projection to Sartre's conception of situated freedom. For Sartre, freedom is always situated, but nonetheless we freely transcend and negate our situations, whereas for Heidegger we are always-already involved with possibilities that are thrown to us by our circumstances and history. However, Sartre's merit is to connect facticity with birth somewhat more explicitly than Heidegger connects thrownness with birth.[11] Sartre also conceives of birth as being more central to the structure of existence than death, and he goes some way towards recognizing that it is from birth that facticity, situatedness, and contingency descend through our lives.

Sartre's discussion of facticity in *Being and Nothingness* is extensive, many-stranded, and distributed across several parts of the book. Facticity figures, first, as an 'immediate structure of the for-itself' (1958: 2.1.II); second, within lived, experienced temporality, as the facticity of the past (2.2.I.A); third, as the facticity of my body as my particular point-of-view on the world (3.2.I); and, fourth, as that which means that my freedom is always and necessarily situated (4.1.II). Overarching these, the concept of facticity is rooted in Sartre's overarching ontology, which we should briefly spell out.

Sartre's basic division is between the 'in-itself' and the 'for-itself'; the latter domain effectively coincides with that of human existents, beings for whom their own being is in question (as Sartre paraphrases Heidegger). Initially, Sartre supports this ontological division with reference to the structure of intentionality, that is, the directedness of all consciousness upon objects—not through any mediating veil of representations, but in a mode of direct access to mind-independent things (1958: xxvii/17). For Sartre, consciousness (*conscience*) is a pure openness onto outer objects, but it directs itself upon these objects in manifold ways—remembering, imagining, perceiving, etc. In all these we are *acting* so as to intend objects in certain ways. But (i) to perform an act, one might think, I must be aware of doing that act (even if I'm not aware of any 'I' who's performing it). For Sartre, however, (ii) ordinary ('pre-reflective') consciousness is fully directed on objects and not on its own activity. To satisfy both (i) and (ii), Sartre maintains that all consciousness of objects presupposes a 'non-thetic' (or 'non-positional') consciousness-of-itself (*conscience (de) soi*)—that is, of the intentional activity in question. 'Non-thetic' means that consciousness does not attend explicitly to its own intentional activity but instead presupposes it, in the background.

Several consequences follow. (1) Consciousness never simply coincides with, but always differs from itself: it is always at least two, thetic and non-thetic. The for-itself is inherently fractured; hence it is *for*-itself, not simply itself. (2) Therefore, consciousness is unlike everything that is just itself, undividedly. The latter comprises the domain of the in-itself, of what is non-conscious (xxviii/18). (3) As such, consciousnesses cannot rightly be reduced to objects amongst other objects, caught in chains of causal determination. (4) Being thus unlike objects, not causally determined either by our own pasts or by interactions amongst objects, we are free to adopt the intentional stances we do. Our practical agency thus has the same source as our agency in conferring particular meanings upon the world through our intentional attitudes towards it. We 'exist' in an interwoven practical–interpretive way, for amongst the actions that we choose to perform are the intentional actions by which we construct meaning. And all these actions have their source in the fundamentally fractured structure of conscious existence.

Let us now home in on facticity with respect to the facticity of the body. To be conscious of objects in the world, Sartre says, is to stand in direct, unmediated relation to them. Such relations are only possible on a perspectival basis: I can only occupy perceptual, tactile, cognitive (etc.) relations with objects from a definite point-of-view.

> *For me* this glass is to the left of the decanter and a little behind it; *for Pierre*, it is to the right and a little in front. It is not even conceivable that a consciousness could survey the world in such a way that the glass should be *simultaneously* given to it at the right and at the left of the decanter, in front of it and behind it.   (1958: 306/368–9)

But to have a point-of-view, I must have a body. To understand Sartre here we need to feed in his account of the body. In the above-quoted passage the body shows up under the first of three dimensions that Sartre identifies in it over the course of *Being and Nothingness*. In this first dimension, one's body is 'the unperceived centre of the field of perception and the unutilizable centre of the field of action' (Morris 2010: 5). The body is thus presupposed in my perceptual and practical experience and, being presupposed, is invisible to me in its bodily character. Later Sartre ascertains that, in its second dimension, my body appears to others as a kind of physical object. That in turn makes possible the third dimension in which I attend to my body as if from an outsider's perspective, regarding it as something physical. Moreover, when the other looks at me, it emerges that I who had been directly absorbed in certain undertakings (such as spying on someone through a keyhole) am the very same as the perceptible, physical object— my body in its second dimension—as which I am now seen and exposed. I am exposed as body (Sacks 2005: 287–8; Webber 2010a: 190). In this retrospective light, we can see that the reason why I could only perceive and act from a point-of-view is that I am a perceiving and acting body, one that is a living physical object as well as the subject of my perceptual and practical experience.

Now having specified that I can only perceive from a perspective, Sartre brings in facticity:

> For human reality, to be is to-be-there [*être-là*]: that is, 'there in that chair,' 'there at that table,' ... It is an ontological necessity .... [T]his necessity appears between two contingencies; on the one hand, while it is necessary that I am in the form of being-there, still it is altogether contingent that I am, for I am not the foundation of my being; on the other hand, while it is necessary that I be engaged in this or that point of view, it is contingent that it should be precisely in this view to this exclusion of all others. It is this double contingency which encompasses a necessity which we have called the *facticity* of the for-itself.   (Sartre 1958: 308/371)

Here facticity applies in two ways. (1) Although it is a matter of contingent fact that any given for-itself does exist, if any for-itself is to exist it must do so from *some* bodily point-of-view or other. Disembodied existence is impossible. (2) It is a matter of contingent fact that a for-itself happens to inhabit the *particular* bodily point-of-view that it does. It must be embodied to exist, but there is no reason why it has the specific body it does.

What body I have is just a fact, then. But aren't there sometimes reasons for our bodies being the way they are? What if I have made a gender transition, or maintained an intensive exercise regime to cultivate a honed, muscular physique? However, all these are alterations I make to the body I already had: I can change the properties of my body but I cannot change the fact that this is the body that is mine to change. Moreover, any alterations I make are to my body in its pre-alteration state. That prior state may already have embodied alterations on which I previously chose, but those alterations too were ones I made to the still-prior state of my body. In the end we come back to the very first states of our bodies, which were not subject to our choices. In two ways, then, a dimension of unchosen givenness runs through my succession of choices about my body over time. The first is that this is the body I have to make choices about. The second is that my body began in a given state, and if I changed it, those particular changes made sense in response to its prior state and would not have occurred had its initial state been otherwise. In this last regard my body retains a dimension of unchosen givenness throughout my life, carried forwards in and through all of my choices.

This sheds light on the general temporal structure of facticity. It is through my past history that facticity—including that of my body, its given states and properties—adheres to me at each temporal point in my life. I am subject to facticity at stages $T_{n...}$ of my life because facticity was present at T_1 of my life and, whatever choices I have made, they have put me into new circumstances which, for me now, are given. Sartre therefore declares that facticity and the past are identical: 'This contingency of the for-itself, this weight surpassed and preserved in the very surpassing—this is *Facticity*. But it is also the past. "Facticity" and "Past" are two words to indicate one and the same thing' (118/162). The whole of my past is part of my facticity insofar as, at any particular moment, this past is given to me, unchosen. What is done is done, is unalterable and fixed, so that it just is what it is, self-identically. And because my past cannot be other than it already is, it is not itself one of my possibilities (116/159), although I can respond to it in different possible ways. Because my past is a given for me at any one time, it belongs to my facticity.

More concretely, my past provides the backdrop against which I envisage possibilities and decide on some of them. That past limits me to a set of possibilities which arise and make sense against this backdrop, and which I envisage as going beyond this given backdrop in determinate ways. My possibilities incorporate a necessary reference to this backdrop, albeit as something that they negate or surpass. Once carried out, my projects fall into my past in turn, becoming part of the facticity against which I choose at the next point in time. My past thus embodies my inherited history of past facticities and past choices, thoroughly intermingled. And although my past includes this quotient of past choice, those choices qua past now belong to my facticity. It is a given that I made those choices, and I cannot now undo what I've done. As Sebastian Gardner thus sums up:

> Facticity . . . is . . . indifferent to choice. Necessarily we begin to make choices under conditions, such as the historical age in which we live, which we have not chosen, but making choices does not *reduce the quantity* of our facticity; the contents of my choices take up particularities offered by the being of the world to my nothingness, and so always presuppose facticity.   (2009: 101)

Facticity is ineliminable, then, for several reasons. (1) I am always in circumstances that are given to me through my prior history and that are 'factical' just in being given. (2) Second, although those (current) circumstances partly result from and so reflect and incorporate (i) (now-past) choices on my part, qua past those choices are now a matter of facticity, while my circumstances always also partly reflect and incorporate (ii) the unchosen facticity of the past circumstances in which I made those past choices. (3) For that reason, those now-given choices that I made in the past already incorporated reference to the previously given circumstances that those choices negated, whose weight was therefore 'preserved in the very surpassing' (Sartre 1958: 118/162). For example, when I get my hair cut, my choice to have it cut in a fairly short bob reflects my reaction against its having previously got over-long and messy, and my determination to have it cut in a way that will make it low-maintenance. What I reacted against— over-long messiness—is incorporated, indirectly, into the chosen haircut as that against which it is set.

In sum, facticity is ever-present because it is conveyed forwards at each moment of my existence from the preceding one—thus, in the end, from my birth. Sartre draws out how facticity runs back to birth in 4.1.II, where he reconsiders my facticity as it furnishes the situation in which I choose. Here, Sartre details four elements of my facticity-as-situation: my *place*; my *past*; my *environment* (*entours*)—the complexes of 'instrumental-things' around me, such as a bicycle, paths, signs, etc., with which I make my way from one village to the next; and *others* (i.e. other subjects), including the references to them that are built into in my place, past, and environment (such as, he mentions, a 'No Jews' sign on a café door).

Regarding my place, Sartre points out that, necessarily, my body—the site of my point-of-view—is always present onto not objects *tout court* but a specific local configuration of objects. Currently I (AS) am sitting in my living room, on the sofa, across the room from my rabbits, and so on.

> [A]lthough this actual place can have been assigned to me by my freedom (I have 'come' here), I have been able to occupy it only as a function of the one that I occupied previously and by following paths marked out by the objects themselves. This previous place refers me back to another, this to another, thus finally to the *pure contingency of my place*; that is, to that one of my places which does not refer back at all to *me*: the place which is assigned to me by my birth.   (490/570)

My place, along with every element of my facticity, is passed down to me along each step of my life, ultimately going back to my birth, when I *received* the first of the ever-elongating series of places I have occupied. My parents may have made choices that led to my being born in the place I was (Bill-ericay hospital). But *their* choices do not belong within the chain of *my* choices, Sartre says (I do not make their choices, for I do not live their lives from the inside, first-personally). Thus, in being born, I came into my first place, which was the start of a distinct series of places—my places—that now began to unfold. My first place was absolutely given to me, with no quotient of prior choice from my side. '[T]o be born is...to *take one's place*, or rather,...to *receive* it' (490/571).

We can now clarify how the concept of facticity hangs together as a whole. *Initial facticity* (my phrase, not Sartre's) refers to (1) the necessity of each for-itself being born as some body, in some place, within an environment and set of social relations; (2) the fact of each for-itself happening to be born as that particular body in the particular place, environment, and social relations that they are; (3) their body, place, environment, and social relations insofar as they are given to that for-itself at birth. At every subsequent step of a for-itself's life, given circumstances have come down to it, directly or indirectly, from its initial facticity; these make up its *ongoing facticity*.

Sartre's concept of facticity only fully hangs together because facticity is connected with birth. He draws this out, again, within 2.*1*.II. I am never 'my own foundation', Sartre says here; I always am-not something that I *already* am. That is, I can only ever envisage possibilities (which reach beyond, 'are not', whatever circumstances I am already in) on the basis of those circumstances as they are given to me (to be determinate, negation must be *of* something antecedent). Unless I were amidst the given, I could envisage no determinate ways of going beyond it. And I am amidst the given because it comes down to me from my birth. When Sartre writes: 'I can ask myself, "Why am I thirsty? Why am I conscious of this glass? Of this Me?"' (82/125), he takes it that I will inevitably come to ask why I am 'this Me' at all, that is, why I was born this particular individual. And I had no choice in that matter. 'Without facticity consciousness could choose its attachments to the world in the way that the souls in Plato's *Republic* choose their condition: I could determine myself to "be born a worker" or to "be born a bourgeois"' (83/126). In reality, Sartre replies, I do not decide whom I am to be born as; rather, that is given to me, and sets into my existence a dimension of givenness that it will never shake off.

Being born, then, plays a major structuring role in human existence, on Sartre's view. Yet he is less than completely explicit about birth's role. Birth comes up intermittently in *Being and Nothingness* because his thinking about facticity leads towards it. But he neither gives the concept *birth* any stable, explicit location in his conceptual framework, nor gives any single, focused discussion of the relations between birth and facticity.[12]

Nonetheless, we can spell out the existential significance of being born as it emerges from Sartre.

1. Birth primarily figures into existence as someone's birth, rather than as a physical and biological process understood in impersonal, third-person terms.

2. From that perspective, an individual's birth is their temporal starting-point, to which their facticity runs back through time in all its aspects. Corresponding to the 'ever-growing totality of the in-itself which I am', ever-accreting as I move forwards in time, are countless backward links in this chain which finally end at my birth.

3. Reception: My birth is absolutely unchosen by me; instead I receive it or, what for Sartre is equivalent, it is given to me. (An alternative view is that it is gifted to me—from Christian perspectives, by God; from some feminist perspectives, by my mother. I'll consider such views in Chapter 7.)

4. Conferral of initial facticity. Through my birth, I am given the several elements of my initial facticity: my particular body in its initial state; my first place, environment, and set of social relations.

5. My first place. Sartre takes one's first place to be the place one came into on leaving the womb (e.g. Billericay hospital). But sometimes he understands birth more broadly, as beginning at conception and extending through intra-uterine life until departure from the womb. In those terms, my first place is the womb of my mother or the person who is gestating me, and my first social and environmental relations are with this person's body and with other events and people in the outer world insofar as the gestator's body mediates my awareness of them.

6. The root source of one's ongoing facticity. From 1 to 5, one's birth is the temporal starting-point from which facticity persists inescapably throughout one's entire existence.

7. Birth plays a greater role in our existence than death. Sartre denies that mortality is the necessary condition of my having situated freedom. I necessarily exercise freedom anyway, whereas my death will cut off unfinished whatever projects I am then engaged in—the more so as it is down to chance, and is unpredictable, when I will die, so that I will unavoidably be engaged in some undertaking or other when death strikes.[13] My death, for Sartre, is thus outside the orbit of my existence

as one of forward projection upon possibilities: if I commit to reading Proust's *À la recherche du temps perdu,* for example, I necessarily envisage continuing to read it across many coming weeks and I tacitly presuppose that I'll remain alive to do so. Thus, not only is awareness of my death not necessary for my freedom, but also my freedom requires that I effectively push the possibility of my death outside my orbit. In contrast, my birth is constitutive of my existence as meaningful, because as the root source of my facticity my birth is necessary to all my exercises of situated freedom. Also, the ramifications of my birth are implicitly carried forward into the present through every such exercise of my situated freedom.[14]

IV. *Nausea* and Groundlessness

I mentioned earlier that, for Sartre, my being born me is not only a pure fact and one that is the source of my life-long facticity, it is also an 'absurd' fact, one that has no ground. This means that groundlessness is an aspect of our natality just as facticity is. We can expand on our groundlessness with reference to Sartre's novel *Nausea.*

Antoine Roquentin, a historian, has begun suffering from attacks of 'nausea'. He records them in a diary to try to make sense of them. The first attack happened on the beach in the provincial town of Bouville: 'There was something I saw and which disgusted me . . . It was a flat pebble, dry all over one side, damp and muddy on the other' (Sartre [1938] 1965: 10/12). Roquentin's attacks proceed to become more and more acute. One time, Roquentin's acquaintance the Autodidact comes to say hello and, Roquentin reports, 'I took ten seconds to recognize him. I saw an unknown face, hardly a face. And then there was his hand, like a fat white worm in my hand' (13–14/16). Another time, Roquentin looks at his face in the mirror and feels perplexed that it can have any qualities at all: 'At bottom, I am even shocked that you can attribute qualities of this sort to it, as if you called a piece of earth or a lump of rock beautiful or ugly' (30/30).

Needless to say, Roquentin's nausea is not a symptom of any physical illness. Rather, it is an 'ontological' affect that discloses fundamental features of the self, the world, and their relation. What exactly these features are, though, only becomes clear to Roquentin over time; until then the nausea's message remains obscure. Roquentin's worst episode of nausea occurs one lunch-time at a café, when he becomes horrified at the sheer material

presence in his hand of a knife he is holding. 'So this is the Nausea: this
blinding revelation?...Now I know: I exist—the world exists—and I know
that the world exists. That's all.... [Since the beach] there had been other
Nauseas; from time to time objects set themselves to exist in your hand'
(176/156). Overcome with horror, he runs out and jumps aboard a tram.
The nausea persists:

> I lean my hand on the seat, but I pull it back hurriedly: it exists [ça existe].
> This thing on which I'm sitting, on which I leaned my hand just now, is
> called a seat. They made it on purpose for people to sit on,...they went to
> work with the idea of making a seat, and when they had finished, it was
> *that* [ça] that they had made.   (180/159)

Roquentin obsessively mutters 'It's a seat', trying to throw off the nausea,
but 'the word refuses to settle on the thing'. He can't attach the word,
meaning, or purpose of the seat to its bare existence. 'Things have freed
themselves from their names. They are there, grotesque, stubborn, gigantic,
and it seems ridiculous to call them seats or say anything at all about them'
(180/159). Roquentin is horrified by the sheer existence and presence of
things; by their materiality; that words are arbitrary human creations; and
that things always have something in them that goes beyond our names,
categories, and efforts to understand them.[15]

Here, though, I want to highlight one thing in particular by which Roquentin is nauseated: groundlessness. He jumps off the tram and hastens into a
park, where he has a long confrontation with his surroundings, especially the
entwined root of a tree. A 'black, knotty mass', 'utterly brute', it is plunged
down into the earth (182/161). This is the book's culminating scene, in which,
in a kind of dark epiphany, Roquentin grasps what has been troubling him
with reference to the root. The tree root is *superfluous* or *gratuitous* (*de trop*);
there is no reason for it to be there. It is therefore *absurd*; as there is no reason
for its existence, we can make no sense of it, can give no adequate explanation
for its being. That it is there at all defies all efforts at explanation. And the root
is therefore *contingent*, in the sense that its existence is groundless, a pure fact
with no grounds behind it. The same goes for everything and everyone,
Roquentin concludes: there is 'nothing, nothing, absolutely no reason for
existing'; 'we hadn't the slightest reason for being there, any of us': 'Every
existent is born without reason' (162/143, 184/163, 191/169).

In this light we can see how Roquentin's previous manifestations of
nausea cohere. There is something in the sheer existence of things which

goes beyond whatever explanations we put forward for them and all our meaning-imposing schemes. What goes beyond all these is the gratuitousness, absurdity, and contingency with which things exist. The tree root, for instance, is not there as part of any teleological system descending from God; it is *just* there. Moreover, the felt bodily qualities of Roquentin's nausea reflect and express its message. That dimension in things of which we can make no sense—their sheer presence—is like an indigestible lump of food sitting in the stomach, resisting all our efforts to assimilate (comprehend, or intellectualize) it. And Roquentin feels dizzy whenever he registers the groundlessness of existence: he has no solid ground to stand on, so that he feels unsteady, liable to fall.

It might be objected that we can explain perfectly well why the tree root is there and is the way it is. A given acorn was borne to this spot in the ground by the wind, and subsequent environmental conditions allowed it to take hold and grow, where the wind was blowing in a certain direction due to prior atmospheric conditions, and so on. In practice, we may never know all the relevant factors because the causal chains at work are so complex, but the reality is that there is no bare contingency here.

In part, though, Roquentin focuses on the root because it symbolizes a locus of contingency that *is* real—the contingency with which each of us is born the particular individual we are. Roquentin himself writes: 'Every existent is born without reason' (*naît sans raison*) (191/169). And he apprehends that he himself simply exists, without there being any reason for it: 'Now I know: I exist...' (176/156). 'And *I*...— *I too was superfluous*' (184/163). He exists in the same way that, as he sees it, the root does. It just surges up, inexplicably, out of the darkness of the earth, standing for the dark impenetrability of the fact that I am me—the mystery at my origin. The root thus stands for birth: the root is the beginning, the basis and source, of the tree, just as someone's birth is the source and beginning of their existence. And the root rises up inexplicably out of the earth, just as, at birth, someone new appears in the world who was not there before, where the utter newness of this existent goes beyond any explanations we may offer for it.

Partly, too, Roquentin focuses on the root as a part through which he apprehends the contingency or groundlessness of existence as a whole: 'the world exists...and that is all' (176/156). We cannot explain why there is anything at all, for any explanation would have to refer to some prior existent, but it is the very fact that there are any existents that has first to be explained. All our explanatory and meaningful schemes meet their limit here, confronted with the sheer presence of the world, for which the root stands.

Roquentin is concerned with groundlessness, then, but neither he nor Sartre distinguishes two different cases of groundlessness that are at issue: (1) the groundlessness of the fact that there is anything at all; (2) and the groundlessness of the fact that we are each born as the particular individuals that we are. The tree root image condenses these cases together.

Regarding (1), Christian thought has often addressed the groundlessness of the world. For example, Zygmunt Bauman says: 'The...hypothesis, that something came from nothing of its own accord with no intervention from a higher power, is...mentally ungraspable' (2014: 44). We bring in God to explain why there is anything at all. Sartre in *Nausea* is re-asserting that the world exists without any ground, even a divine one. This gives rise to certain similarities with Schelling's unconventional theological approach in his *Investigations into the Essence of Human Freedom* (the *Freiheitsschrift*) ([1809] 2006).

For Schelling, prior to God's creation of the ordered world is the ground-lessness with which God himself is born. Distinguishing between God's existence and his ground, Schelling argues that God cannot exist or exercise creative agency unless he has a ground of possibility, namely in his own upsurge into existence. While Schelling understands God to be a personal saviour, he also equates God with the Absolute: the whole in which all finite things are contained and which they express and manifest. In saying that there is a ground of God's existence, then, Schelling is simultaneously affirming that the world's existence has a ground in a brute appearance or upsurge by which this world comes about. This upsurge is non-rational and chaotic—the ground of God or the world is itself groundless—since there is no reason why this upsurge occurs: rather, the upsurge is the prior condition of there being anything at all that can serve as a causal and explanatory factor. The fact that there is a whole cannot be explained, because until that whole appears there are no explanatory factors to be invoked. As the ground is thus inexplicable—it simply bursts forth—Schelling calls it 'the incomprehensible basis of the reality in things, the indivisible remainder, that which with even the greatest exertion cannot be resolved into the understanding but remains eternally in the ground' (2006: 359). The ground (*Grund*) is an abyss (*Abgrund*), a darkness the depth of which reason cannot plumb. And this imbues all things with an aspect of groundlessness insofar as they participate in and instantiate the Absolute or God and, within it, its own ungrounded ground.

Schelling links the ground with birth and gestation: 'it is the yearning [that] the eternal One feels to give birth to itself... [And] the yearning wants to give birth to God' (28). 'All birth is birth from darkness into light' (28). Seeds come to fruition in the darkness of the earth; likewise, the human being is 'formed in the maternal body; and... from the darkness of that which is without understanding (from feeling, yearning, the sovereign mother of knowledge)' (29). Thus, God's ground is associated with a maternal body—out of which God, child-like, comes forth—as well as with the dark earth in which plants germinate, prefiguring Sartre's root plunged into the ground.[16]

Sartre's concerns in *Nausea* are akin to those of Schelling's *Freiheitss-chrift*. For both philosophers, it is a matter of sheer contingency and gratuity that anything exists at all. They both interpret the brute fact that things exist (Sartre) or the upsurge by which they exist (Schelling) on the model of birth as emergence from darkness to light.[17] However, in terms of *Nausea*, the resulting problem is that Sartre does not distinguish (1) the contingency of there being anything at all from (2) the contingency that it is in each case inexplicable why I am born in the particular life that I am. These two problematics are run together, partly because birth counts at once as a source of our individual groundlessness and as a model for the groundlessness of all existence. To this extent, Sartre in *Nausea* does not so much succeed in thinking about what it is to be born as treat birth as a mystery that is a model for the mysteries of the universe.

V. Situatedness, Freedom, and Sense-Making

Let's now return to situatedness and its connections with being born. For Sartre, the same elements of our facticity that are given to us, ultimately by birth, also serve as the elements of our situation insofar as they are enabling conditions of our freedom. Thus, for him, facticity and situation are strictly correlative and they also correlate with freedom: facticity, specifically as providing the enabling conditions for free choice, constitutes situation. The elements that make up my facticity on any occasion—my past to this point, the state of my body, my place and environment—at the same time make up my situation just insofar as they provide the circumstances to which I must choose how to respond. For Sartre, then, to be situated is to be in a set of given circumstances which provide the background for my choice, but where I can always choose how to react to these circumstances because I am never simply identical with them.

In Chapter 3, I introduced situatedness along lines informed by both phenomenology and feminism, suggesting that our situations right through our lives come down from our initial natal situations. Sartre agrees on this last point: because we occupy particular situations in the world at the outset, so too we inescapably remain in determinate situations at every subsequent point in our lives—however much agency we may exercise. If I am born in situation S1, and then effect some change in my circumstances, that change is nonetheless wrought on my prior situation to place me into S2, where I am in S2 only because I was in S1. S2 may incorporate aspects of S1, or have its meaning from its relation to S1, or be as it is because of its relation to S1. Likewise, for S3 in relation to S2, and so on. The situating force of my birth thus remains ever-operative in my life, across the series of choices I make, which would not be *this* series had it not been for the specific first situation into which my birth placed me.

Despite Sartre's merit in highlighting the role of birth and facticity in situatedness, there are problems with his understanding of situatedness as situated *freedom*. These problems concern (1) unchosen values, (2) the social-relational conditions of freedom, (3) the genesis of the for-itself, and (4) the weight of the past. These problems raise the question of whether (5) Heidegger's conception of thrownness is preferable to Sartre's conception of facticity.

1. *Unchosen values*. To make choices, Charles Taylor argues against Sartre, we must have reasons to choose, where these reasons are supplied by a background of values (Taylor [1976] 1982: 117–22). Sartre certainly accepts that we make day-to-day choices, generally pre-reflexively, in light of deeper, longer-term projects and the values they embody. For example, Mathieu Delarue in *The Age of Reason* ([1945] 2001) strives desperately to obtain money for his pregnant mistress Marcelle to have an abortion *because*—as Mathieu only realizes later—he does not want to marry her. For Sartre, however, our projects and values are themselves chosen—mostly pre-reflexively, over time, through the successive micro-choices that presuppose and realize these longer-term commitments. (Mathieu has all along been continually committing himself to staying unmarried in his efforts to procure the abortion fee.) Only occasionally do circumstances call on us to make a reflexive and conscious choice of our guiding values, as happens to Sartre's imagined young man in *Existentialism and Humanism* who must choose between staying with his dependent mother and leaving her to fight with the Free French.

Taylor objects that our background values cannot be entirely chosen, for at least some choices require prior values to motivate them. Even if I modify and adjust those values over time, that is because I revise my beliefs about what has value, not because of some arbitrary decision to change values. The overarching point is that we can only make choices insofar as we have a never-fully-chosen background of values and commitments. Initially, these values are ones I inherit and take on from the world around me. I may modify these inherited values, at least by adapting them to my specific circumstances. But there always remains a dimension of facticity about what I value. My givenness thus informs and shapes my values and choices and is carried forward in and through them. Givenness is thus internal to choice and not merely a background against which spontaneous choice occurs.

2. *Social-relational conditions of freedom.* Sartre's strong understanding of freedom makes it virtually identical with autonomy, that is, deciding how to act based on self-chosen values. However, as we saw in the last chapter, feminist theorists of relational autonomy argue that the capacity for autonomy actually consists in a complex bundle of capacities involving imagination, empathy, attention, reflection, and criticism, capacities that are constituted and maintained in and by one's social relationships. Given these multiple components of autonomy, individuals can have it to varying degrees, depending on how far their social relationships support them in developing and maintaining the relevant capacities. Sartre does not identify social–relational conditions as being necessary for us to develop capacities to make either short-term or deeper, longer-term choices; rather, for him, these capacities are built into the structure of the for-itself. He is wrong here: we develop these capacities, with social support, to varying degrees as social conditions permit. In this way, again, a dimension of givenness is built into these capacities, as well as—from (1)—into the specific choices in which our exercises of these capacities may result.

3. *Genesis of the for-itself.* Sartre's denial (from 2) that our capacities for freedom undergo a process of genesis beginning at birth and continuing through infancy, childhood, and beyond is connected with his view that one cannot rightly be said to *become* a for-itself. To be sure, temporality is a necessary part of the structure of the for-itself. Because the for-itself is fractured and self-negating, its experience is necessarily articulated into the (past) givens that it is not, the (future)

goals it is oriented towards, and the (present) negation of the former in favour of the latter. But since temporal articulation thus depends on the for-itself's self-negation, temporality cannot obtain outside of or prior to the for-itself and there can be no temporal genesis of the capacities constitutive of being-for-self.

On this basis Sartre denies that it makes sense to ask how an individual's consciousness emerges during their gestation *in utero*. He says:

There is a metaphysical problem of birth in that I can be anxious to know how it can be from *such an* embryo that *I* was born; and this problem is perhaps insoluble. But it is not an ontological problem;... for consciousness can appear to itself only... *as being already born*.... To be For-itself is to *be born*.

(139/185)

That is: we might ask how a material organism, the embryo, becomes conscious. But that would be a 'metaphysical' inquiry, not the 'onto-logical' type of inquiry that Sartre favours. 'Ontology' investigates how our conscious experience of the world is possible and how it is struc-tured in view of these possibilities, whereas 'metaphysics' investigates reality on the taken-for-granted assumption that reality is a given way independently of consciousness. From the ontological perspective, it is only once there is some particular for-itself that it has a past, *its* past, about which it can inquire. The past is only ever there *for* a present existent that has this past as what lies behind it, as its facticity. 'If there is a *Before*, it is because the For-itself has arisen in the world, and it is from the standpoint of the For-itself that the past can be established' (139/185). Before that conscious for-itself has arisen, then, we cannot legit-imately assume that there are temporal processes that produce it, for the whole meaning of 'temporality' is moot here.

By the same token, Sartre argues that because the for-itself must have its past as its facticity, as soon as anyone exists they have a past—the most minimal content of which is just to have been gestated and born. Here, Sartre again builds having-been-born into the basic char-acter of the for-itself:

What originally constitutes the being of the For-itself is this relation to a being which *is not* consciousness, which exists in the total night of identity, and which the For-itself is nevertheless obliged to be, outside itself, behind itself. The For-itself, which can in no case be *reduced* to this being, represents an absolute newness in relation to it, but the For-itself feels a profound solidarity of being with it and indicates this by the word *before*.

(138–9/184)

Here, Sartre also conveys the groundlessness and contingency of my being born—the 'total night of identity', of my being who I am, where no reasons or causal claims can find purchase and only acceptance, not explanation, is possible. Whatever story I tell about myself, an element of mystery ('night') will remain in my existence because of my birth, which no narrative can fully incorporate. Thus, Sartre's denial that we can meaningfully talk about the genesis of the for-itself contains some truth insofar as it speaks to my birth being radically contingent, a sheer fact, that of the brute upsurgence by which I came into first-person existence. However, *pace* Sartre, we can also say that, viewed from a third-person perspective, the foetus's material formation and development in the womb enable it to acquire sentient experience and then start making sense of things (in the same way that post-natal social processes may enable that same subject to acquire some level of autonomy); there is nothing insoluble about these real processes of emergence.

4. *The weight of the past.* From (1)–(3) we see that Sartre gives insufficient weight to the past. Both my capacities for autonomy and my motivating values arise as I internalize my personal and social relationships with others. These capacities and values are the sedimentation of my past history of relationships (contrary to Sartre, who does not have a concept of sedimentation at this stage in his thought).[18] For Sartre, sedimentation is ruled out by our translucency in the face of the given, which therefore can only ever be inside us as that from which we are also at an internal remove. But we are not translucent: rather, we are thick, dense, heavy. Less metaphorically, my past persists in and as my present, for even when I re-appraise the more-or-less given values and capacities that have come to me from my past, I do so by exercising powers and being motivated by values that embody and carry forward the effects of that same past.

It may be objected that Sartre's view has an advantage when it comes to moral, social, and political criticism. If we always can stand back from, evaluate, and decide how to act in our circumstances, then given, say, circumstances in which oppressive gender norms are upheld, we can always take a critical distance from those norms and decide to act contrary to them or to enact them differently or subversively. Yet we need not appeal to translucency to explain our possibilities of resistance, social criticism, and subversion. We can instead explain these possibilities, as I suggested in Chapter 3, from the fissured, fractured, unstable characters of the cultural and relational inheritances sedimented within us, and the legacies of previous challenges and contestations which are part of what we inherit; as well as from the capacities for autonomy that we develop to varying degrees through our relational histories, and the motivations that these histories may give us for questioning and changing some our inherited values.[19]

Being born is at stake in problems (1) to (4). (1) Insofar as—contrary to Sartre—our values are always at least partly given to us, they have come down to us from our births. (2) Insofar as—again contrary to Sartre—our capacities for freedom are constituted by our relationships with others, those capacities too have come down to us from birth. (3) *Contra* Sartre once more, those capacities undergo a process of genesis, which means that our ways of navigating through life from birth are not intrinsically autonomous ones; they may or may not *become* autonomous, but if so, this necessarily remains a sub-form of some broader way of navigating in which we are always and already engaged. (4) And—still *contra* Sartre—our past relationships with others are carried forward in and as our present capacities—for example capacities for making free choices, re-evaluating our practices, re-interpreting their meanings. In this way the past prolongs itself in and as the present, giving any present moment its depth. The same past that continues into my present runs back to my birth. Inhabiting a present imbued with the thickness of the past is thus part-and-parcel of being a natal being.

5. Perhaps these problems could be solved by adopting *Heidegger's conception of thrownness* rather than Sartre's conception of facticity. Admittedly, Heidegger's comments on thrownness (*Geworfenheit*) in *Being and Time* are scattered and brief. His only dedicated discussion of thrownness is in the short section 'Falling and thrownness', which is mostly on fallenness (1962: 219–24/175–9). Still, broadly, just as facticity and situation are correlative phenomena for Sartre, so are thrownness and situation (*Lage, Situation*) for Heidegger. I am situated insofar as I always make sense of things in a particular context—in terms of my location, point in my life, and prior life-history, culture and tradition, etc. As we saw in Chapter 3, these factors shape both (i) what is around me to be made sense of—my surroundings—and (ii) my available ways of making sense of these surroundings, including through my moods, emotions, personality traits, and concerns and through the web of inherited meanings and values with which I operate (Withy 2014). The last point means that our ways of

responding to our surroundings are themselves situated, having been formed and sedimented in us over time. For Sartre, in contrast, we are always free to respond to our circumstances in ways that do not themselves embody any sedimented values, because there is invariably an ontological gap between ourselves and our past. This exposes an important difference between Heidegger's and Sartre's views of situatedness.

Now, for Heidegger, insofar as I have not chosen either (i) or (ii), I am thrown into them: 'thrownness' highlights my passivity and lack of choice with respect to the variables entangled in my sense-making. And (i) and (ii) always are unchosen insofar as, at any given time, I am always-already caught up in them prior to any possible choices about them which I may now make. Moreover, crucially, (iii) my very possibilities for how to respond to these factors are ones that I am thrown into. 'In every case Dasein ... has *already got itself involved in* definite possibilities' (1962: 183/144; my emphasis). I am now sitting on the sofa, typing; I might go for a walk, but I shouldn't if I am to get some writing done. Walking and staying at work are (as per iii) determinate possibilities that only obtain for me given both (i) my surroundings (in the house, on the sofa) and (ii) my received ways of making sense of them (wanting to get work done, but also to enjoy some sun). I can take one possibility forward and not the other, or try to realize first one then the other. I may reject both and do something else. But all these are possibilities into which my situation and sense-making history have thrown me.

For Sartre, in contrast, my possibilities in a given situation arise because I freely negate its facticity. I entertain and project forwards possibilities which incorporate reference to the pre-given elements of the situation but always go beyond them (in the mode of determinate negation). One's choices certainly reflect the circumstances to which they react, but they reflect those circumstances as something that those same choices negate. For Heidegger, conversely, my possibilities are themselves given to me, or thrown, although as these are possibilities they have an open character such that I can carry them forward in various ways that are not guaranteed in advance. This view does better justice than Sartre's to the receptivity of human existence—both the receptivity of the horizons within which we make sense of our surroundings, and the receptivity of the possibilities that arise for us in this relation between horizons and surroundings.

To put all this together, there is a more basic way that we navigate through our lives than by doing so autonomously. Namely, we find ourselves again and again in surroundings of which we make sense in determinate ways stemming from the sedimentation within us of our own life-histories so far, our inherited values and horizons of meaning, and our personality structures and relational histories. For each of us, the chain of our circumstances (surroundings, patterns of sense-making, possibilities), choices, new circumstances, etc., descends from birth. Through this history we may acquire more or fewer of the capacities pertinent to autonomy, and so we may come to navigate through our lives more autonomously—reflecting on how we got here, coming to conscious judgements about what to do, etc. But insofar as I don't come to act autonomously—and no one is ever totally autonomous all the time—it is not that I am totally unfree and propelled along by forces outside my control. In making sense of my circumstances as I move through life, I already exercise to some degree the capacities—to interpret meanings and imagine options, for instance—that can be further developed and brought together in the shape of autonomous choice. This everyday mode of navigation still falls short of autonomy, for when I make autonomous choices I bring together and use the relevant capacities in a reflective, critical, and focused way. But equally in my everyday navigation I go beyond being a mere puppet pushed along by the force of events. This is what is right in Sartre's idea of our practical–interpretive agency; where he errs is to equate that agency with full autonomy. Whether or not we exercise autonomy, our more basic way of moving through life is by making sense of things in inherited and sedimented ways. In the end, then, Sartre's idea of radical freedom is best replaced with an idea of *sedimented sense-making*.

Let me sum up where this leaves facticity, situation, contingency, and groundlessness. Facticity is the givenness of the many circumstances in which I exist at every temporal point of my life. These circumstances include my surroundings in the corner of the world where I am, my inherited way of making sense of those, and the possibilities that arise thereby. But this does not mean that facticity has swallowed up situatedness. Facticity and situatedness remain correlative phenomena: I am situated, or am in a situation, insofar as I am making sense, at one and the same time, of my corner of the world, my meaning-laden inheritance, and the resultant possibilities. They are given to me—in that respect they comprise my facticity—but I am also engaged with them in a mode of sense-making—and, as the materials and conditions of my engagement, they make up my situation.

All of these factors that have been given to me are one manifestation of the whole dimension of givenness that has run right through my life, coming down in the end from my birth. Our existence is run through with facticity because we are born; thus, our facticity is part of our natality. And as facticity derives from birth, so does situatedness. Depending on my natal circumstances, of which I make sense in certain ways, I come into a certain new situation, and in turn a determinate chain of further situations, depending where I was before. My birth does not narrowly determine my future, but the life I move through nonetheless unfolds on the basis of my birth.

As for contingency—at birth I come into a unique set of circumstances. And I come into them as this particular individual that I am, leading my own life and none other from the inside. This can occasion puzzlement: why was I born as this individual? There is no answer to be had and, as no explanation can be supplied for why I was born me, there is a basic groundlessness—an inexplicable fact—at the root of my existence. To be born, then, is to have an element of mystery at the core of our being. This mystery can provoke anxiety in us, and I turn to this in Chapter 5.

Notes

1. Other critics of Sartre's account of radical freedom include Beauvoir (1964), 1972)—at least as she is interpreted by, e.g. Sonia Kruks (1995)—as well as Bell (1999), Green (1999), and Hoagland (1999).
2. The question here is not how consciousness can emerge in a previously non-conscious foetus, i.e. through the development of its nervous system, sensory apparatus, etc. Rather the question is why, given that there are very many conscious individuals in the world, I am this particular one.
3. Nagel argues that the difference in perspectives is real and not to be dismissed as merely reflecting confusion about indexicals. '"Hello, I'm TN" or "I own that car" convey information that others can express in the third person . . . But even when all that public information about the person TN has been included in an objective conception, the additional thought that TN is *me* seems clearly to have further content' (Nagel 1986: 60).
4. Kierkegaard likewise contrasts the objective and subjective domains, anticipating Nagel. For Kierkegaard, objective thinking works fine for certain impersonal matters, including history and mathematics. But subjective thinking is ineliminably required for an agent leading their own life (Kierkegaard [1846] 1992).
5. Beauvoir's belief in this fundamental ambiguity is shared by Merleau-Ponty ([1945] 2012). Prefiguring Nagel, Beauvoir shows—focusing on ethics, politics, and history—that we cannot avoid taking both objective and subjective perspectives, e.g. on individual human beings as mere quanta in a calculus and as ends in themselves of no calculable value. '"Rational animal", "thinking reed", he [i.e. "man"] is still a part of this world of which he is a consciousness. He asserts

himself as a pure internality against which no external power can take hold, and he also experiences himself as a thing crushed by the dark weight of other things' Beauvoir 1964: 7).

6. As I noted earlier apropos of Dan Zahavi (Ch. 3, n. 12 of *Being Born*), one might say that just in being sentient I have a stream of first-person experience that is already implicitly mine, i.e. presupposes a sense of self. I prefer instead to say that acquiring a sense of one's 'core' self depends on one's antecedently having a particular stream of embodied experience, just as acquiring a richer self—a personality—depends on one's antecedently having a core self. Each later stage transforms but presupposes the earlier ones, while the earlier ones do not yet contain all that is in their successors. Or so I argued in Chapter 3. In addition, we might recall here the distinction that I made in Chapter 1 Section IV, amongst various respects in which each of us is unique: *at* birth, (i) from one's unique placement in relationships, (ii) from one's unique natal situation more broadly, (iii) as a unique locus of experience, and (iv) from one's unique bodily constitution; *from* birth, in the series of relationships, situations, and bodily states that flow down from one's first natal ones to make a unique life-history (and self and personality). Thus, already at birth we are unique in some respects; amongst those respects it is (iii) that concerns me here: i.e. my being the locus of a specific stream of (embodied) experience.

7. Sometimes 'ensoulment' was held to occur once the foetus was formed, rather than at conception; see Jones (2004).

8. This is by now very familiar from the non-identity problem, best known from Kavka (1982) and Parfit (1984). Kripke is crucial for this way of thinking about the necessity of origins ([1972] 1980: esp. 113–14).

9. One might adduce a third way in which my birth involves contingency—namely that, given the same genetic materials but a different intra-uterine environment, some of the properties with which I was born would have been different, say if folate deficiency had caused me to develop a neural tube defect. In that case I might have been born with different properties (e.g. with the defect), while still being me because composed from the same genetic materials. This third type of contingency pertains to intra-uterine environmental conditions. One might add that post-natally, too, there is often a degree of contingency in how someone's inborn genetic predispositions become actualized given contingent environmental effects. Whereas causal contingency is such that I might never have been born at all, environmental contingency is such that I might have been born with, or come later in life to acquire, different features from the ones I in fact have, while remaining me. (On this see Cooper 2015.)

10. For a variety of feminist responses to Sartre, see J. S. Murphy (1999). Sartre's critics include Collins and Pierce (1976) and, targeting his example of the woman on a date whose flirtation ostensibly exemplifies 'bad faith', Hoagland (1999) and Le Doeuff ([1989] 1991: esp. 72–4). Fullbrook and Fullbrook (1993) re-evaluate

the Sartre/Beauvoir relationship. Other feminist critics, some of them mentioned in n. 1, target Sartre's belief in radical ontological freedom, and I share their objections. Despite these problems, Sartre's account of facticity still has much to offer.

11. For Heidegger, I am always thrown both 'whence'—*from* somewhere—and 'whither'—*towards* somewhere, that somewhere being the possibilities arising for me in my situation. But whence I am thrown is obscure to me, necessarily so (Heidegger 1962: 174–5/135–6). This is because I am always looking forwards towards possibilities, not backwards. But in addition, Heidegger perhaps takes it that the chain of throws leads back to past beginnings that I cannot remember, including above all my conception, gestation, and (narrow) birth, so that I cannot understand 'whence' I was thrown into existence. And this is also the case because my having been born me admits of no explanation; along with that, for Heidegger, there is also an element of mystery as to why I have been thrown into this family, culture, point in history, and so on (see MacAvoy 1996 and Staehler 2016b: 163). Ultimately, then, Heidegger largely agrees with Sartre on the role of birth, but he makes this role less explicit than Sartre does. I thank Kate Withy for discussing this aspect of Heidegger with me.

12. Sartre does discuss for some two pages the 'shocking' fact that we are born (1958: 138–9/184–6). What he finds shocking is the idea that I might have *become* a for-itself from having been merely an embryo, a non-conscious body—although ultimately he denies that this is the right way to look at the matter; see Section V.

13. This may change if, for example, someone has a terminal illness and knows they have a short time to live (Howie 2016), or is a prisoner awaiting their execution scheduled for a given date. But such cases modify our more typical relation to death.

14. Actually, I think that Sartre underestimates death's significance. But I mention his views here because they reverse the usual emphasis on death and not birth.

15. For some interpretations of *Nausea*, see Rolls and Rechniewski (2005).

16. Schelling has been praised for recognizing the importance of birth and, indeed, elevating it to stand for the inscrutable contingency of all existence. Thus Alison Assiter says that for Schelling, the 'whole of Being' is 'conceptualized in terms…both of a body that can birth and…of a force that longs to give birth to itself' (2015: 1). And birth is thereby seen as an active process, something that Assiter also regards favourably.

17. As far as I know, Sartre was not directly influenced by Schelling. But he may have been indirectly influenced, possibly via Kierkegaard, Heidegger, or other theological sources; see Kirkpatrick (2017). Comparing Sartre and Schelling, see Gardner (2006).

18. He developed an understanding of sedimentation later; see Sartre ([1971] 1981).

19. Furthermore, from Sartre's belief in translucency it is a worryingly short distance to the charge that anyone who fails to oppose oppressive norms is in bad

faith—thereby effectively blaming oppressed people for their own oppression. Hence, again, the feminist criticisms of Sartre's view of radical freedom noted earlier; and hence Beauvoir's claim that women are *not* at moral fault if they follow oppressive gender norms, because their freedom is compromised in several ways by the oppressiveness of the circumstances (1972: 29). Beauvoir still allows that there can be cases where agents act in bad faith, though, whereas I prefer to abandon the notion of bad faith.

5

Birth Anxieties

Historically, mortality and not natality has been our central preoccupation. Françoise Dastur argues that one reason for this is that our mortality is a source of fundamental anxiety for us: 'The question of the origin of things is indeed a source of disquietude for our understanding, but the question of their end constitutes the torment of our entire being' (1996: 36). Likewise, Zygmunt Bauman argues that the thought of my death horrifies me and fills me with worry, dread, and anguish which reason cannot placate (1992: 3). This anguish or 'death-anxiety' is universal, he claims, and motivates us to create culture as a source of permanence and therefore of a degree of immortality. Likewise for Ernest Becker, we all have a basic anxiety, the terror of death, which motivates us to pursue immortality by constructing cultural and symbolic systems (1973: xii). However, I aim in this chapter to show that natality, as well as mortality, is a source of fundamental anxiety for us. A more balanced picture of human existence will take account of both ends of human life along with the anxieties they provoke.

Philosophers in the existentialist tradition have tended to distinguish anxiety from fear. Under this distinction, fear is of specific entities or events, whereas anxiety is directed towards our existence as a whole or its organizing structural features—its meaningfulness or meaninglessness, or our freedom and responsibility. On this basis, Heidegger argues that anxiety, not fear, is the mood that properly attests to death in its full import: namely, that everything loses meaning in the face of my mortality, which therefore threatens the world as a whole—the totality of interwoven meanings amongst which I live.[1] I feel anxious at this slipping away of the world, of the entire realm of meaning, in the face of my death. Heidegger disagrees, then, with those who hold that our central feeling about death is fear—that, as Colin Radford put it, 'men fear the endless, dreamless sleep of death and fear it for all that they will miss' (1975: 79).

It does not make emotional sense to feel fear to have been born, though, since one's birth is in the past but fear is of events that are either in the future or imminently present.[2] In addition, fear of birth makes no sense because

Being born: Birth and Philosophy. Alison Stone, Oxford University Press (2019). © Alison Stone.
DOI: 10.1093/oso/9780198845782.001.0001

one's birth has not deprived one of good things as one's death will do. On the contrary, having been born made it possible for me to enjoy whatever good things I've enjoyed in life.

Anxiety, though, *is* perhaps an affect we can feel about having been born. Philip K. Dick suggests so in *We Can Build You* ([1972] 2008). The novel's main characters run a scheme building electronic simulacra of figures from American history and have just activated a newly made simulacrum of Abraham Lincoln. 'We were, beyond doubt, watching a living creature being born,' the protagonist, Louis Rosen, says (76).

> And, as I watched the Lincoln come by degrees to a relationship with what it saw, I understood something: the basis of life is...the fear which I saw here. And not even fear; much worse. Absolute *dread*. Yet the Lincoln stirred, rose out of this. Why? Because it had to.... That state, by its own nature, could not be endured. All the activity of life was an effort to relieve this one state.... Birth, I decided, is not pleasant. It is worse than death; you can philosophize about death – and you probably will. Everyone has. But birth! There is no philosophizing, no easing of the condition. And the prognosis is terrible: all your actions and deeds and thoughts will only embroil you in living the more deeply.   (77–8)[3]

What, for Rosen, is so terrible about birth, aside from philosophers having ignored it and therefore bequeathed us few intellectual resources with which to deal with it? It seems to be arrival in the world in its total unfamiliarity that induces dread, along with the unfathomable mystery of the event by which one has come into experience—come, like the Lincoln simulacrum, to have a relationship with what one sees, not having been there before. Earlier another simulacrum, Stanton, admitted to feeling dread on different grounds. 'When I consider the brief span of my life, swallowed up in the eternity before and behind it, the small space that I fill, or even see, engulfed in the infinite immensity of spaces which I know not, and which know not me, I am afraid.... I am afraid, sir, and wonder to see myself here rather than there. For there is no reason why I should be here rather than there, now rather than then' (60).[4] Dick, thus, points towards various grounds on which one might feel anxiety and dread at having been born.

In Section I of this chapter, I shall identify some grounds of birth anxiety overlapping with those indicated by Dick. In Section II, I'll look semi-critically at accounts of birth anxiety from psychoanalysts, who historically have been the main theorists to address birth anxiety. However, Sartre, taking up suggestions in Kierkegaard, maintains that anxiety is necessarily directed towards future possibilities of action, seemingly implying that one cannot possibly be anxious about one's birth. In Sections III and IV, I'll argue that, actually, both Sartre's and Kierkegaard's views leave room for certain kinds of birth anxiety, features of which we can therefore tease out from their work, particularly Sartre's.

Some initial clarifications about my goals in this chapter are in order. First, one might expect me to start by defining anxiety, but my approach is different. I take anxiety to be multifaceted, coming in many shapes and sizes, and having already been multiply interpreted by philosophers, psychoanalysts, and others. An opening definition risks either being unduly restrictive or unhelpfully vague. So, instead, I'll proceed by looking at some substantive anxieties about birth. What makes them all forms of anxiety I consider en route, treating these forms as overlapping along a spectrum rather than exhibiting strict unity.

Second, I am not claiming that we are constantly consumed with overt, explicitly felt anxiety about having been born—that claim would hardly be plausible. But neither, in our everyday lives, are we all consumed with explicit anxiety either about our freedom of action or our mortality. When Heidegger and Sartre discuss our fundamental anxiety about mortality and freedom respectively, they take it that this anxiety only occasionally or intermittently becomes acute and manifest but otherwise subtends our lives in an implicit, background way.[5] Anxiety has this subtending presence because it attests to structuring features of our existence—mortality or freedom—which are always with us; consequently, so too at some level is the mood or emotion, anxiety, that testifies to these features. Because anxiety has this continual background presence, it can sometimes move right into focus, but it is also possible—and indeed regularly happens—that some people never explicitly feel any existential anxiety at all. The same considerations apply to anxiety about birth. Third, then, I will also take it, as Heidegger and Sartre do, that anxiety is disclosive or revealing about our condition.[6] But unlike them I am concerned with our condition as natals, beings who have been born.

Fourth, though, given my concern with natality one might question whether anxiety is the right mood to look at. Perhaps anxiety does disclose our freedom or mortality or both, but some *other* emotion is revealing about our having been born. In this vein, Klaus Held ([1992] 1993) and Tanja Staehler (2007) suggest that wonder discloses our natality, whereas anxiety discloses our mortality.[7] Ricoeur suggests joy rather than wonder.[8] However, I do not claim that it is *only* in anxiety that we register features of our natality. Other emotions or moods may well attest to other features of our natality than the predominantly troubling ones that occupy this chapter. Nonetheless, I concentrate on anxiety because I want to challenge the view that we must orientate ourselves around death and not birth because only death provokes deep anxiety. Birth may not provoke exactly the same anxieties as death, but it still engenders anxieties of its own, ones that subtend our existence and play various kinds of organizing roles in our lives.

Fifth, I've referred to anxiety as a mood, an emotion, and as felt. But there is considerable debate on how to distinguish such arguably distinct affective phenomena as moods, emotions, and feelings (see, for example, Sizer 2006). It may be that anxiety is a mood and not an emotion—for arguably moods, unlike emotions, have no definite object while, on existentialist and psycho-analytic views, anxiety differs from fear precisely in having no definite object. I might fear, say, dogs or wolves, but anxiety is more diffuse, global, and directionless. For our purposes here, though, it does not really matter whether such characteristics make anxiety a mood, an atypical emotion, or a member of some other affective class, or indeed whether different forms of anxiety fit into different classes. What matters here is not how anxiety is best classified emotionally but whether we feel birth anxiety, in what forms, and what about.

I. Strange to Ourselves

Some of the aspects of being born which we came across in Chapter 4 of this book can provoke anxiety. It is a brute fact admitting of no explanation that I was born into the life I am leading and none other. I could not possibly have been leading any other life, for then it would not be me leading it. Nonetheless, that this particular life is the one I inhabit from the inside is something that cannot be explained and presents an insoluble mystery—the same mystery with which the Stanton simulacrum wrestles in Dick's novel. We come up against a parallel mystery when we confront the first-person existence of others.

> We might be telling someone of a memory or event and then realize that, at that time, the person in front of us did not even exist! Someone who is real and significant in our lives, who is the centre of his or her own story,... once did not exist. If we seriously consider the existence and the beginning of any one particular human being,... we realize that it is something

strange and profound. Many philosophers have recognised that the existence of the world is something mysterious... However, if we truly grasp
the existence of any one person we see that this too is mysterious.

(Jones 2004: 1)

Moreover, the groundlessness and mystery of whom we are born as persists
right through our lives for as long as they last. This is disconcerting: my
particular existence defies comprehension in respect of its contingent beginnings; and the whole universe is mysterious insofar as it contains many
people each of whose particular existences is likewise contingent.

The sorts of anxious feelings in which we register these disconcerting
realities are uneasiness and discomfiture: feelings of the presence of the
uncanny. What is uncanny (*unheimlich*), Freud argues, is something *both*
familiar, known, and homely (*heimlich*) *and* unfamiliar, unknown, and un-
homely (*unheimlich*) ([1919] 1955a). One of his examples is a severed hand
(244): as a hand, it is familiar to us, but only as part of a body. As severed, it is
unfamiliar. It seems as if the hand might at any moment spring back to life and
movement, because this is how we are familiar with it: as a functioning, living
organ. But we also know that is not what the hand now is, so that it would be
'wrong', unnatural, if it moved. This conjunction or superimposition of its
familiar and unfamiliar modes makes the severed hand uncanny.[9]

Likewise, it is our everyday, familiar, taken-for-granted world that has
dimensions along which it is *un*knowable to us and mysterious. Indeed, my
own existence, inescapable and utterly familiar as it is, also has a mysterious
dimension, under which there is no explaining why it is the way it is and why
I am in it at all.[10] In our own homes—our world, our selves—we are never
fully at home. A point of contrast is with Hegel's view that the world is a
home for us, if we could but recognize it (Hardimon 1992: 1–2). For Hegel,
the world in itself is rational and intelligible, and so it admits of being
understood rationally by us. We and the world share in the same rational
structure, so that we can be at home in it (122). *Contra* Hegel, though, in
exploring birth we have come upon respects in which the world and our
existence in it do not admit of ever fully being understood. To this extent, we
can never be entirely at home in the world or even in our own individual
existences—and this is discomfiting.

There is also something mysterious in the fact that I have *begun* to exist
at all. I was not always there; for aeons, events in the world unfolded without
me. This is scarcely comprehensible or imaginable: as soon as I try concretely to imagine events in one of these past eras, I surreptitiously presuppose

my own presence as their imagined observer.[11] Moreover, the transition from non-existence to existence may appear to be so absolute that it seems incomprehensible that I can have crossed it.[12] Yet, to compound the difficulty, there *was* no single crossing point. In reality, we don't begin in the faux-Cartesian way announced by Ruby Lennox, the narrator of Kate Atkinson's novel *Behind the Scenes at the Museum*: 'I exist! I am conceived to the chimes of midnight on the clock on the mantelpiece in the room across the hall' (1995: 13). When first conceived, I was a single cell (a zygote), by no means the kind of conscious, speaking, self-narrating agent that, fictitiously, Ruby Lennox was from the start. From having been a zygote I developed a formed body, began to have a rudimentary level of intra-uterine experience, and through gestation and then departure from my mother's womb I gradually became a participant in culture and in relationships, with a structured personality and history. Yet the zygote in question was still me, even though it had none of this.[13]

Another factor in my difficulties in making sense of my own origin is the fact that I cannot remember being born. Ordinarily, people talk of not remembering their birth in its narrow sense of the passage out of the womb, but we cannot remember the intra-uterine period either.[14] This may not seem important: much of what I've lived through, I cannot now remember. Perhaps being born is no different to countless forgotten days out, books read, and television series watched. However, an important difference is that my birth—in the broad sense beginning with my conception—was not just one event in my life amongst others but was the beginning of that entire life. The fact that this beginning is shrouded in mystery therefore imbues all that comes out of it with an element of mystery as well.

Moreover, as Bernhard Waldenfels puts it, 'one's own birth...is never fully one's own, as it is never actively experienced and is never a subject of free choice. An "absolute present," which would gather in it all sense, belongs to the phantasms of traditional orders that deny their origin' (2011: 18). Similarly for David Farrell Krell, although I was present at my birth, it is outside the field of presence known as consciousness (see Krell 2015: esp. 104). Whatever I may have undergone and experienced in being gestated and born, I as an adult cannot now bring any of that to consciousness. But this is no accident. Birth is *necessarily* unrememberable in some way bound up with the very nature of my beginning. We might think that this is because I did not unequivocally experience being born in the first place (for Waldenfels, it is never 'actively experienced'; Krell suggests a kind of presence that is outside of consciousness).

One perspective here is that of Christina Schües, for whom being born is a necessary precondition of having experience in the first place, so that it cannot itself appear *in* experience (1997). Earlier, though, I argued against Schües that within intra-uterine life we already begin to have experience and so to partake in a nascent way in the field of meanings in the world around us: we hear voices spoken in a given language; we detect changes in levels of light, corresponding to the day-and-night cycles that regulate human life. Having undergone *gestation* up to a certain point is a precondition of experience, as the foetus must first acquire its corporeal structure including a nervous system, sensory apparatus, etc., before it becomes sentient. But being born in the *narrow* sense of leaving the gestator's womb is not a precondition of experience: rather, we can already experience by the time we leave the womb. Schües accepts this when she reconstructs sympathetically how a baby must experience things having just left her mother's womb: feeling the weight of her limbs yet the possibility of free movement, the in- and out-flux of breath, and tactile sensations as she is touched and feels things; feeling the air temperature; being bombarded by visual sensations (2016: 271–5). Since we were already sentient late in gestation and when we left the womb, then, there must be an alternative explanation for our inability to remember being born.

It is worth bearing in mind here that that inability is part-and-parcel of our broader lack of memories of infancy—'infantile amnesia', in Freud's phrase. Scarcely anyone remembers anything of their first two years; most people remember little from their first six years, sometimes longer. This is not because of the lapse of time as such, because teenagers usually remember little from their early years whereas 60-year-olds usually remember a good deal from their teenage years. The amnesia affects our first years specifically; there is a caesura between them and all that comes later.

On one influential set of explanations for infantile amnesia, at around ages 6–8 our memory system changes and we begin to form and lay down memories in new ways. The older and newer memory systems have been categorized, respectively, as implicit/explicit; general/specific; schematic/episodic; non-linguistic/linguistic; and non-narratival/narrative.[15] More-over, given that human babies are born as immature as they are, even the earlier 'implicit' memory system must take shape and become established over the baby's first year.[16] Prior to that process, any memories that babies formed within the mother's womb, or of exiting that womb, will be relatively indeterminate, unstable, and liable to be rapidly lost. Then, during our childhood, a systematic change occurs in how we remember, making most of the memories of the older system unavailable to us. Some of them may actually be destroyed, and only a few will be incorporated and remodelled into the new system. Ironically, then, it is the development of our own cognitive systems that prevents us from knowing about our early lives. Infantile amnesia is thus a consequence of birth in the shape it has for human beings, where we begin life very immature and unformed yet, over the years, ascend to high levels of mental functioning.

Our inescapable ignorance of our early years is significant because of (i) the extent of the period of lived time that becomes lost to us, (ii) how irretrievably it is lost, and (iii) because these are our formative years. Because of (iii), infantile amnesia leaves us in the dark about fundamental features of our personalities, about why we have the traits and dispositions we do. Why do we fall in and out of love with the people we do? Why do we sometimes greet terrible events with calm indifference and then react to much more minor setbacks by becoming greatly upset? Why does a certain song move me to tears and leave you cold, and vice versa? Infantile amnesia puts the rationale for much of our emotional and relational lives out of our reach. In important respects, we are left strangers to ourselves.

However, the very fact that our early years are formative presents a challenge for the idea of infantile amnesia. How can our early experiences shape us in ongoing ways, remaining active within our personalities, unless we are in some sense remembering them? If I am disposed to criticize myself harshly in a way that embodies my internalized image of my father, am I not thereby remembering him? *How* I remember him here, though—in my patterns and dispositions of action, response, and reaction—conforms more with the earlier or archaic memorial system than the later one. For it involves implicit, practical, enacted remembering done at a bodily, habitual, affective level, not that of explicit consciousness.[17] Thus in our bodily habits, emotional dispositions, and patterns of response and reaction, we keep our infantile history alive. Every time I feel scared of a dog approaching me, I exhibit an emotional response I first formed in childhood. As I walk along with a particular gait and style of movement, I re-enact habits I established in childhood. Yet I cannot bring to consciousness any determinate memories of learning to walk in this fashion or being accosted by dogs. We relive the past continually in ways that escape our powers of explicit recollection, narration, and cognition.

It appears, then, that after all we do not entirely cease to use the archaic memorial system, but rather that the newer memory system overlays its predecessor without altogether ousting it. Yet, typically, we re-enact early experiences without having any overt memory at all of what we are thereby re-enacting. This suggests the following. Under the early memory system, we remembered events in implicit, vague, schematic ways bound up with practical behaviour and affects. But now the specifically mnemonic functions of that early system are taken over by the later system, as explicit remembering. What remains relatively intact of the early system is its specifically affective and practical side, but this now persists in us separated from our explicit memory system.

The net result is that our infantile past lives on in and through us without being directly knowable by us. Once again, this places us in the domain of the uncanny, for what is so familiar to us that it constitutes our very being— our everyday, routine habits and emotional dispositions—is just what we cannot comprehend in ourselves. It is our very selves, and our own life-histories, which are in major respects strange and alien to us. This is all the more so because infantile amnesia sets limits to how far we can reconstruct our early life-histories retrospectively, in narrative. Of course, I can in fact construct narratives about my early life, drawing on what others tell me and what I can piece together from manifold sources (family photographs, the historical record, documents dating from that time). But no such narratives can ever be fully adequate to the period they narrate, because during that time I did not remember and experience in a narrative mode. A kernel of opacity will always remain.[18]

Overall, as Jean Laplanche says, '[T]he primacy of infancy decenters us as irremediably . . . as the unconscious or the id' (quoted in Butler 2005: 76; see Laplanche [1999] 2015: Ch. 6). To be born, and so begin life as an infant and child, is to be 'decentred': destined to forget much of my earlier life, even while it still lives on within me; limited in how far I can understand myself and the wellsprings of motivation from which I act and react; limited in my ability to narrate or reconstruct my life-story retrospectively. In these several ways, 'the lapse of time between myself and my birth disrupts in advance the possibility of a completely masterful, unified selfhood' (Guenther 2006: 10). I act and react in given ways that are inscribed within me without my ever being fully able to understand them or, therefore, control or regulate them.

Moreover, I chose neither to be born nor whom to be born as, or into what situation, body, and set of relationships and historical context to be born. Passivity precedes agency, as reception precedes creation: the greater part of what I am, I was made to be by other people and by countless broader forces exceeding my control. This undermines our favoured self-image as independent agents steering the course of our own lives. And the recognition of how far we are passive and receptive even in regard to our own being can, again, be disconcerting.

However, all these considerations might seem to be compatible with Dastur's view that we feel only intellectual disquietude about birth but existential torment about death. Yet that distinction need not be sharp: disquietude can become tormenting, especially when it rises into the feeling that our very existence is uncanny and that we can never be completely at home in the world or in our own skins. We can feel troubled to think that we once did not exist, or that others did not: how can someone so necessary to the world, around whom everything revolves, ever not have been in it? And sometimes, like Harry Kent, the fictional police surgeon mentioned in Chapter 4 of this book, one can feel tormented to be leading the particular life that one is, no-one else's, where one can find no grounds for this state of affairs that would offer reconciliation: like one's life or not, one is stuck in it and no other life is available to one.

Feelings of torment can also arise with respect to the other aspects of being born considered in this section. We can feel tormented by our inability to remember our early years, especially when we suspect that they harbour important clues to our current situation. In *Behind the Scenes at the Museum* much in Ruby Lennox's life and relationships, especially her mother's apparent lack of love for her, makes no sense to her until she eventually recovers a swathe of repressed memories and realizes that she was born a twin and that her twin sister Pearl drowned, as an infant, in an accident for which Ruby was unjustly blamed. Suddenly, a great deal falls into place. At other times we can feel tormented by the inexplicability of our own behaviour. Take the character Martin Lynch-Gibbon in Iris Murdoch's *A Severed Head*, who launches a drunken attack on his recent acquaintance Honor Klein. Afterwards, he writes her three separate letters of apology accounting for his behaviour in various ways, but feeling that none of them provides an adequate explanation or self-defence. He can only describe himself variously as a madman, a wild beast, and a beast *and* a madman ([1961] 2001: 114–17). He had been gripped by deep-seated forces within himself which go beyond his comprehension, and this distresses him, as do his failures to craft an apology that can satisfactorily make sense of these forces.

In short, being born presents us with existential difficulties in its own right, and these occasion feelings in us that can reasonably be seen as anxieties: discomfort at the pervasiveness of the uncanny in our lives;

perplexity at the mystery of our own beginnings; unease and distress to be in the particular lives we are and to be driven, against or beyond our explicit wishes, to act as we do.

II. Psychoanalysis and Birth Anxiety

I've said that we do not remember being born, and that this is discomfiting. But some psychoanalytic authors have taken a different view: that being born—in the narrow sense of exiting the mother's womb—is traumatic, and that we have troubling memories of it which we repress, leaving us with a pervasive sense of anxiety. This is Otto Rank's view in *The Trauma of Birth* ([1924] 1973). Some subsequent therapists have applied and developed this view: notably Arthur Janov, the founder of primal scream therapy (see Crosby and Crosby 1976); and Stanislav Grof, for whom in certain crisis experiences we can psychically recapitulate aspects of the physical birth process (1988: 1–36). But here I want to focus on Rank and one other key psychoanalytic treatment of birth trauma and anxiety: that of Freud in *Inhibitions, Symptoms and Anxiety* ([1926] 1959).

We might feel dubious at the outset about psychoanalytic views of birth trauma. Even so, it is worth considering them, firstly because they are the main place where birth and anxiety have been thought about together historically. And, secondly, these views deserve attention because, although they have problems, there are insights about natality that we can glean from them.[19]

Freud repeatedly remarked that birth is the 'source and prototype of the affect of anxiety';[20] this remark formed Rank's starting-point. ('Birth' is meant narrowly here, a narrow usage to which I'll adhere while expounding Rank and Freud.) Rank elaborated on Freud's remark as follows. Exiting the mother's womb is the original traumatic event, because with it the blissful peace and unity of intra-uterine life end. All subsequent anxieties trace back to this first trauma, and so 'the trauma of birth [is] the explanatory key to human suffering' (Pizarro 2012: 693). This trauma is also key to 'the history of the development of the human mind and of the things created by it' (Rank [1924] 1973: xi). The whole history of culture plays out our unconsciously preserved trauma about being born as well as our concomitant, equally unconscious wish to return into the mother's womb. Effectively, then, Rank establishes a new psychoanalytic framework that prioritizes our relations to birth. The castration and Oedipus complexes which for

Freud were the principal forces in human personality and culture are, for Rank, only secondary and derivative.

How is exiting the mother's womb traumatic? First, on leaving the womb the baby is flooded with a mass of sensations that it cannot master or accommodate. For Rank, this is traumatic in the sense Freud had established, where trauma occurs when a flood of intense sensations absolutely overwhelms an individual's sense-making capacities. A traumatic event, then, is one that breaks down our sense-making capacities and horizon of meaning.[21] For Rank, the trauma of being born motivates one to repress one's experience of birth, and do so more severely the more difficult and traumatic one's birth was. In addition, because leaving the mother's womb was traumatic, we form a primary wish to return into that womb and regain our pre-traumatic state. But we repress that wish as well, because it reminds us of the very trauma to which it reacts.

Rank also sees leaving the womb as traumatic in a second sense: it is 'the first separation from the first libido object, namely ... the mother' (4). Children's subsequent separations from their mothers—in weaning, potty training, starting school, etc.—re-enact the original separation of birth: These 'situation[s] remind the child, who is still close to the experience of the primal trauma, of the womb situation—with the important difference that the child is now consciously separated from the mother' (11–12). Separations from the mother provoke anxiety, then, because they recall the original separation that the baby underwent at birth, which threatens to bring to consciousness the child's repressed memory of the birth trauma. Anxiety, for Rank following Freud, is the affect that signals imminent danger (Freud [1915-17] 1963: 487–511), in this case the danger that the repressed complex of memories surrounding birth will reach consciousness. For Rank, then, we are prone to become anxious whenever our repressed memories of being born threaten to regain consciousness. And as they always might do so, birth anxiety pervades our lives—*anxiety* and not fear for, since the memories in question are repressed, we do not consciously know what danger is being signalled (if we did—for example, if the danger to which we were reacting was a nearby fierce dog—then we would be feeling fear).

Rank detects the influence of these repressed memories and wishes concerning birth everywhere, from psychopathology to politics, art, religion, and philosophy.[22] He claims, for instance, that we make substitute wombs whenever we clothe, shelter and comfort ourselves and create buildings. Even language, as our symbolic home, is a womb-substitute. Such behaviour is healthy for Rank: it shows that we have not repressed our fantasies of returning into the maternal womb too severely but are allowing them sublimated expression. When we *do* repress those fantasies too severely, women become devalued by their association with birth and society becomes patriarchal (Rank 1973: 94). This, for Rank, is pathological and undesirable. Rank wants us, then, to reduce our levels of repression—and correspondingly of anxiety—so that we can find pleasure by giving our wishes for the womb and the mother partial, substitute kinds of satisfaction. We do that, supposedly, in heterosexual intercourse and child-bearing for women and in cultural sublimations for men (189). That last claim notwithstanding, Rank may be considered a proto-feminist insofar as he criticizes patriarchy and stresses the paramount importance of our first relations with our mothers.

Rank also argues, prefiguring Cavarero and Jantzen, that anxiety about death is only a derivative consequence of birth anxiety. For Rank, death is dreaded partly because it has the meaning of 'being *separated*—and this directly touches on the primal trauma' (24), and partly because death is conceived as 'an everlasting return to the womb' (114). This seems contradictory, but Rank's view is that although unconsciously we wish to return into the womb, the thought of death threatens to make us conscious of this wish and, with it, of the dreaded birth trauma against which the wish reacts. We therefore react to death with anxiety. But our attitudes about death are not really about death itself, for Rank; instead they concern birth.

Now, Rank's account has many problems. He reduces all emotional difficulties to birth trauma, denying them independent weight. He also overestimates newborn babies' levels of understanding of their situation: a newborn cannot be aware of her birth *as* separation from the mother, for she is not yet aware of her mother as an individual (as Freud points out; 1959: 130). Moreover, in holding that birth-traumas and womb-wishes lie behind all adult pathologies and cultures, Rank assumes that we have memories *both* of the peace of intra-uterine life *and* of leaving the womb, albeit that all these memories are repressed. But, as we've seen, we do not have such memories, certainly not as adults and probably not for long in infancy either.

When *The Trauma of Birth* came out Freud responded with *Inhibitions, Symptoms and Anxiety*, in which he sought to offer a better account of birth trauma and birth anxiety than Rank's.[23] Freud identified birth, as he had before, as the 'source and prototype of the affect of anxiety'. Leaving the womb is traumatic for babies, for it floods them with sensations that overwhelm their capacities for meaningful experience. This sort of overwhelming of the sensory apparatus is traumatic generally, for Freud, as when soldiers at war are overwhelmed by experiences of violence, death, deafening noise, shock, pain, and horror. In its mundane way, being born is traumatic too: it entails a massive influx of sensations and a 'vast disturbance' of the baby's psycho-physical 'economy' as new sense-organs are stimulated and the lungs are activated (1959: 135, 137). But in its traumatic nature, birth can be made no sense of. Hence, when we are newborns, we do not and cannot understand birth as separation from the mother. We, nonetheless, find birth traumatic because it dramatically ends our previous, familiar mode of intra-uterine experience. The birth-experience becomes installed in the psyche as the prototype of an experience we want to avoid—specifically a chaotic, disturbing, overwhelming one.

What happens here, Freud thinks, is that the lived, embodied experience of being born comes to stand in the psyche as the symbol or form under which the psyche signals any further dangers of undesirable experience. When we apprehend any such danger, we therefore reproduce the felt experience we had of being born: heightened sensory awareness, motor tension, tightened breath, painfully constricted stomach and chest, etc. To feel anxiety, then, *is* to relive in miniature the embodied experience of being born, and we do this in reaction to a danger of having a bad experience. It is as if the psyche says to itself: 'Look! Potential bad experience! Remember what that was like before', but this 'remembering' of the birth trauma is not explicit remembering but occurs on a visceral bodily level, conforming to the archaic memory mode. Whenever we feel anxiety we therefore 'remember' being born, but without knowing that we do so. In this way, Freud explains the somatic and affective quality of anxiety in terms of how this affect recapitulates the lived departure from the womb.

Freud details how the birth-trauma bears on our subsequent emotional lives. At different times and stages, he maintains, we are anxious about different dangers: of being separated from our mothers, in infancy; of castration, in childhood; of losing the approval of our own super-egos, during older childhood and adulthood. We react to these several types of danger-situation with anxiety—not, say, anger or misery—for the following reasons. Being born was traumatic and was laid down in the psyche as the prototype of not merely a bad experience but also a specifically traumatic one. But in all successive danger-situations, the ultimate danger is that of trauma (1959: 137). For instance, when parted from her mother, an infant can fulfil neither her wish for her mother's presence nor her wishes for those things for which she depends on her mother: food, drink, rest, and comfort, etc. Thus, the danger is that unsatisfied wishes will build up to the point that they flood the infant's sense-making apparatus (151). We get anxious about these situations that threaten us with trauma because they are 'reminiscent of birth', the first trauma (Freud 1959: 138). In effect, we are anxious that we may be about to suffer another trauma of the sort we suffered at birth.

But here Freud goes back at least part-way to Rank's reductive approach of treating all our emotional difficulties as really concerning birth trauma, however manifold they may seem to be. To be sure, for Rank, when an infant is anxious about being separated from her mother, what she is really anxious about is that traumatic birth memories will surface. For Freud, in contrast, we are anxious about the prospect of undergoing *another* trauma, which would be bad directly, and not only because it recalls and threatens to resuscitate the previous birth-trauma. Thus, for Freud, unlike Rank, birth-memories are not the object of the anxiety but only supply its somatic form (as James Strachey notes, in Freud 1959: 83). Even so, for Freud, one does not want to avoid separations and other potential dangers in their own right—that is, just because one doesn't want to be separated from one's mother. Rather one wants to avoid such separations because they threaten to bring about a traumatic flooding of one's own mental–bodily apparatus. For Freud as for Rank, one is anxious about a potential undesirable psychical state on one's own part, not about a potential undesirable state of affairs in the world between oneself and others.[24]

A simple way to avoid this problem is to acknowledge that what we are anxious about at different times in our lives is just the dangers that they present in their own right. For example, in infancy, we are anxious about being separated from our mothers or our other care-givers. We are not, *pace* Freud, anxious about the expected causal *effects* of these dangers, that is, unsatisfied wishes building up. In feeling separation anxiety, the infant is anxious that his mother has gone and might not come back, and that even if or when she does come back, she might go away again, in ways the infant cannot control. The infant is also anxious because he apprehends that his mother is an agent in her own right, with her own mind, who cannot be guaranteed to conform to the infant's fantasies.[25] This is troubling because the infant acutely depends on his mother, whose absence and independence therefore threaten his entire being. That is, given their dependency and helplessness, infants are particularly vulnerable to the absence and loss of their care-givers; separation anxiety registers that vulnerability.[26] Furthermore, the infant is struggling to come to terms with the mother's status as an independent being, which is part-and-parcel of a fundamental aspect of our natal condition: plurality.

Separation anxiety is thus a consequence of our natal dependency and vulnerability in combination with our plurality, which is also connected with our natality. And the anxiety arising here is not confined to infancy. For Freud:

> Adult emotions are ... built up from and out of childhood emotions; both the usual distinction between them, and the notion that adult emotions are more 'mature' than infantile emotions, have less importance in psychoanalysis than in common understanding.... [Rather] the germs of all important adult emotions from love to anger to sexual desire are found in children.... [This] means that the emotion in question [e.g., anxiety] has a strong antecedent relating to a person's childhood, and that this childhood pattern is of primary importance in the structure of this emotion and its expressions today.   (Chapman 1989/2007: 49)

After all, we depend on others throughout our lives; we therefore remain vulnerable to them hurting us because, being distinct individuals, they will not necessarily do what we want or even remain alive and well enough to do so. As we did in infancy, we continue to register our dependency and vulnerability, our relatedness with others and their difference from us, in anxiety. For the adult emotion is built and modelled on the infantile one, just as we reproduce infantile patterns of relationship and behaviour generally throughout our lives. Separation anxiety persists to degrees throughout our lives, as a way that we register fundamental tensions between our difference and togetherness with which we began to grapple as infants.

Let me sum up what we can take and not take from these psychoanalytic positions. It is plausible that being born has the traumatic quality described by Freud, but *pace* Freud I suspect that any somatic memory formed of the experience does not persist for long. And we need not suppose that it does to explain our anxiety about such subsequent dangers as separation from the mother, especially when we remember that the specifically bodily manifestations of anxiety can be explained as the effects of hormones such as adrenalin and cortisol released in response to the perception of danger. Subsequent dangers and the anxieties they provoke *may* connect with and take up residues and fragments of very early memories of birth trauma. But even if so, those residues would be just part of the whole past history that infuses our difficult emotional encounters with weight and depth. In this regard, both Freud and Rank rightly highlight how our very earliest experiences and emotions feed into the later ones and provide the initial basis out of which more complicated emotions are built up. And they also highlight the importance in this process of our earliest experiences of separation anxiety—albeit that Rank mislocates these at the time of exiting the womb, whereas they actually begin from around 8 months onwards. Nonetheless, in this way Rank, like Freud, registers that separation anxieties are connected with birth—but this is not as directly as Rank and Freud have it, but by way of our natal dependency, vulnerability, and plurality. In their ways, then, Rank and Freud apprehend that by birth we come into a natal condition that has troubling aspects and presents us with deep difficulties with which we start to grapple as infants, in ways that have lifelong ramifications for our personalities, relationships, and cultures.

III. Anxiety, Freedom, and Conflicting Attachments

I have explored some ways in which we may feel anxiety about having been born and about features of our existence that obtain insofar as we are born. Yet the existentialist tradition provides reasons for doubting that anxiety about having been born is even possible. These reasons may be taken from Kierkegaard's *Concept of Anxiety* ([1844] 1980), a text that is the starting-point for the views on anxiety of Sartre, Beauvoir, Heidegger, and others.[27]

For Kierkegaard, (1) anxiety centrally differs from fear. Fear is directed towards particular objects, where 'objects' includes events, persons, states of affairs, etc.—anything on which our attention is focused. We fear harmful objects that are either actually present (e.g. a perceived dog) or potentially contained in my current situation (e.g. the potential for a fierce dog to be just around the corner) (42). (2) Anxiety has no definite object. We feel anxiety without knowing what it is about, and where the anxiety exceeds anything we try to pin it down to. The challenge, then, is to identify what anxiety means. Kierkegaard's answer is that it is about one's own freedom.

> Anxiety may be compared with dizziness. He whose eye happens to look down the yawning abyss becomes dizzy. But what is the reason for this? It is just as much in his own eye as in his abyss, for suppose he had not looked down. Hence anxiety is the dizziness of freedom, which emerges when... freedom looks down into its own possibility.   (61)

My freedom is not an object; rather it is the core of my subjectivity, which for Kierkegaard contrasts with the entire domain of objects and objectivity.

Anxiety lacks an object because it is directed upon a non-object, indeed that which is most non-objectual: my free self (76–7). I experience anxiety, then, just when I register my freedom emotionally. (3) But why should my freedom make me anxious? For Kierkegaard, 'anxiety is the vertigo of freedom'—'freedom . . . showing-itself-for-itself in the anxiety of possibility' (61, 77). That is, I feel anxiety when confronted with the freedom to choose between different possibilities. High on a mountain path, next to a precipitous drop, I could choose to jump over the edge into the abyss, or not. Either option is open to me. I feel anxious because I apprehend, tacitly, that there is nothing solid and determined, either in me or the world, to secure me against the option of jumping which I may always choose to take. Indeed, even if all the available options are benign, I still apprehend my freedom to choose between them with anxiety as long as I grasp that there is nothing to push me either way. The choice rests entirely with me. And along with this the future is radically open: depending how I choose, it will go one of many possible ways. At every moment, as it were, I stand at a fork where roads branch starkly apart. I cannot take both, but neither can I see what is down them, for that depends on actions I have not yet taken. All this makes anxiety future-oriented in a radical way that fear never is, for unlike potential events the possible consequences and ramifications of my actions are not contained in the world, even potentially, in advance of my deciding on one or other of them (91).

In contrast with all this, my birth lies in my past; I face no choices about it, as it has already happened and cannot now be other than it already is. But, Kierkegaard seems to say, one cannot be anxious about the past. 'When it is sometimes said that one is anxious about the past, this seems to be a contradiction . . . [But actually] this is only a manner of speaking and . . . the future in one way or another manifests itself' (91). On one reading here, if someone appears to be anxious about some event in her past it is only because she still has a choice about how and whether to take some aspects of that event forward—how, or how not, to 'repeat' that event (91).[28] If I feel anxious to remember a past altercation with my next-door neighbour it is because I still have choices with respect to it: whether to belatedly apologize, remain aloof, act as if nothing happened. Thus, it may seem that Kierkegaard holds that anxiety always pertains to possible actions and futures, not to the past just qua past, so that birth anxiety is ruled out.

Kierkegaard can be read somewhat differently, though, such that I can be genuinely anxious about my past insofar as it never *is* exclusively and entirely past: a person's past always remains ongoing right through their life. My past always prolongs itself into my present in memory, perception, emotion, and various forms of transference. As I am always taking my past forward, every choice that I face is necessarily, in part, a choice about how to take my past forward, which parts of it to pursue and which to leave behind, and under what meanings.[29] So understood, Kierkegaard holds that anxiety is always both future- *and* past-oriented. And, since my past comes down from my birth, the latter is always involved in my anxiety about possible actions and futures. The anxiety about possibilities which pervades my existence is thus, in part, a form of birth anxiety. In its birth-facing aspect, this anxiety is about how to take forward my birth and its ramifications; what meanings to give to my birth and its consequences; and how to go on with my life specifically as it has been unfolding on the basis of my birth.

Sartre, however, appears to read Kierkegaard in the first, narrowly future-oriented way. For Sartre, I register my facticity—that is, what is given to me—in *nausea*, not anxiety, whereas in anxiety I register my freedom: 'the existential grasping of our facticity is Nausea, and the existential apprehension of our freedom is [Anxiety]' ([1983] 1984: 132–3). But in Sartre's work, matters are less clear-cut than this, as we see from his imagined man who has to choose, in anxiety, whether to fight with the French Resistance or help his ageing mother.

Sartre uses this character to exemplify *abandonment*, one of three phenomena—abandonment, anxiety (*angoisse*), and despair—treated in 'Existentialism and Humanism' ([1946] 2001b). The man is 'abandoned', for Sartre, in that he has to choose what to do for himself, without divine guidance—and, anyway, he would first have to decide to believe in and follow such guidance—and without guidance from any other secular agency since, again, he would first have to choose to follow it anyway. The man feels 'anxiety' because his choice about what to do is radical: any reasons he might invoke to justify the choice are ones he must already have chosen to find compelling. Perhaps he finds it compelling that 'the Free French need more fighters' in light of his deeper-level values or goals—for example, 'I must serve my country when called'—but he has already chosen those goals as well, even if he did not realize it until now. His responsibility for his choice therefore rests entirely with himself. Further, in choosing, he chooses 'for everyone': if he opts, say, to stay with his mother, he effectively declares 'staying with loved ones is the right thing to do'—*for anyone*. (If he replies, 'no, it's right only for *me*, because I deeply love my mother', then he is still choosing to treat deep feelings or relationships as generating compelling reasons for action for anyone who has them.) Finally, the young man is in 'despair' as he cannot rely on others to carry out the options that he chooses not to take, say combat the German occupation; others may opt not to fight either; so, he cannot reassure himself that it does not really matter which option *he* takes.

As we saw in Chapter 4, this example is central to Taylor's criticism of Sartre's idea of radical choice. Taylor argues that the young man faces a terrible dilemma just because there are competing claims on him which are *not* created by his choice. If they were so created, he could dissolve the dilemma at a stroke: just by choosing to care for his mother, he would make it the case that the Free French cause is valueless (Taylor 1982: 119). So the young man is in a genuine dilemma because both his mother and Free France have claims on him, yet he cannot honour both.[30] These are not claims that he creates but ones that arise out of his ongoing relationship with his mother, on the one hand, and on the other, the history of relationships and experiences out of which his political beliefs have precipitated: in particular, his brother was killed by German soldiers. The man's dilemma, then, arises because of values and attachments that he has inherited and received through his relationships, context, and history. As inheritances, these values and attachments are part of his facticity, given to him as effects and sedimentations of his past.

Insofar as Sartre's example is compelling, it shows—*contra* Sartre—that our values, meanings, and reasons for action are fundamentally inherited and only derivatively chosen and created, if at all. This becomes apparent when our values and relationships conflict, so that we become aware of the competing demands they impose on us prior to any choices on our part. Arguably the same is true throughout our lives at a lower level, for we are always caught up in manifold relationships and values which are not in seamless harmony. For Sartre, the challenge here is how to act authentically, in full and non-evasive admission of one's freedom and responsibility. But as our values are actually inherited, the primary ethical challenge here is how to act most *faithfully* to our multifaceted relational histories. When we feel anxiety faced with their conflicting demands—be it overt anxiety or lower-level unease—we are registering the conflict and the impossibility of satisfying all the claims that our attachments make on us.

While Sartre offers a compelling description of the torn young man, then, he misconceives what his description shows. It shows not that anxiety reveals our radical freedom but that anxiety arises in situations where we cannot possibly honour all our attachments even though they all press claims on us; our anxiety registers the force of these unmet claims as well as our awareness that we cannot meet them. This may not seem to be, directly, an anxiety about my having been born. But it is a form of anxiety that arises on account of a feature of our existence as natals—our status as inheritors and receivers—where we are attached to and value what we inherit and so wish to carry it forward, but where the complexity of what we inherit makes it impossible to honour all of its elements.

We can think further about conflicting attachments by considering the plight of the main character, Tambu, in Tsitsi Damgarembga's novel *Nervous Conditions* (1988), set in the late 1960s in Zimbabwe, then the British colony Rhodesia. As a girl, Tambu has to resist both her father and elder brother to obtain an education, and finally—after her brother's untimely death—she succeeds him to study at a missionary school run by her uncle. Leaving her family's homestead to board at the school, Tambu leaves her broken-hearted mother behind, but Tambu tries not to think of her and focuses entirely on her schoolwork. Tambu studies extremely hard and two years later wins a scholarship to a more prestigious Catholic missionary school, where she moves in turn, leaving behind her uncle's family, including her troubled aunt and cousin. Thus, Tambu can gain an education under the colonial system only by making a series of emotional, geographical, and cultural breaks with her family, birthplace, and ethnic origin, ending up at a school run by white nuns, where nearly all the pupils are white and the teaching is in English.

Tambu has had to make successive choices between different values to which she is attached—education *and* love of her mother and mother tongue; gender equality *and* family bonds. Nor is it only that in practice Tambu cannot pursue her education without having to neglect her family's indigenous agricultural way of life. More than that, to pursue her education under the colonial system, Tambu has to take up and participate in a system of values which is actively opposed to those of her family. The values between which Tambu has to choose are not merely irreconcilable in practice but positively antithetical to one another, as the entire system of colonial values is predicated on opposition to indigenous life.

Steeling herself against indigenous values in the name of educational ones, Tambu lives in a constant 'nervous condition', shielding herself from, yet buffeted by factors that make her nervous: the attachments she has had to leave behind and—worse—repudiate to advance her education.[31] Tambu is nervous, anxious, and uneasy, not only because she cannot be faithful to all the values she has inherited, but also as the register that she is violating some of these values in adhering to others. Her situation constrains her to do wrong not merely by omission but also by action. Tambu's anxiety reflects her awareness of the values and attachments she is dishonouring, which press back upon her with their rejected claims, reminding her that she has wronged them. It falls to Tambu's mother, near the end of the novel, to spell out the source of Tambu's anxiety: Tambu is becoming too English, and 'you [can't] expect the ancestors to stomach so much Englishness' (1988: 207). Ancestral claims that come through one's family, birthplace, and background can be repudiated, but those claims remain real and rejecting them is wrong; unfortunately, though, under colonial conditions, Tambu cannot avoid acting wrongly.

The anxieties dramatized by Sartre and Dangarembga are anxieties about how to take forward one's past and inherited attachments when these attachments conflict—as they always do to some degree, given the fissured and complex nature of inherited cultures and relationships; and as they sometimes do sharply, as in the colonial society Dangarembga portrays. We feel anxiety in these cases as we register the conflict amongst attachments that cannot all be honoured, although they all press claims on us.

To bring this back to Kierkegaard, he described the anxiety we feel at the vertiginous way that our choices create the roads we take and cut others off from ever even existing. But that anxiety has a natal or birth-facing dimension as well. Whatever road I take, some of the inherited luggage I've been carrying, rich with history, memory, and attachments, will have to be left behind or sometimes even thrown away and torn up. There is no way to avoid being in the wrong.

This form of anxiety is not, directly, about one's having been born. Yet it arises because of aspects of our natality—inheritance and reception—where, given the complexities of intergenerational transmission and the many dimensions along which we inherit values and meanings, all inheritances are fissured and fractured to at least some degree. Anxiety about conflicting attachments is thus a form of anxiety to which we are subject as natals, and that registers aspects of our natal condition: that, being born, we have attachments that make claims upon us, prior to our choices; and that the complex history of these attachments means that we cannot possibly honour them all.

IV. Anxiety and Wrong Life

Existentialism appeared to preclude the possibility of birth anxiety, but on closer inspection matters are less black and white: one of the most compelling existentialist descriptions of anxiety, Sartre's in 'Existentialism and Humanism', has shed light on a form of natal anxiety. Another of its forms comes into view, again against Sartre's intentions, from his memoir of his childhood, *Words*. He reports a recurring dream he had as a child:

> Stowaway traveller, I had fallen asleep on the seat and the ticket-inspector was shaking me. 'Your ticket!' I was forced to admit that I had not got one. Or the money to defray the cost of the journey there and then .... I could save myself only by reversing the situation; so I revealed that I was summoned to Dijon by important and secret reasons which concerned France and possibly humanity. Looked at in this new light, there was no one to be found in the whole train with as much right to occupy a seat in it as myself.   (1964: 70)

One interpretation of the dream is metaphysical: none of us has any justification for existing, taking up space and resources in the world, for our lives have no inherent value beyond what we create in them. We are born lacking value or justification, and we create value in an endless, Sisyphean effort to give our existence the vindication it inherently lacks. On this view, we feel a root sense of anxiety as the register of our existential lack of any intrinsic justification for existing, where the anxiety motivates us to try to give ourselves that value. This is another way that anxiety is important in existentialism: as registering that our existence lacks value or justification in itself. This view is expressed not only in Sartre's *Being and Nothingness* but also in Camus's essay *The Myth of Sisyphus* and his novel *The Plague* ([1947] 2001), to which I now turn.

In this novel, the people of Oran succumb to a modern-day strain of plague. As the epidemic consumes the town, it undoes people's usual preoccupations with trade, routine, and personal drama, and their unthinking expectation that the future will be like the past. The plague brings death, and so as the epidemic takes hold we see the power of death to unravel human meanings. This fictional plague has been construed in various ways, notably as representing the German occupation of France, while the devoted group of doctors and volunteers combatting the plague together stand for the Resistance. But on another level the plague is a metaphysical or existential affliction. It is latent in everyone, always dormant and never finally eradicable: the epidemic has only brought into the open a corruption that was already there (Camus 2001: 237–8, 15). This makes the plague sound like original sin, but at several points the text suggests that the plague stands not for sin but death. The protagonist, Doctor Rieux, says that 'the order of the world is governed by death, . . . [but we should still] struggle with all our strength against death' (98). Death comes to us all and threatens to make all our undertakings meaningless and futile, just as the town's ordinary life and relationships have ground to a halt, having lost their point. The only way to restore meaning is to combat the plague, that is, to try to create meaning and value where death threatens them.

Camus thus attributes our inherent lack of meaning and value to our mortality. Ordinarily, we believe unquestioningly in the customary values around us, but death (the plague) exposes that these have no inherent value; we are left to create for ourselves any value that we want these (societal) values to have. However, the lack of value is also natal, for we are born without value and must create it, or so *The Plague* suggests. As an infection passed on from person to person, the plague is bound up with processes of reproduction and transmission, and so it is associated with biological reproduction and by extension birth. As the infection spreads from one person to the next, so does each generation hand down the lack of inherent value to the next one. Thus, *The Plague* suggests that by being born we come into a condition devoid of inherent meaning or worth.

In *Words*, Sartre gives this a moral–social–political twist. The context of his recurring dream, he tells us, was his privileged childhood. He was well-off, comfortable, bourgeois, with a doting family who indulged his every conceit and gave him access to his grandfather's extensive library of classic literature, fostering his dream of becoming a 'Great Artist'. But no 'reasons'—no 'ticket'—justified Sartre in occupying this privileged social and cultural position (his seat in the train carriage). He was born into privilege, but he was not thereby justified in enjoying it. Sartre's anxiety lest he be caught without a ticket is that he enjoys inherited privileges and powers without having any right to do so. As a bourgeois, Sartre is in the wrong, as by extension are all those who are born into privilege.

Birth figures twice here. First, it is by birth that we come into either powerful or disempowered situations in the world, or into situations where we are empowered along some axes of social power and disempowered along others. Second, the radical contingency of whom we are each born as implies that these inequalities of natal power and privilege are illegitimate. To see this, consider by contrast that, on some explanations of whom we are each born as, the inequalities between our different natal situations are basically just. Plato appeals to choices we made before birth, as disembodied souls, to explain whom we are born as: the more virtuous we were in earlier lives, the better are the new lives that we choose. Consequently, we are each born in the social niches we are as the working-out of justice, the proportionment of happiness in this life to past-life virtue.[32] Similarly, on certain views of *karma* we are reborn in locations that repay us for good and bad actions and dispositions in past lives. As John Hick sums up, on all such views: 'There is no arbitrariness, no randomness, no injustice in the inequalities of our human lot [into which we are born], but only ... the reaping now of what we ourselves have sown in the past' (1976: 301). One might consider it an advantage of such views that they portray the world in a redemptive light, as essentially just. Against such views, however, I've proposed that it is sheer contingency, pure fact, that we are each born where and when we are. But if there is indeed no explanation in terms of, say, accumulated past-life *karma* for Sartre's advantageous birth, then his natal advantages are *un*justified: he has no grounds for enjoying them when others do not. This is reflected in his anxiety that he is on the train illegitimately, without a ticket. This anxiety is about one's illegitimacy in a moral–political rather than metaphysical sense. The anxiety is not that one lacks inherent value existentially, but that one is in the wrong on account of one's unjustly advantageous social and political location.

A person might reply that she did not choose to be born, or be born where she was: because birth is an absolute given, not susceptible of being chosen, it's no fault of the one born if it is privilege that she is born into. Having no choice here, one is neither responsible nor blameable for one's natal circumstances and so cannot be in the wrong with respect to them, however advantageous they are. Sartre replies that I *am* responsible for having been born where I was, even though I did not choose it (1958: 556). This seems to conflict with the standard assumption that we can be held responsible only for actions that we've freely chosen to perform. But Sartre's statement, like his train dream, hints at another kind of responsibility that is not so straightforwardly dependent on freedom. Walter Benjamin speaks of it too as 'the guilt-context of the living' ([1919] 1996: 204), and Adorno as the fact that 'Wrong life cannot be lived rightly' ([1951] 1978: 39). And Beauvoir restates it again: 'You can't draw a straight line in a curved space.... You can't lead a proper life in a society which isn't proper' ([1954] 1991: 508).

To elaborate: By and from birth, we all become caught up in different ways in inequalities that, given the radical contingency of our births, are unjust. When I am born in a given social location I am also born into the relationships, practices, and meanings which sustain the social inequalities into which I've arrived. As I gradually come to participate in the world, this web of meanings comes to constitute who I am. For, as we've repeatedly seen, my social situation and relations are not accidental to but constitute my self. Because the self is relational, then, I become entangled in an illegitimate order in my very being. What I do, feel, and think inescapably comes to carry something of this order forwards. To that extent I come to play a part in perpetuating this order and to be responsible for doing so, even though I had no choice over the place at which I entered this order or the aspects of it to which I thereby became attached and which have shaped my ingrained activities. The same remains true even if I come to criticize the order in question, for my capacities for criticism arise out of the same social space that I am in, with which I therefore remain caught up even when criticizing it. So, after all, a degree of residual connection between agency and responsibility persists here: even though I became attached to my habitual, entrenched activities before I had any choice in the matter, I am still responsible for them to the extent that I exercise and have been exercising sense-making agency in carrying them forward.[33]

There is, then, a form of anxiety in which we apprehend that we are caught up in a context of wrong life and are 'in the wrong' not by choice but birth. This form of anxiety registers a tension in our natal condition. It is contingent where we are each born, so that natal inequalities are unjustified; yet, as inheritors, we become thoroughly constituted by and attached to the unequal arrangements into which we are born, unable to extricate ourselves from the wrong or avoid contributing to it.

One might object that this is not really an existential anxiety, because it arises only contingently given an unjust social world. In contrast, an existential anxiety would be one that attests to fundamental features of the human condition and that can arise in any context just because the features it attests to are fundamental and universal. However, the anxiety in question *is* at least partly existential insofar as it does attest to a fundamental tension in our natal condition. This is the tension between the radical contingency of our starting-points in life, and the depth at which we nonetheless become attached to the social relations and conditions that are at work in and flow out of these starting-points. It is a radical contingency that I started where I did, yet that start has come to shape and pervade me through and through. When we feel anxious to be caught up illegitimately yet intimately in a social context of wrong life, that existential anxiety has been refracted into a specific form that pertains to an unjust society. But it is still a refracted form of an anxiety that pertains to basic features of our natal condition—contingent birth, deep attachment—and that as such remains existential.

Sartre's focus was on anxiety to have been born into privilege. But I might also feel distressed and frustrated to have been born in a deprived and disadvantaged location in the social world, or with a body that has conferred inherent disadvantages on me, say by genetically predisposing me to a chronic illness. That might look like a sense of grievance or injustice rather than anxiety, but actually it is another shape of the existential anxiety about contingent birth and deep attachment. For my distress registers how deeply my life has been shaped, disadvantageously, by the bodily and social place in the world into which I was born, *and* that my birth there was radically contingent, so that there is no justifying or redemptive light to be shone on the situation.

To the extent that these forms of anxiety are socially refracted, they can motivate us to criticize the social inequalities whose injustice has contaminated us. This yields another route, in addition to those I've identified earlier, by which we may come to criticize our natal inheritances, despite the depth at which they have shaped us. Indeed, in these cases it is partly our recognition of the depth of that influence, combined with frustration and unhappiness about it, which motivates our criticism. And as part of that criticism we may start trying to participate in inherited practices differently, in ways that depart from, rather than reinforce, the surrounding inequalities.

Overall in this chapter, I have sought to counteract the view that only death and not birth arouses anxiety. I've argued that being born is also a multifaceted source of anxiety for us: of discomfort at our lack of sovereign control over our lives and feelings; distress that we are leading the particular lives we are; bafflement at the mystery of our origins; and in other ways. Being born thus presents anxieties of its own, distinct from those aroused by death; and in this way being born has negative aspects for us as well as positive ones. When we attend to birth as well as death, we can do better justice to the full range of existential anxieties and difficulties with which these two ends of life present us.

Notes

1. The Heideggerian term I am glossing as 'mood' is *Stimmung*, although debate continues about how his linked terms *Befindlichkeit* and *Stimmung* are best translated (see, e.g. Staehler 2016b: 140).

2. On fear as future-directed, see Svendsen (2007: 39, 43), who refers inter alia to Aristotle's *Rhetoric* where he defines fear as pain arising from the expectation of a coming evil.

3. Thanks to Angus Taylor for alerting me to this passage.

4. Stanton's comment recalls the view evoked in Pascal's *Pensée* n. 194: 'I see those frightful spaces of the universe which surround me, and I find myself tied to one corner of this vast expanse, without knowing why I am put in this place rather than in another, nor why the short time which is given me to live is assigned to me at this point rather than at another of the whole eternity which was before me or which shall come after me' ([1670] 1958: 55).

5. Heidegger's term is *Angst*, which Sartre, along with other French authors such as Beauvoir, translates as *angoisse*. Both are equivalents of Danish *Angest*. In English, they can be translated as *anxiety* or as *anguish*, *angst*, or *dread*. Nonetheless *anxiety* and *anguish* differ etymologically. According to the Oxford English Dictionary, *Angst* and *angoisse* are rooted in Latin *angustia*, meaning tightness or narrowness, or severe bodily pain or mental distress. *Anxiety*, however, comes from Latin *anxietās*—worry, solicitude, extreme care. This suggests that perhaps *anxiety* does not best convey what Heidegger and Sartre mean by *Angst* and *angoisse*. Nonetheless, I retain 'anxiety', but without confining it to meaning undesirable worry or stress and while broadening its meaning to take in the connotations of anguish.

6. Emotions have intentional structures: a given type of emotion is characteristically directed upon an 'object' of a certain type in respect of certain properties. For instance, admiration is typically directed towards impressive things or towards things in view of their impressive qualities. An 'object' here is anything that is the focus of awareness: an event, a possibility, a person, a material thing, etc. How do emotions intend objects? One answer is that emotions respond to objects *represented* in a certain way, that is under certain judgements, beliefs, etc. For example, I feel fear of the lion because I judge it to be capable of killing me. Thus, here, intentional content is equated with propositional content (Deigh 1994: 848). With Deigh, I find this overly intellectualist. While I won't offer any rival account of the nature of emotions, I'll assume that anxiety bears witness to certain features of our existence in some immediately felt and holistic way, and I'll talk about 'disclosure' and its cognates to convey this.

7. The wonder is at the fact that there is something rather than nothing; at the fact that I am there, and that there is anyone there at all; at our plurality; at the mystery of beginning; at the way that someone radically new appears with each birth who was not there before; and at our uniqueness.

8. See Ricoeur ([1965] 1986: 161) and Macquarrie (1981: 386).

9. Freud also suggests that the female genitals are uncanny because they recall our now-repressed wish to return into our first home, the womb—a wish that, being repressed, is both familiar and unfamiliar (1955a: 245).

10. Compare Heidegger's view of the uncanny in his *Introduction to Metaphysics*, which Tanja Staehler expresses as follows: 'We experience the world as uncanny on some basic level because we did not bring it about, but were born or "thrown" into it, and into a particular time and space, without ever being able to fully grasp this...world. However, we do not stop at this encounter with the world as uncanny, but try to make ourselves at home in the midst of this uncanniness' Staehler 2016a: 373; and see Heidegger [1935] 1959: 156ff). In his earlier book *Being and Time*, Heidegger had connected both anxiety and the uncanny with thrownness. In anxiety, the world emerges as strange to us and no longer makes sense, and one way that the world is strange is that we inhabit our specific places in the world without there being any accounting for our being where and when we are. Having made these promising connections, though, Heidegger narrows down anxiety's scope later in *Being and Time* so that anxiety only properly concerns mortality (see MacAvoy 1996: 69–70).

11. Freud says the same about how one cannot concretely imagine one's own death: 'whenever we attempt to do so we...are in fact still present as spectators' ([1915] 1957a: 289).

12. As Staehler observes, giving birth can also provoke anxiety in those who are pregnant because the coming event seems incomprehensible: 'How would one finite creature be able to release another finite creature from itself?...[W]e do not yet know what will emerge and cannot even imagine it, and that we cannot ultimately imagine that there will indeed be a living creature' (2016b: 149–50). This parallels the difficulty we can feel when thinking, retrospectively, about having been born ourselves.

13. As we saw in Chapter 4, Sartre finds it shocking that I was ever a mere non-experiencing, material embryo (1958: 138-9/184-6). In Anglophone metaphysics, Eric Olsen (n.d.) argues that the fact that I was once a foetus poses a problem for many standard approaches to personal identity in terms of psychological continuity. As I see it, though, I have the experience I do *as* the particular body I am, and I was still that body even when it had not yet formed the capacities to have experience.

14. Admittedly, some people claim to remember being born and even being in the womb. See Salvador Dalí's autobiography ([1942] 1993)—although this is hardly intended as a reporting of straightforward facts. And in, for example, *Behind the Scenes at the Museum*, Ruby's alleged memory of her conception proves deceptive, for she was in fact a twin: at conception, she was not yet the 'I' she says she was, but a 'we'. In short, these apparent memories are especially unreliable, for they tend to project an experiencing self back into the time before it had emerged.

15. See, e.g. White and Pillemer (1989), Nelson (1993), and Bauer (1996).

16. Indeed, for some evidence that this system only becomes established at around 8 months, see Cromie (2002).

17. Edward Casey speaks of 'body memory': 'memory that is intrinsic to the body, to its own ways of remembering: how we remember in and by and through the body...being in the situation itself again and feeling it through our body' (1987: 147).

18. I am informed by Butler's rejoinder to Cavarero's account of the narratable self. 'The one story the "I" cannot tell is the story of its own emergence as an "I" who not only speaks but comes to give an account of itself.... [T]he "I" who tells the story...constitutes a point of opacity and...induces a break or interruption of the non-narrativizable in the midst of the story' (Butler 2005: 66).

19. Rank and Freud are concerned with the trauma of being born, not that of giving birth. Of course, it has since become recognized that giving birth can be traumatic too. See Moyzakitis (2009), who dates the first reference to childbirth (i.e. childbearing) trauma to 1993.

20. Or *die Quelle und das Vorbild des Angstaffektes*. See, e.g. Freud's *Introductory Lecture on Psychoanalysis* 25, 'Anxiety' ([1915–17] 1963: 492–4) and *The Interpretation of Dreams* ([1900] 1958: 400).

21. For Freud, a trauma is 'characterised by an influx of excitations that is excessive by the standard of the subject's tolerance and capacity to master such excitations and work them out psychically' (Laplanche and Pontalis [1967] 1989: 465). Freud's classic statement is in *Beyond the Pleasure Principle* ([1920] 1955b: esp. 29–30). The literature on trauma, psychoanalytic and not, is of course huge. Caruth (1996) offers one very influential account. I confine myself to Freud's specific understanding of the links between trauma and being born, on which Rank draws.

22. Thus for Rank, reversing Bauman/Becker type views on which death-anxiety drives culture, birth-anxiety fuels culture; here Rank prefigures Irigaray, Cavarero, and Jantzen.

23. In *Inhibitions*, Freud also sought to resolve his long-running difficulties in theorizing anxiety. His first theory of anxiety (Freud [1894/5] 1962) was that the repression of sexual wishes causes anxiety because, strictly, only the ideational component of these wishes—our ideas about wished-for sexual acts and scenarios—is repressed, while the associated erotic energy remains conscious and, being now set free from any accompanying ideas, assumes the guise of free-floating nervous energy, that is, anxiety. Anxiety, on that view, is a directionless energetic surplus, unlike fear, which has a definite object. In *Inhibitions* Freud adopts the opposite view—the core of his second theory—that anxiety motivates repression, not vice versa. (Dividing Freud's thought on anxiety into these two stages is standard—see, for example, Salecl 2004: 18–23—although for a three-stage classification, see Morris 1973: 190ff.)

24. This reflects Freud's tendency, at worst, to reduce others to our mental representations of them, rather than address intersubjectivity and its difficulties.

25. On this anxiety in babies from around 8 months old, see Winnicott [1971] (2005) and Jessica Benjamin (1988).

26. I am departing somewhat from mainstream thinking about separation anxiety, which descends from Bowlby [1969] (1997), and on which separation anxiety is a developmental stage that children normally move beyond, both endogenously and given appropriate parental care. Thereafter the anxiety reduces to a small part of a person's emotional landscape, except in cases of pathology. In contrast I regard anxiety, including separation anxiety, as attesting to fundamental and lifelong features of human existence.

27. On Kierkegaard's view of anxiety, see esp. Pattison (2005: Ch. 2).

28. On repetition, see also Kierkegaard ([1843 1983) and Carlisle (2006a: Ch. 5).

29. On the role of the past in lived time for Kierkegaard, see Christine Battersby (1998: 182–4).

30. There is a rich literature on whether moral dilemmas are ever genuine (see McConnell 2014). Broadly, I side with those who argue in the affirmative.

31. Dangarembga's phrase 'nervous condition' comes from Sartre's preface to Fanon's *The Wretched of the Earth*: 'The status of "native" is a nervous condition introduced and maintained by the settler among colonised people with their consent' (Sartre [1961] 1967: 17). Here, Sartre was taking up Fanon's diagnoses of colonialism's harmful psychological effects. Fanon thought that colonized people typically suffer from neuroses because of their repressed memories of traumatic experiences of colonial oppression, violence, and insult. See Bulhan (1985) and Hook (2004).

32. Origen takes a related view. Influenced by Plato, he interprets the Fall as having occurred when different souls, having the power of free choice, chose to 'depart...from the good in varying degrees' (Wiley 2002: 48; see Origen [*c*.220–230] 1936: II.9.1–6). God then banished each soul into the material world in a particular body and social niche, more or less healthy, wealthy, and powerful depending on the extent of the evils that soul had chosen.

33. Consider the furore after anti-racist activist Munroe Bergdorf posted on Facebook: 'Honestly I don't have energy to talk about the racial violence of white people any more. Yes ALL white people' (Fortin 2017). Many white people objected that they were not racist, or were actively anti-racist, or that there are actively anti-racist white people. But as Katherine Craig replied: 'Too often, we seem to think that racism means actively doing or saying something racist. Not so. We live in a society that is built on the spoils of racism, and that continues to benefit from inequality in all its forms.... if you grow up in a racist society, *through no fault of your own*, some of that racism is bound to stick subconsciously. It's an unconscious conspiracy in which we are all complicit' (Craig 2017; my emphasis). For a theoretical framework for making sense of this, see Mills (1997).

6

Natality and Mortality

In this chapter I turn to our mortality, the fact that we will die and our awareness of this fact as it structures how we exist. Despite my overall focus on natality, I do not deny that mortality remains important for our existence. As natality is also important, though, I want to reconsider mortality in view of its connections with natality.

In Section I, I differentiate my approach from those of Cavarero and Jantzen, who want us to re-orient our lives and cultures around birth and not death. In contrast, I advocate re-balancing rather than reversal.[1] In Section II, I suggest that our deaths are *relational*.[2] Our deaths shade into each other: because we are relational beings, when someone dies who was important to us, we lose part of our own selves, part of the unfolding web of relationship, meaning, and value of which we were constituted. Here we undergo a degree of death, even in life—a part of the same loss of relationships, meaning, and value which we will undergo totally when we die. Furthermore, there are grounds for me to fear our deaths, as they spell the end of our relationships, to which I am deeply attached. In Section III, I suggest that another reason to fear death is that at death I will cease to be in the world that I share with others, with whom I want to be together. Thus, much of what death will deprive us of is relational in character and matters to us on that account. This reflects the fact that we are relational beings, and are relational as thoroughly as we are—with deep attachments to others, our own histories of experience, and the shared world—because we are born. Given these attachments, it makes sense that we would not want them to be severed by death. In these ways, our mortality is that of natals. I draw out these ideas with reference to two works by Simone de Beauvoir: *A Very Easy Death* and *All Men are Mortal*.

In Section IV, I situate this relational view of death in contrast to Heidegger's explicitly 'non-relational' account of mortality in *Being and Time*, according to which the prospect of my own death bears both negatively and positively on the meaningfulness of my existence as the deaths of others cannot. Although I disagree about this,[3] I use Heidegger's analysis of

Being born: Birth and Philosophy. Alison Stone, Oxford University Press (2019). © Alison Stone.
DOI: 10.1093/oso/9780198845782.001.0001

the implications of Dasein's supposedly non-relational mortality to draw out what implications instead follow, given that our mortality is in fact relational. One implication is that mortality loses the priority over natality that Heidegger accords it. Another implication is that fidelity, as well as authenticity, is important in our ethical lives.

As is no doubt apparent, in discussing death and our fear of it, I will be focussing not on dying but on being dead or no-longer-existing, and not on our fears of dying but our fears of non-existence. Admittedly, many people's most pressing fears around death are about becoming fatally ill, growing old, losing their capacities, and undergoing protracted, painful, difficult, and burdensome processes of dying. Many of us go to our deaths through illness, ageing, incapacitation, and decline, and how people undergo these processes of dying matters very much to them and the people around them. The history of philosophy has neglected these matters, tending to dismiss them as not properly philosophical and to concentrate instead on death as non-existence. Plausibly, this is part and parcel of philosophy's tendency to sideline dependency, vulnerability, and embodiment. So it might seem that, as I want to reconsider death in connection with birth, I should attend to dying more than non-existence.[4] I focus on non-existence, though, in order to show how death *as* philosophy has mainly addressed it— as non-existence—looks different in light of our natality; and, specifically, how in this light it looks less radically individual and more relational and communal.[5]

For purposes of this discussion, I assume that death is final—that there is no afterlife, rebirth, or post-mortem survival. I don't believe that we are epistemically qualified to rule out these possibilities, but evaluating them is beyond my scope here. For the time being I take it that for each of us death is the end, permanently.

I. Rebalancing Death and Birth

Irigaray's, Cavarero's, and Jantzen's criticisms of the historical preoccupation with death and mortality have been important for me, and I agree that we should correct the historical over-concentration on death.[6] However, it does not necessarily follow that we should re-orientate our attention towards birth exclusively rather than re-balance our attention to both ends of human life. At times, though, Cavarero and Jantzen endorse the former goal— wrongly, I'll now argue regarding Cavarero.

According to Cavarero in *In Spite of Plato*, fear of the maternal body led Western culture, in the classical Greek period, to establish a counter-reaction and become preoccupied with death. To be born is to begin life in a state where one's mother has the power to give or take one's embryonic and foetal life, and one's infantile life too, say by refusing to breast-feed, or committing infanticide (Cavarero 1990: 64–5). This power is particular to women, for Cavarero. But if we look away from our status of being born towards our mortality, and treat death alone as being central to human existence, then the power of the maternal body is eclipsed. Women and mothers die, as everyone does (68–9, 104–5); death has more power than mothers. The power of mothers to kill their children or let them die becomes absorbed and subsumed into the broader, universal power of death.

However, Cavarero argues, once the prevailing attitude is that 'all men are mortal', death becomes frightening, because it expands to fill our vision. Hence, we become motivated to imagine an afterlife or eternal realm unaffected by death into which our selves can potentially escape, as when Plato holds that death releases the immortal, immaterial soul from its bodily prison. By implication for Cavarero, if we defined ourselves instead as natals and not mortals, we would cease to fear death, or at least fear it less. For if death were not treated as central to human existence, then we would be less troubled by it; it would recede from view.

Cavarero cements that conclusion from another argumentative direction. Once death and not birth is seen as central to human existence, she argues, birth becomes understood by comparative reference to death. But to die is to pass from being into nothingness (at least as we intuitively apprehend death, prior to postulating any afterlife). Reciprocally, birth becomes understood as the passage from nothingness into being—entrance into existence out of nothingness. The role of the mother is thereby eclipsed once more. We regard birth, now, not as coming into the world out of the mother's body but rather as coming into existence where before we did not exist (53). After I die endless non-existence will follow; likewise, until I was born an eternity of non-existence rolled by.

Reversing this position, Cavarero approaches death in comparative relation to birth regarded as coming into existence from out of one's mother's body. Reciprocally, death is not annihilation, passage into non-existence, but passage into a new bodily form: 'from the point of view of...living matter, one's own death is a metamorphosis' (114). This passage occurs as one's dead body loses its organization and its organs break down into component materials that disperse and become incorporated into new material forms.

Cavarero interprets this disorganization and re-incorporation of bodily matter as a participation in cycles of super-individual, cosmic life.

Cavarero appeals here to Lispector's *The Passion According to G.H.*, whose influence on Cavarero we've noted before. We recall that G. H. comes to apprehend and celebrate a single, immemorial process of life flowing through the liquids seeping out of the cockroach that she has killed. She says:

> The narrow passage had been the daunting cockroach ... And I had ended up, all impure myself, embarking, through it, upon my past, which was my continuous present and my continuous future— ... and my fifteen million daughters, from that time down to myself, were also there. My life had been as continuous as death. Life is so continuous that we divide it into stages and call one of them death .... I had always been in life.   (1998: 57)

G. H. (and/or Lispector)—and Cavarero—take the life-process to be universal, yet also specially linked to the female body in that life passes in and out of its successive forms through females giving birth to females giving birth to females, and so on.

Ultimately, for Cavarero, each person's death is just part of this cosmic life-process, so that dying is 'conquered' by life (1995: 116). We would no longer have grounds to fear death, she suggests, if we took this view of death, not as one's personal annihilation but as merely another phase in life's overarching cycle. 'Since there is no nothingness in the incessant and internal labor of life's metamorphoses', we would experience 'disinvestment from death' and undergo 'conciliation' with it, seeing that on death we will not cease to exist but only be re-incorporated into a set of processes which is larger than us and continuously existent (114, 119).

G. H. suggests something similar. Normally, our membership in infinite life is concealed from us insofar as we are finite, organized bodies. Totally identified with her organized bodily form, ignorant of the larger life that this form organizes, G. H. says that she is 'afraid to understand, the matter of the world frightens me, ... with its cockroaches' (1998: 52). G. H. fears death because she falsely believes that on death she will lose 'everything I have had ... what I am'. But when she comes to apprehend and embrace the deeper life-process suffusing her, her fear gives way to joy: a future of continuous life beyond her current finite form awaits her.

I find this picture of joyful conciliation with death implausible in several ways. First, we may at times feel our participation in broader, infinite life-processes. But the fact that these processes run through me does not make me immortal; and apprehending these processes at work, I may be apprehending the eternity or infinity of life or the whole cosmos, but this is not an eternity of the finite embodied individual that I am. As such, my perception of these larger processes should not take away my awareness that I as a finite embodied individual will die, and any joy I take in these larger processes should not take away such fear as I may feel about my own death.

Second, if I do fear my death—as many people do—this, contrary to Cavarero, need not be solely down to my inhabiting a cultural horizon that foregrounds death. We are meaning-making beings, whose lives are of significance and concern to us, yet this first-personal existence of mine will cease when I die. At the same time, the biological materials that made up my body will continue to circulate and be re-arranged and recycled in the natural world—as Hamlet says, 'a king may go a progress through the guts of a beggar' (Shakespeare 2003: 200, 4.3.28–9). But that these third-person material processes will occur does nothing to keep me going first-personally. And the fact that when I die the first-person existence that concerns and matters to me will end provides me with grounds to fear death, independent of the cultural horizon I inhabit.[7]

Third, Cavarero's proposal that we should regard death symmetrically with birth conceived as passage out of one's mother's body relies on an equivocation between broad and narrow senses of birth. Taking birth narrowly as departure from the womb, I already existed before my birth—which yields the conclusion Cavarero wants: that death is not disintegration but re-integration into a bigger (and quasi-maternal) body. However, if we take birth more broadly as a process extending back to conception, then before I was conceived, I didn't yet have a formed body, nor was I sentient; I didn't exist at that point at all. So, there *is* an important sense in which I did not exist before being born, and if death is compared with birth so understood it emerges that after all, *contra* Cavarero, I will cease to exist when I die.

Insofar as Cavarero hopes to remove or reduce our fear of death by showing it to be poorly founded once death is viewed as symmetrical with birth, her intent is almost Epicurean. In his 'symmetry argument', the Epicurean philosopher Lucretius reasons that I do not fear the indefinitely long period of non-existence that preceded my birth; but my endless non-existence after I die will be no different to that earlier non-existence; so, as I do not fear the former, rationally neither should I fear the latter (2007: 3.823–42 and 3.972–5). In Cavarero's revised version: before (narrow) birth, there was not nothing, but my material pre-formation; after death there will be, not nothing, but my material re-formation. Some of the problems with Lucretius's argument arise from the temporal asymmetries between birth and death, which also bear on Cavarero. Contrary to Lucretius, I do have grounds to fear my death and not the time before my birth because the latter is in my past, whereas my non-existence after I die lies in my future, and fear as an emotion is directed towards bad things expected in the future. The same temporal asymmetry also means that, as Nagel argues, when I die I will be deprived forever of existence and its good features, whereas I could not be deprived of these before I had them in the first place (for something to be able to be taken away from me, I must first have it; Nagel 1979: Ch. 1).[8] These considerations suggest, against Cavarero, that we do have grounds to fear death. We do not all in fact fear it, but those who do fear it have reasons for doing so; it is just that we are not all responsive to these considerations.

II. Relational Death

How does our mortality look once it is considered together with natality, not in isolation from it? In this section I explore one way in which we are mortal *as* natal beings: relationally. Because we are relational, the deaths of distinct individuals are intertwined and shade into one another.

To throw into relief this thought that our deaths are 'relational', let's note by contrast Heidegger's view that each Dasein's death is its own, its 'ownmost, *non*-relational, unsurpassable possibility' (*eigenste, unbezügliche, unüberholbare Möglichkeit*; 1962: 294/250; my emphasis) which 'individualizes Dasein down to itself' (*vereinzelt das Dasein auf es selbst*) (308/263). For Heidegger, my own death can never be an event *within* the world for me, as the deaths of others are. Rather, from my first-person perspective, my death threatens my *entire* world, exposing its fragility and throwing the meaningfulness of everything into question.[9] So my death and the deaths of others are of different orders, radically asymmetrical.[10] I therefore relate to my death inauthentically if I envisage it as just one more finite future event like other people's deaths—which, however, just is the average everyday way we each do tend to treat our deaths. I think that Heidegger is right to see death as a more radical threat to meaningfulness. But, against him, I want to suggest that our deaths are continuous with one another and not radically different in kind, so that 'my' death is always 'ours'.

To be sure, when I die I will cease forever to have any first-person experience, which is a fearful prospect, not only because of all that I will thereby lose but also because it defies comprehension or imagining. I can frame the abstract thought of 'my permanently ceasing ever to have any first-person experience' but I cannot substantially comprehend what this will consist in—not least because there *is* nothing, experientially, that it will consist in. Here I run up brutally against the limits of my understanding.

In addition, when I die, all my relationships will end. But it is not that I will cease to have experience, fundamentally, and that *because* of this my relationships with others will cease, derivatively. For I am not a bare subject of first-person experience; rather, I have experience as a self-with-others, whose relationships with these others have become organized over time into a concrete personality. And the way I personally experience and make sense of things has long since become enfolded by the horizons of meaning I've imbibed from others. Furthermore, to have experience is not to be in a private realm of representations but to be in relation with the world and as one intrinsically shared with others. Thus, when I cease on death to have any first-person experience I will also cease (1) to be with others, (2) to participate in a shared horizon of meaning, and (3) to inhabit the shared world, especially as shared with those whom I care about. All of this is not derivative of some more fundamental cessation of my experience. Rather, these several factors along with that cessation are all part of what my death will consist in.

Now, in this section I want to look at (1). As we have seen in earlier chapters, my concrete personality consists of a web of unfolding relationships with others. When I die these relationships will end—each of them individually as well as their total web. Relationships, though, take place between at least two participants. The relationships in question were also parts of the webs that constituted the concrete selves of the others involved. So, if the permanent ending of my relationships is part of my death, then the equally permanent ending of each of these people's relationships with me, an ending that will occur when I die, must also be part of each of those people's deaths. And in that case their deaths occur, to a degree, *already*, even while those individuals remain alive. Something of each of these individuals dies, during their lives, as and when I die. Correlatively when others die, part of me dies too. And so our deaths are not after all separate from one another.

This may seem odd and counter-intuitive. We might prefer to say that when someone with whom I was related dies I have lost them, and lost a strand of my relational make-up, but that *I* have not thereby undergone any degree of death. This may reflect an assumption that death is all-or-nothing.[11] Then again, we do not share one single, internally consistent set of intuitions and assumptions about death. For John Donne, it made intuitive sense that: 'If a clod be washed away by the sea, Europe is the less... [and] any man's death diminishes me, because I am involved in mankind, and therefore never send to know for whom the bell tolls: it tolls for thee' ([1624] 1999: 103). What more can be said for the Donne-type view?

First, when someone I love dies, the whole way I was disposed to act and feel with them ceases to be available to me. This can be very far-reaching; large swathes of my self may be taken from me at a stroke. Second, those strands of my internalized relational history which were kept alive through these dispositions are put out of count as well. Third, my history together with the loved one is lost. Of course, I can remember it from my side; but it existed for us both, from our distinct perspectives, and unfolded between us in the interplay between these perspectives. I have lost this really unfolding history and am left with only my partial memory of it. That loss is a loss of part *of* me—not of a history that was extraneous to me—because, all along, my own self has existed partly outside me. One instance of this exteriority is that the actions I perform over time are the actions they are, with the meanings they have—meanings that constitute what these actions count as—partly in virtue of how these actions are perceived, responded to, and taken up by others. A flirtatious advance that is favourably received and responded to is that, but if it is unfavourably received it is already on the way to being a distressing nuisance and, if pursued regardless, is sexual harassment. To give a different example of shared history, my family knows what my academic writing means to me by the time and worry I expend on it, the time that it takes me away from them, and so on. If my family was no longer there, the meaning of what I am doing would be that much diminished. And these activities and projects in which I engage contribute to making up my self in the thick, concrete sense, so that when someone dies and I cease to be able to engage in a project under the meaning it had for me hitherto—in that other person's eyes—it is my self that is thereby attenuated.

A person's death is never solely his or her own, then, because it is never the case that *only* this person who dies, dies. Always it is *we* who die: the death is shared, communal, or collective. This emerges in Beauvoir's narrative of her mother's death, *A Very Easy Death* ([1964] 1966). At times in this memoir Beauvoir inclines towards a Heideggerian view that we must each die alone, existentially if not in empirical fact. She declares that: 'The misfortune is that although everyone must come to this, each experiences the adventure in solitude. We never left Maman during these last days...

and yet we were profoundly separated from her' (1966: 87). She is alluding to Heidegger's claim that, although we all encounter dying others—which is how we first become familiar with the phenomenon of death—nonetheless the 'dying of Others is not something which we experience in a genuine sense. At most we are always just "there alongside"' (Heidegger 1962: 282/239).

Yet Beauvoir's narrative also implies a different view on which our deaths are relational. The memoir begins when Beauvoir's mother is admitted to hospital after a fall. The doctors discover that she has intestinal cancer, on which they operate. Beauvoir is frustrated that the doctors persistently deceive her mother about her condition and prolong her mother's life with drugs and operations although she is terminally ill and in great pain. The doctors insist on treating her mother's death merely as a physical process befalling a 'defenseless carcass' (Beauvoir 1966: 10), failing to recognize her mother as a meaning-making subject. The threat posed by Mme Beauvoir's death is that it will undo her meaning-making projects, and the doctors' behaviour exacerbates, rather than allays, this threat.

Beauvoir feels powerless to step in and exert control: 'One is caught up in the wheels and dragged along, powerless in the face of specialists' diagnoses, their forecasts, their decisions' (50). In overtaking Mme Beauvoir, the medical establishment overtakes Beauvoir too: they are objectified and rendered powerless together. Finally, overpowered by the joint forces of medicine and illness, Mme Beauvoir dies unwillingly, painfully short of breath, but having roundly declared that she does not want to die. This is the very point when Beauvoir declares that we each die alone, ontologically.

Beauvoir's narrative undermines these claims, though. Immediately after making them, she writes of how closely bound up in body with her mother she has always felt. Her mother's body was her first love; it was her mother with whom she first identified, as an infant. She loved to be intimately joined with her mother's nurturing body. Unconsciously, she remains caught up in this early loving identification with her mother: in her dreams, her mother 'blended with Sartre, and we were happy together' (89). Beauvoir's dreams restore her mother to life in the body of Sartre, reassuring Beauvoir that they are still together, not separated by death after all. Her intense attachment to her mother's body also leads Beauvoir to describe her mother's illness and dying in meticulous, gruesome, physical detail: her mother's 'flayed body was bathing in the uric acid that oozed from her skin', she writes; it was 'rotting alive' (71, 73).

This identification and attachment overcome the supposed solitude of Mme Beauvoir's death. She resists death, doggedly clinging to life—a bodily clinging, which for Beauvoir is rooted in her mother's intense organic vitality: '[S]he clung ferociously to this world, and she had an animal dread of death'; 'Her vitality filled me with wonder' (14, 17). Beauvoir, then, admires the vitality with which her mother defies and resists the processes of illness that are overcoming her. Beauvoir joins in this defiance: 'in every cell of my body I joined in her refusal, her rebellion' (91). Beauvoir shares in the refusal because she is so closely bound, psychologically, with her mother; the refusal is theirs, shared. Beauvoir's resistance to the death is her mother's resistance continuing in and through her, so that exactly when Beauvoir is stating that her mother has to die alone, she finds her face copying her mother's movements, crying her mother's tears—'I had put Maman's mouth on my own face... Her whole person, her whole being, was concentrated there' (28).

With Mme Beauvoir's death, a part of Beauvoir dies too. So just as Mme Beauvoir resists dying, Beauvoir too resists both her mother's death and the death of the part of her self that will be lost with her mother. Insofar as the death that is coming to them is shared, the two of them resist together. Mme Beauvoir has an animal, vital attachment to her body staying alive; likewise, Beauvoir has a a vital, deep-seated attachment to her mother's body, even in its sickness and decay. This is at the same time an attachment to her whole relational history with her mother. Not surprisingly, therefore, Beauvoir answers her self-addressed question 'why was she so moved by her mother's death?' by writing first of her unconscious identification with her mother and then of their shared vital spirit, their corporeal entwinement. All this leads her to concede that death is not so solitary after all, for 'love, friendship, or comradely feeling overcomes the loneliness of death' (91). When we are deeply attached to one another, we suffer death together, not alone.

A Very Easy Death puts death at the centre of human existence. But we can re-read it as approaching death from a natal perspective, on which we are constitutively related with one another by virtue of being born, so that our deaths always shade into one another, just as our selves do. Here it is no coincidence that the text revolves around Beauvoir's *mother's* death. After all, it is generally our mothers of whom we are born and, very often, who care for us in infancy (notwithstanding complications around maternity, gestation, child-caring, and parenthood). Because our relationships with our mothers are, especially clearly, natal relationships, the death of a mother spotlights how death affects us as natal beings.

It may be objected that our deaths remain different from one another: for example, that when Mme Beauvoir died, Simone only underwent a degree of death, a partial and temporary death from which she could resurface into new life-giving attachments, whereas her mother died totally and unequivocally. Indeed, our deaths do differ in this regard, just as each of us is constituted by a total web of relationships which is unique in each case. Our respective webs overlap without ever completely coinciding. But these points remain consistent with our deaths shading into one another by degrees. When someone I love dies, I undergo only a *partial* death. But it is still a partial *death*. For my death will be the end of the multi-stranded set of meaning-laden relations I have had with the world and others; and single strands of this web can already end, during my life, through the deaths of the others who were essential to them.

III. Death and the Shared World

I've suggested that we have grounds to fear death: it will end forever my relationships with those whom I care about; and when I die I will cease to be in relation with the world, to which I am attached as well. Yet my attachment to the world is not separate from my attachments to others; rather, I am attached to the world because it is intrinsically shared and is the medium of our lives together. Let me explore this by drawing on Beauvoir's novel *All Men are Mortal* ([1946] 1995).

In this book Beauvoir carries out a fictional thought-experiment revolving around Raymond Fosca who, centuries ago, drank an elixir that gave him immortality. Initially we meet Fosca through the actress Regina, who is tormented by the thought that her death will erase her presence from the world as if she had never lived. For his part, Fosca is already as if dead to the world; he doesn't eat, barely moves, neither sleeps nor speaks, and struggles even to see people or hear their utterances. Regina is drawn to the challenge of capturing his attention and then, learning from Fosca that he is immortal, she comes to desire his love so that her memory at least can be preserved eternally. Fosca, though, tries strenuously to persuade Regina that immortality is 'a terrible curse', partly by telling her his life-story since his birth in 1279.

Beauvoir intends to convey that Fosca's existence is meaningless—before it becomes temporarily re-animated through his infatuation with Regina—because he cannot genuinely commit himself to any projects. Having already thrown himself into numerous enterprises already and seen them through to completion, and often subsequent dissipation or reversal, Fosca now sees no point in doing anything. This is also because he has endless time ahead in which he can pursue any project he wishes. Beauvoir's point seems akin to that which Bernard Williams (1973) makes with reference to the 'Makropulos secret', an opera by Janáček which in turn was based on a play by Karel Čapek ([1922] 1999). Elina Makropulos takes an elixir giving her three hundred more years of healthy adult life, after which she can decide whether or not to take another such elixir; at that point she elects to die. Williams endorses Elina's decision on the grounds that, to have a meaningful life, one must have a set of categorical desires that define who one is. But, given endless time, all those desires would be satisfied. One's life would either become essentially and pervasively meaningless and boring, a torment (as Elina says her life is); or, if one adopted a new set of categorical desires, then that life would not remain one's own in any substantive sense, as that depends on continuity of character. Williams's argument has been variously criticized, defended, and qualified.[12] But in any case, there is a quite distinct line of implicit argument concerning immortality in Beauvoir's text, which appeals, not to categorical desires, but to our constitutive sociality.

Ultimately, Fosca says, the reason why all his potential undertakings seem pointless is that he can no longer form any deep relationships with others with whom he could share these projects. 'You'd [soon] lose interest in everything', he tells his friend Carlier at one point, 'because you'd be alone in the world' (Beauvoir 1995: 253). Fosca's destiny is to endure the 'bitter taste of solitude and eternity' (271). Forming significant, affecting bonds with others has become impossible for Fosca because he knows that these others will die, something he has already suffered many times before. When Regina says to him 'we'll do great things together', his face falls and he says: 'A lot of people have told me that' (52). He has already lost sons, wives, grandchildren, and many others—with whom, moreover, all his relationships had already failed, having been blighted by the awareness that Fosca does not share the mortal condition of these others. Fosca embraces the relationship with Regina as an illusion in which he can temporarily immerse himself, but it very quickly crumbles away.

Beauvoir's picture, then, is that without meaningful relationships Fosca's endless life shrivels to emptiness. He cannot commit himself to any projects because he has no one with whom to share them. He knows that anyone with whom he might share a project will die, leaving him to carry it onwards alone. But that would be pointless, since the project had its purpose as a shared undertaking. Moreover, since the project had part of its meaning in the eyes of those with whom Fosca shared it, he cannot even carry it on as the same project it formerly was: most of its meaning has fallen out of it. Thus, Fosca's problem is not so much that he cannot be himself without a finite set of fundamental projects, but that no projects can matter to him at all unless he can share them with others. And he cannot do that because he does not share their mortal condition.

Fosca's condition is undesirable, though, because he is the only immortal. Thus, despite her intention of showing that mortality is the condition of meaningful existence, Beauvoir leaves open the possibility that Fosca's world might become meaningful again, and his immortal life become worth living, if other human beings were immortal too. And despite her intention of showing how our projects and possibilities depend on our mortality, her literary thought-experiment actually illuminates how my projects and the things around me have value and significance for me insofar as I share them with others. It also illuminates the importance to us of the world's being shared.

This comes out when Beauvoir suggests that Fosca has ceased to be human—his former wife Beatrice exclaims at one point that he belongs to another species. The world has shrivelled in Fosca's eyes to a domain of bare, meaningless facts: he is 'alive and yet lifeless', he says (29). He finds the world empty, affectively dead; thus, he has ceased even to inhabit the same kind of world in which mortals live, an affectively rich and meaningful one.

We might think that Fosca's alien mode of experience arises out of his lack of possibilities. Whenever Fosca decides to do A and not B now, he can always come back to B later; thus picking A does not rule out B as it would if Fosca were mortal. But by the same token A is not genuinely possible either, for picking A involves no commitment on Fosca's part. As there is nothing at stake in his choices, no possibilities can be meaningful or emotionally salient to Fosca. Perhaps this is why he finds the world affectively dead.[13] But perhaps instead—I suggest—it is because Fosca cannot have relationships with others that he experiences the world in this denuded way. Ordinarily, the world we experience is intrinsically shared; but since Fosca cannot share the world with others, it becomes empty and meaningless. Thus, Fosca says that only if Regina can bring him back to life, draw him back into a loving relationship, then 'the world [will] return to its original shape' (29)— although unfortunately Regina cannot do this, as she cannot restore him to mortality.

Beauvoir's suggestion that Fosca's world is devoid of meaning and affect because it is unshared and unshareable is borne out from a perhaps unexpected source, Lisa Guenther's study of solitary confinement. This practice, she finds, dramatically reduces and undermines the capacities of prisoners even to perceive and make sense of the everyday items around them. Typically, prisoners so confined move through a phase of sustained hallucinations and acute anxiety into a final, persisting state of blank deadness and dullness. Guenther concludes: 'Without the concrete experience of other embodied egos oriented toward common objects in a shared world, my own experience of the boundaries of those perceptual objects begins to waver' (2013: 35). Why is this so?

We know from Arendt that by birth we come into the world amongst a plurality of others, all apprehending things around them from their particular embodied perspectives. More concretely, in infancy, we learn to make sense of things around us and of our embodied streams of experience and agency in a context where the others who care for us are there more or less continually. We begin, for example, to develop powers over our bodily movements as we see and imitate others exercising the same powers in their own movements, speech, and gestures (Meltzoff and Moore 1983). We make sense of our being in the world, then, by coming to appreciate that others occupy locations in it too and that the world is intrinsically open to apprehension from these multiple embodied locations.

Directly from birth we also begin to imbibe the meanings and values of a given culture. The world, then, immediately starts to become cultural, a realm not of bare material objects but of things, events, bodies, actions (etc.) which are pervaded with communal meaning. This raises a question about whether members of different cultures are best described as inhabiting one single, universally shared world from their distinct cultural vantage points or as inhabiting different worlds. Maria Lugones takes the latter view, claiming that those who move between different cultures, whether uncomfortably or creatively or both, are 'world'-travellers (1989). One worry about this view, Mariana Ortega observes (2001: 10–11), is that it may follow from it that, as each individual inhabits a unique location within their culture in turn, each individual lives in their own private world. Ortega's alternative proposal is that our individual 'takes' on our physical circumstances are shaped by our shared cultures, so that 'worlds' continue to exist at the level of cultures, not of individuals—but not at the level of the single set of physical objects and spaces on which we have our cultural 'takes'. Indeed, on one view, developed by Husserl in *The Crisis of European Sciences* ([1936] 1970), those objects and spaces conceived in impersonal physical terms are merely an abstraction from the cultural–historical worlds (life-worlds) in which we immediately live. Even so, those abstractions may still provide our best understanding of how the world around us is mind-independently. In that respect, all of us, everywhere, inhabit a single shared 'world' just in that there is a common physical substrate to our various cultural 'worlds'. In our lived experience as it unfolds from infancy, though, physical objects are all along imbued with relational and cultural meanings, with memory and history, and with affective significance and reference to the possible actions they enable.[14] In everyday life, the cultural enfolds the physical, so that the physical stratum can be identified in isolation from its cultural import only by abstraction. Furthermore, cultures are not self-contained. Different cultures have common and overlapping elements, especially in respect of certain basic factors such as 'the concrete experience of other embodied egos oriented toward common objects in a shared world' (to quote Guenther). To the extent that cultures overlap and include shared dimensions, we cannot easily decide whether we live in different worlds or one single world. It is more that the world is internally variegated and differentiated, uneven and mottled.

To return to *All Men are Mortal*, Beauvoir intended it to dramatize why immortality would be bad, and hence to show that death is not unequivocally bad because mortality is a condition of our lives being meaningful. I have taken the novel differently, as illuminating how deeply the world we live in is shared, thereby shedding light on part of what *is* bad about death: that when I die, I will be deprived of any experiential relation to the world as shared. If I fear death, this reflects my attachment to the world as a 'with-world'. Fosca feared death, so he drank the elixir that made him immortal. Unfortunately, as it made him the only immortal, he failed to achieve his goal—which was, in fact, not merely to remain a living being in experiential relation with the world as such but rather to remain in experiential relation with the *shared* world. Tragically, Fosca only realizes this when it is too late and he has come to inhabit an alien, dessicated world, one that, having been deprived of its shared meaningfulness, is only a pale shadow of the world we normally live in.

The concept of the 'with-world' that I've just invoked is one which Heidegger puts forward in *Being and Time* and which offers another lens on the world's intrinsically shared status. The concept captures how the co-involvement of others is the precondition of my maintaining the everyday practical, meaningful, equipmental relations in which I am engaged.

> The Others who are thus 'encountered' in a ready-to-hand, environmental context of equipment, are not somehow added on . . . to some Thing which

is…just present-at-hand; such 'Things' are encountered from out of the world in which they are ready-to-hand for Others.   (1962: 154/118)

My involvements can take place only on the presupposition of a set of practices to which they belong—hammering presupposes carpentry, building, the use of certain types of buildings and objects—all maintained collectively. And my involvements necessarily take place against the background of a web of meanings—hammering being for making chairs for sitting in, for instance in school classrooms, to be used by teachers and children, and so on. This entire web of practices and meanings comprises a world, within which other Daseins are presupposed—not as objects, however, but as those who co-maintain this web. Concomitantly, our everyday relation to others is to take them for granted as we follow the norms encapsulated in this web of practices and meanings.[15]

For Heidegger, then, my world is all along and necessarily shared. However, Heidegger tends to picture the with-world in terms of the public sphere—broadly, the realm outside the family.[16] But we only become able to participate in publicly shared norms and practices through our long histories of care and education from birth, usually in families. Our primary relationships with others are with our first care-givers and are intimate, unique, and emotionally intense. So, we do not share the world with *all* its other inhabitants in flat indifference. Some of those with whom we share it matter most to us and stand out. Thus, insofar as what Fosca actually wanted—unknown to himself—was to remain in the shared world, those with whom he most wanted to share it were the close others he has loved. Instead, he is condemned to outlive them all.

My suggestions in these last two sections by no means exhaust how our natality affects our mortality. It does so in many other ways too. For instance, one came up before in connection with Beauvoir's *Pyrrhus and Cinéas*: the meanings, values, and projects to which we are attached are ones that we value having inherited them from loved others. Thus, if my death cuts off my projects from fulfilment and continuation, I am not the only one who is thereby deprived. So are the others whose projects I was continuing (possibly after they have already died themselves). The deprivation afflicts us together.

However, Beauvoir's point that we can carry forward others' projects after they die might seem to suggest that death is less bad than I have been arguing. For if others will take forward my projects after I die, then perhaps my death does not utterly deprive me of the prospect of my projects coming to fruition after all. In a related vein, Samantha Brennan suggests that, according to 'deprivation' accounts of death's badness such as Nagel's, death is a deprivation from the perspective of a 'career self' pursuing its individual projects (Brennan 2006a, 2006b, following Nelson 1999). But a self whose central good is the good of the others with whom they are in relationship, such as their children—thus, a conventionally feminine self—is 'invested in something robust enough to withstand their death' (Nelson 1999: 124). In short, insofar as our values and projects are shared, they can perhaps transcend our deaths as individuals. However, my attachment to the others who share my values and projects makes my death bad in another way: it will permanently sever these relationships. That others may take forward projects they have shared with me is a consolation, but it mitigates rather than removes death's badness. Moreover, these others who take our projects forward are relational beings too, attached to me, and so they will be diminished by my death; while, if they take forward our shared projects, those too will be much reduced by my absence. My daughter will, I trust, outlive me; but, offsetting the goodness of this, my death will indelibly scar her and cast a shadow over her life. All this gives me grounds to fear my death and those of others *as* a relational, not a 'career', self.

However, if others can carry my projects and values forwards after I die, then perhaps this opens up a route along which I can to a degree survive my death. Others who outlive me will carry forward my projects or other aspects of me internalized as traits within them, or in patterns of feeling and action which they shared with me. Surely then, one might think, parts of me will thereby survive my death. For example, although my mother has died, a part of her—her love of reading—lives on in me, as I am attached to reading in part as an activity I shared with and inherited from her. Because part of me exists outside me, in other people, it follows that (1) part of me dies when someone I love dies, but also that (2) when someone I love outlives me, part of me lives on in them. If part of me can die while I (otherwise) remain alive, then conversely part of me can live on after I have (otherwise) died.[17]

That said, it is only a small part of my mother that survives her death in my reading activity, and even that part is heavily depleted, for my reading activity cannot maintain all the meanings it formerly had for my mother or that she and I sustained between us. Given the loss of my mother as a meaning-making subject, the reading in which I remain engaged has correspondingly diminished meanings. And the more my reading gains new meanings over time, the further it departs from what it meant to my mother, and the less she survives. Such survival as we can attain through others, then, is very attenuated, and concomitantly when we suffer a bereavement we undergo an irreparable loss. We will carry onwards parts of those whom we have lost, but this does not undo or overcome the loss, which remains.[18]

IV. A Brief Engagement with Heidegger

I contrasted my relational view of death with Heidegger's view that death 'individualizes Dasein down to itself' and is each Dasein's 'ownmost, non-relational possibility'. I now want to use Heidegger's analysis of the implications of Dasein's non-relational mortality to draw out, in partial contrast, some implications that follow from our mortality in fact being relational. Of course, the literature on Heidegger on death, as on all of *Being and Time*, is voluminous.[19] My discussion will admittedly be brief and partial, intended only to indicate some ways to think both with and against Heidegger in exploring natality.

But first, a question that *Being and Time* raises is whether I have gone astray in saying that it makes sense to *fear* one's death. As I mentioned in Chapter 5, Heidegger contrasts fundamental moods and more superficial everyday moods; his contrast between anxiety and fear, which owes much to Kierkegaard, is the central instance (see Staehler 2007). For Heidegger, fear is directed towards specific entities within the world, such as fierce dogs (1962: 179/140), whereas anxiety is indefinite, and this is because it is directed towards the world as a whole (231/186). Thus, for Heidegger it is anxiety, not fear, that attests authentically to my death, not as a prospective event within the world, but as threatening my entire world as a meaningful one. For Heidegger, fear is the inauthentic version of anxiety: by transposing anxiety into fear, I make it manageable by reducing its object to a definite entity that I can deal with (230/185–6; 234/189). I displace my global anxiety about death onto a finite object—fatal car accidents, say, or cancer—from which I can take practical measures to protect myself—by not driving or by doing things that I hope will reduce my cancer risk. If I feel fear in the face of my death, then, this indicates that I am misconstruing my death inauthentically as a mere everyday event that will occur in the world as the deaths of others do. I am treating my death as something akin to a manipulable object, rather than confronting its full challenge to the meaningfulness of my existence.

However, perhaps fear of my death *is* appropriate insofar as my own death is actually continuous with the deaths of others, at least if these are potential events in the world about which, as such, it makes sense for me to feel fear. For the death of any individual other person is, to a degree, an event 'in' my world, since my other relationships and attachments persist beyond it. At the same time, though, these deaths are not merely events 'in' the world, for they also deprive me of part of myself and of my horizon of meaning, and they impact upon the fabric of the shared world that persists—depleting it, draining it of affective richness, narrowing and contracting it. The deaths of others therefore cut ambiguously across the division between the whole world and events or entities within it, and so across Heidegger's division between anxiety and fear. By the same token, so does my death, insofar as the deaths of others are part of it. To this extent I can appropriately feel fear of my death, with the proviso that this will be an anxiety-like and radical form of fear insofar as this embodies a genuine apprehension of the magnitude of what my death involves—and in this I include the magnitude of what it involves relationally, for all those whom it affects and who are bound up in it.

In Chapter 5, though, I accepted a version of the division between fear and anxiety when I took it that anxiety attests to fundamental structures of human existence. So, I now want to qualify that division. In particular, saying that fear is only ever of finite objects or events does not capture the full spectrum of forms of fear. For instance, there is also nameless fear: an indefinite mood that goes beyond fear of any particulars onto which it may become focused, just as anxiety goes beyond specific worries or anxieties onto which it may temporarily be localized. Consider an amorphous fear that overcomes someone entering an office at night where the atmosphere feels oddly wrong (they might suppose that a ghost or supernatural presence is there, in an attempt to pin down the object of their fear). In such cases fear, like anxiety, is unfocused, global, and directed towards some unspecifiable, all-pervasive danger. Thus, there are varieties of fear which shade into some varieties of anxiety. This means that we *can* appropriately respond to our deaths in ways that range continuously along the fear–anxiety spectrum. I fear the deaths of those whom I love partly as prospective events in the world but also as events of a peculiar, liminal type which will reshape and deplete that entire world and in which I will lose part of myself, so that my fear rises towards the nameless and global and shades into anxiety. And I feel both fear and anxiety about my death too insofar as it blurs into the deaths of others and so, again, crosses the boundary between the whole meaningful world and events within it.

Let me move on to how Heidegger prioritizes mortality over natality based on his analysis of death. (1) I'll summarily reconstruct his analysis of mortality's role in human existence,[20] then (2) I'll revisit how it follows, for Heidegger, that natality can play the structuring role it does only by virtue of the prior role of mortality. Criticizing his reasoning, (3) I then trace how the natality–mortality relation instead becomes more balanced if our deaths are in fact relational.

(1) Prescinding from numerous interpretive puzzles and controversies, the broad line of Heidegger's analysis of mortality is this. We begin the interpretation of Dasein's existence based on its average everyday way of being, in which it is more-or-less fallen into uncritical going along with shared norms and practices, doing the done thing.[21] Anxiety in *Being and Time* is the hinge-point at which Dasein begins to gain the possibility of existing more authentically. In anxiety, I find myself unable to go on taking part; the everyday world falls away and loses its meaning; things cease to make sense for me; I am left alienated, disconnected, and isolated. But ordinarily the world had the meaning it did as a *whole*, an inter-referring web of meanings and purposes. Thus, in anxiety it is the world as a whole which is exposed as having crumbled and as being fragile, ever-capable of so crumbling: 'the *world as world* is disclosed first and foremost by anxiety' (1962: 232/187). This exposure makes it possible for me to apprehend authentically what my own death means: it threatens the world as a whole. Third-personally viewed, my death may be just another event in the world, but this cannot properly be how it presents itself to me first-personally. Furthermore, experiencing the world's precariousness and instability in anxiety makes it possible for me to apprehend not only that my death is certain to come at some point but also that—just as the world is always fragile and liable to crumble—my death is always possible at any moment, maybe the very next one. Inasmuch as I take this insight fully on board and incorporate it into my existence, I treat it as constitutive of that existence that it will inevitably, and might always, cease. Whatever my possibilities in a given situation, my death is always possible too; it is the necessary shadow around the light cast by my other possibilities. In turn, realizing this allows me to embrace several other features of my existence and thereby exist more authentically. These features are as follows:

(a) The ever-present possibility of my death is a *pure* possibility in that it can never become actual for me, first-personally: my death will never be an event that I can experience (1962: 306–7/262).[22] This highlights the fundamental difference between possibility and actuality, which Heidegger thinks the metaphysical tradition has denied, treating the possible merely as a deficient form of the actual. For Heidegger, as for Kierkegaard, genuine possibilities are radically distinct from actual objects, events, and potentials that already actually exist as germs or tendencies within what is. What is most genuinely possible is not already contained in the actual but is radically non-actual. That is (I take it), genuine possibilities can come about only through my free action in view of my projection and anticipation which reach beyond everything that is already given: a possibility in the true sense of the word needs *my* action to make it happen.[23]

(b) Further, as I may always die, whatever possibilities I am acting on or considering acting on, I should commit to now. If I postpone and avoid deciding and acting on them, they may never come to pass at all.

(c) In addition, for Heidegger, and as we've seen earlier, my death is my own: I cannot share it, nor can anyone else save me from it by dying themselves. If someone jumps between me and a rapidly approaching car, that heroic person goes to their own death earlier that they would have otherwise, but my death has thereby only been postponed, not averted. This highlights the mineness (*Jemeinigkeit*) of my existence: it is *I* who have been and am living this particular life; the possibilities it throws up arise only for me, where I am situated, and so as ones that only I can ever actualize. Others may 'leap in' on my behalf, trying to make my decisions for me, but this is not fitting to existence in its actual *Jemeinigkeit*.

Possibility, commitment, responsibility, and mineness are only one side of the coin, though. The other side is situatedness and thrownness, so that together Dasein's existence is '*thrown possibility* through and through' (*geworfene Möglichkeit*) (1962: 183/144). That is, once more, what possibilities arise for me depends on and is constrained by my situation. Consequently, what is possible for me at any point depends on my past and ultimately comes down to me from my birth.

(2) We can now appreciate why Heidegger explicitly prioritizes mortality over natality. He does so, in *Being and Time*, after having asked whether he has concentrated too exclusively on death and not either on birth or on existing in a way that stretches between birth and death (425/373). He admits here that 'factical Dasein exists as born' (*existiert gebürtig*), and that its birth is in its past (426/374).[24] This is not in that one's birth took

place at a chronological point that lies in the past and is over and done with. Rather, my birth is in my past in such a way that it always figures into my ongoing existence—albeit such that I look away from it at whatever situation it has thrown me into and at the possibilities towards which I am thrown in this situation (174–5/135). Thus, my birth is the ultimate source of the thrownness that characterizes my existence at every point. Nonetheless, Heidegger maintains that it is our being-towards-death which accounts for how we stretch between our two 'ends' in thrown projection, and therefore for our existing as born (1962: 425/373). How is this so?

We can identify stronger and weaker understandings of Heidegger's reasoning. To start with the weaker one: it is in light of the authentic apprehension of my death that I experience my existence as requiring me to choose responsibly from the possibilities open to me—maybe choosing between them, or choosing how to take them up, or how to reject them and find other wellsprings of possibility. Only in light of authentically being-towards-death can I appreciate my responsibility for choosing between just *these* and no other possibilities, these ones that arise out of my thrownness. For I accept that as it is I alone who is to make a choice here, I can only choose from the particular place where I am, and this is from what has already come down to me, over which I no longer have any choice. Thus, I also accept that I must embrace these unchosen constraints on my action, as its conditions of possibility. In short, only if I exist-towards-death can I appreciate my thrownness in full. Hence authentic being-towards-death is the condition of authentic being-from-birth. Dastur sets out this version of Heidegger's reasoning when she argues that:

> The assumption of [Dasein's] being assigned to something already given, which refers to the existential phenomenon of birth, demands ... the free-dom of an authentic ability-to-be supposing the assumption of mortality. It is only in terms of this future ... which is death, that *Dasein* can assume the absolute past of its birth.   (1996: 72)

However, Dastur then continues, 'the condition of birth is shown in this way to be death' (72) and 'dying is the condition of being born and death the condition of life' (76). This is the stronger claim, which is not merely that an authentic relation to mortality is the condition of an authentic relation to natality as thrownness, but, more than that, that being mortal is the condition of being natal. One cannot be born unless one can die—indeed, Heidegger endorses the adage that as soon as one is born one is old enough to die (e.g. 1962: 426/374). He does not mean this in the biological sense that one cannot come to life without thereby also becoming capable of dying. Rather, for Heidegger, the point is that I can only exist as thrown at all on condition that I am also a being of possibilities, and so am capable of relating in advance to the possibility of my own death. For to be thrown is necessarily to be both thrown-whence *and* thrown-whither—that is, towards possibilities, possibilities that are always shadowed by my possible death. So, it is only insofar as I am thrown towards my possible death that I can also be thrown from somewhere, and ultimately from my birth: the latter is possible only on condition that the former also holds.

Yet the same is true in the other direction too: I can only have an advance relation to the possibility of my death if I am already thrown into existence, 'whence' somewhere, in the first place. I can only relate to my death from where I already am—and this is wherever I have come to be from birth. Indeed, in this chapter I have effectively spelt out some of what this means. Being thrown flows down out of being born, and being born means that we come into and are constituted by relationships with others from the start. So, it is from within and on the basis of these relationships that we relate to death. Hence, we relate to *our* deaths, *as* ours, shared, and not exclusively mine. Being thrown, I relate to death as shared and not individual.

The problem, then, with Heidegger's argument for mortality's priority to natality, if construed strongly, is that it overlooks how natal thrownness and mortal possibility affect one another. Thus, although he tries to justify giving mortality priority, ultimately he takes this priority for granted, for in arguing that we can be natal only as mortals he neglects the fact that (as his own work implies) we can be mortal only as natals, and therefore relationally. If on the other hand, his argument is construed more weakly, then it presupposes his account of an authentic relation to one's death, on which we relate to it authentically just when we approach it as non-relational. But since we are relational beings through-and-through, that approach to death is not obviously the most authentic one. If our deaths are in fact shared as I have suggested, then the more authentic relation to death is to apprehend it in that way, as shared.[25]

(3) What else follows if our deaths are relational rather than non-relational? To the extent that I fear my death and those of the others I love, I am fearing our permanent separation. This is a way that I relate in advance to death as someone who is already embedded in given attachments which have come down to me from my birth: thus, it is a way of being mortal natally, of responding to death as a natal being. Reciprocally, the way I anticipate our

deaths, as undoing our relationships, can draw me to embrace these same relationships more fully. It can bring home to me how deeply I am attached to those I love and to the values, meanings, and histories that we share and that matter to me on that account. Confronting the prospect of death can thus 'relationalize' me, casting me into a more vital appreciation of the value that my relationships have for me.

This alters the character of my responsibility as it is thrown into relief here. For Heidegger, insofar as I anticipate my death authentically, this brings out the fact that I am ultimately responsible for myself. It is exposed that I am a being of choice and possibilities: that I am, and do not merely have, my possibilities. The more authentically I exist, the more I embrace my own character of choice and possibility, and so choose myself and my character over time.[26] On my alternative picture, when I apprehend authentically that our deaths are shared and will affect us together, this throws into relief the value and meaning to me of the relationships that I am already inhabiting, and of how deeply I am indebted to others and how much I owe to them. I feel the weight of the claims that these relationships have on me. From confronting our shared mortality, then, I come to appreciate with new depth that I stand under obligations to carry forward what others have given me: to be faithful to them and to their horizons of value and meaning, and press them onwards against the threat of death. Fidelity to others, more than responsibility for myself, is exposed as holding centre stage in our ethical lives.

Notes

1. Some other feminist philosophers likewise favour re-balancing rather than reversing the importance of birth and death: see Heinämäa (2010: e.g. 90, 101, 110) and Clack (2002—who focuses, however, on balancing death and sex, treating birth as included within sex and reproduction; criticizing Clack's view; see Jantzen 2004).
2. Butler also takes a relational view of death: 'if I lose you … "I" have gone missing as well'; 'grief … [can] bring to the fore relational ties' (2004: Ch. 2, esp. 22). Likewise Havi Carel argues that the death of a loved one, particularly as experienced in grief and mourning, constitutes a non-metaphorical loss of part of Dasein (Carel 2006: 154).
3. So does Levinas ([1979] 1987), but I set out my criticisms of Heidegger independently of him.
4. Thus, one way to treat birth and death symmetrically might be to look at the processes by which we gradually fade out of the world by becoming increasingly

dependent, helpless, and vulnerable—the counterpart of the earlier processes whereby we gradually entered the world through gestation, leaving the womb, and becoming inducted into relationships and communities. That said, we should bear in mind that, while death and birth are both important and structure our lives, they are in key respects *not* symmetrical: as I've mentioned before, they are asymmetrical temporally (on this, see also Chapter 7, Section I of this book) and in their relations to value (Chapter 2, Sections. IV and V).

5. Also, the end result of the process of dying—if it is truly that—is non-existence. Thus, arguably, some awareness of impending non-existence is inevitably bound up in experiences of dying, so that understanding them as experiences of *dying*—rather than, say, of becoming ill or incapacitated—requires prior consideration of non-existence.

6. A largely independent set of discussions of death has taken place in Anglophone feminist philosophy. See, e.g. Brennan (2006a, 2006b), Nelson (1999), and Overall (2003).

7. For Heidegger, one feels anxiety, *not* fear, about one's death if one is relating to it authentically. I'll instead suggest that fear and anxiety about death shade into one another. This need not undermine my picture of birth anxiety. Fear of having been born does not make sense as fear of death does. Thus, our feelings about birth belong to the anxiety spectrum, as per Chapter 5, whereas our feelings towards death overlap between anxiety and fear.

8. To the rejoinder that once I am dead I will no longer be there to be deprived of anything, Nagel responds, first, that I can undergo harms, such as loss of reputation, without having to experience or be aware of them; and, second, that the one who is and has been deprived of good things by death is the person who used to exist.

9. For some, Heidegger's term 'death' differs from our normal notion of death as the end of a life. For Blattner, Heidegger instead means 'existential death': anxiety-cum-depression, feeling dead to the world (2009: 146–51). For Carel, Heidegger means 'finitude'—thus, 'being-towards-death' means so existing that one admits and embraces one's finitude in various respects (2007). Certainly, Heidegger distinguishes death from perishing (biological) and demising (inauthentic death), but his entire set of arguments about non-relationality, finitude, mineness, etc., only go through if he does mean by 'death' not, indeed, the end of a biological life or a third-person event, but that same phenomenon re-considered in its first-personal import.

10. 'Radical asymmetry' is Gillian Howie's phrase (2016).

11. Heidegger explicitly denies that death can be undergone in degrees (1962: 307/262). In this connection Dastur reprises another of his arguments (made at 1962: 282/238–9) that there can be no continuity between different people's deaths. If 'the experience of mourning is indeed the experience of being authentically with another, this does not mean that it is therefore an authentic experience of death

"itself".... Certainly, the death of a loved one...condemns me to a desolation the *experience* of which can be like the disappearance of all *Dasein*.... [But] the experience of such an "emptying", of the melting of that horizon of meaning constituted by the world, can in no way claim to be a true assumption of death "itself". As Heidegger observes, if the death of someone close is lived as an irreparable loss, the loss suffered by the other has not thereby become accessible' Dastur 1996: 46–7). But why hasn't it, given that as Dastur says one's loss involves at least a degree of melting-away of the meaningful world altogether? Dastur's answer is just that for each of us, one's existence is one's own: 'this untransferable character of existence...is a great gulf fixed between us' (46). Thus, for Dastur, I cannot share in or experience your death, just because it is yours. But what needed to be established was why it is exclusively yours in the first place, given that the same melting-away of the world afflicts us both—you totally, and I partially.

12. Critics include Bortolotti and Nagasawa (2009), Bruckner (2012), and Overall (2003: Chs. 5 and 6). Smuts (2011) is more sympathetic.

13. In Blattner's (2009) terms, then (see n. 9), Fosca has undergone 'existential death', succumbing to a state of anxiety-cum-depression in which he has no sense of the salience of different possibilities. Fosca exists in the thin sense of being biologically alive, but not the thick sense of pursuing projects and choosing between possibilities. My point, though, is that such projects and possibilities depend on relationships with others.

14. For evidence of this, and of how children learn to make sense of the world by participating in it alongside others who are also inhabiting it from their own standpoints, see Simms (2008).

15. It is a matter of debate whether Heidegger's analysis of being-with-others should have complicated his distinction between one's own death and the deaths of others as events in the world. That distinction seems to entail that being-in-the-world is *prior to* being-with, such that with-relations occur in the (prior) world. Tina Chanter criticizes Heidegger for presuming this (2001: 97–8). However, arguing that Heidegger at his best does treat being-with-others as just as funda-mental to our existence as being-in-the-world, see O'Brien (2014).

16. This is apparent from Heidegger's various examples from the world of work and his conception of *das Man* as the anonymous *public* by whose norms we are levelled down; his critique targets the public, not the private, sphere. This is connected with another limitation of Heidegger's view of the with-world: in conceiving it in terms of shared practices and practical abilities, he overlooks how these practices have typically been structured in ways that build in exclu-sions of young, ill, elderly, and disabled people. For example, when a shelf is set too high to be reached by a wheelchair-user, they cannot share in the shelf's meaning as a place to store books (Toombs 1995: 16; on the loss of shared meanings in somatic illness, see also Carel 2016: Ch. 3). Historically, then,

with-worlds have rarely been shared 'with' everyone. Instead, they have been based around the presumed normality of an idealized adult male, healthy, independent body—the body of a head of household, hence the link with the public/private division.

17. Indeed, this is Guenther's argument (2008).

18. Heidegger speaks to this in terms of our being with those who have died as-dead (1962: 282/238–9): an authentic relationship with these people is as-dead, not as if they were still alive. We can accept this point without having to conceive death non-relationally as Heidegger does. I can try to keep something alive of a person who has died, all the while acknowledging that this is a very poor something compared to the formerly living person, and that my keeping something of them going does not suffice to undo their having died.

19. On Heidegger and death, see, amongst many others, Blattner (1994), Carel (2006, 2007); Dastur (1996), Derrida (1993), and Pattison (2013). Feminist critics of Heidegger on death include Guenther (2008), MacAvoy (1996), and Secomb (1999). Guenther and MacAvoy criticize Heidegger for focusing on death rather than, or in priority to, birth. Secomb in contrast criticizes him for taking a masculine view of death 'as a future event anticipated by an isolated individual' (1999: 112); she explores an alternative feminine way of dwelling with and caring for the dying. Notwithstanding these problems, *Being and Time* can still illuminate natality, as authors such as MacAvoy (1996: pt. III), O'Byrne (2010: Ch. 2) and Schües (2016: Part 1, Ch. 3) explore.

20. To recall, I treat 'human' and 'Dasein' as coinciding in scope.

21. Heidegger often suggests that everydayness itself tends towards fallenness: for example, 'Dasein has, *in the first instance* [*zunächst*], fallen away from itself' (1962: 220/175); '*in no case* is a Dasein... untouched and unseduced by this [public, anonymous] way in which things have been interpreted' (213/169; my emphases). This creates a puzzle, as it seems that everyday going-along with what others do is both essential and structural to Dasein *and* is fallen and inauthentic—the puzzle being that if both apply then Dasein cannot possibly be authentic, in which case moreover the very notion of 'inauthenticity' loses its purchase. Dreyfus's solution is to distinguish falling (structural) and fleeing (inauthentic) (1991: Ch. 13). Blattner's broadly similar solution is to say that average everydayness is neutral but can become modified either towards the authentic or—if one flees—towards the inauthentic (2009: 130; and see Heidegger 1962: 275/232). Instead, I'm taking it that Heidegger thinks that a tendency towards inauthenticity is inherent in being-with-others (as falling) but that that tendency can also be actualized in fleeing.

22. One might try to square the circle and observe one's own death, as Poe dramatizes in his story of Monsieur Valdemar, put into a hypnotic trance so as to observe his own death ([1845] 1986). But as long as Valdemar is observing

himself, he cannot fully die. Once the trance ends, his body, having been held in limbo unable to die, disintegrates on the spot into a putrescent mass.

23. Controversially here, Heidegger says that my death is the 'possibility of the absolute impossibility of Dasein [*die Möglichkeit der schlechthinnigen Daseinsunmöglichkeit*]' (1962: 294/250). I understand this formulation thus. The total absence of any possibilities that will obtain for me when I am dead is nonetheless a 'possibility' (i) in that it can always come about, albeit not as an experience I can have, and (ii) where I can take up and embrace (i), that is, accept that my ever-possible death co-determines my existence, (iii) which further brings out the possibility-character of my other possibilities, and so (iv) enables me to embrace my own status as a being of possibilities. See also Derrida (1993) and McNeill (2009). Notably, this way of embracing the 'possibility' of my death, which Heidegger endorses, is different from making my death a (possible) project by committing suicide.

24. MacQuarrie and Robinson say 'exists as born', Stambaugh 'exists as being born' (2010: 357).

25. Here I agree with Havi Carel. Following Dreyfus, for whom genuine authenticity means authentically being-with others, Carel argues that we can relate authentically to the deaths of others when we experience these not as mere 'external' events in the world but rather as losses to and of oneself, as we do when we grieve and mourn for loved ones who have died. Thus, 'against Heidegger's emphasis on my own death as the only way to understand mortality . . . experiences of grief and mourning for others can also intimate mortality. This opens the way to an authentic attitude to the death of others' (Carel 2006: 111).

26. This is contested, but I take Heidegger's conception of authenticity to be broadly ethical or evaluative: it is good for us to exist authentically as far as we can— albeit that we can never do so completely or consistently. Existing authentically requires no particular course of action but a more appreciative and engaged attitude towards what one was involved in anyway; see Varga and Guignon (2017).

7

Temporality, the Gift, and Being Born

In this chapter I take up two threads that have come out of the preceding discussions but remain to be explored in their own right. The first thread is what the preceding account of being born implies regarding the temporality of lived human experience. I consider this in Section I. The second thread is whether we are not only given birth but are also, more strongly, *gifted* it, and if so in what senses. My discussion of this in Section II leads into an exploration of the ethical implications of our natality, drawing in some of my earlier suggestions on these matters. Finally, Section III offers a very schematic summary of the main claims I've made in this book.

I. Temporality

Some connections between birth and temporality have emerged in the preceding chapters. For instance, I've said that we begin to exist at birth—where a beginning is something that comes first in time—and that the subsequent course of our lives and the succession of situations in which we find ourselves flow down out of our natal beginnings—where that flow is partly temporal in nature. I've also said that our lives elapse between birth and death, unfurling from birth at the start towards death at the end. I now want to elucidate these and other temporal aspects and consequences of being born which have remained largely implicit so far.

My focus is on lived temporality: temporality as it structures the overall contours and character of human existence and figures into human experience. In the last respect, temporality does not figure primarily as an explicit focus of attention but rather as the taken-for-granted background qualifying what our experience is like. Ordinarily, experience has duration; it elapses. In this elapsing, what is already past is continuously prolonged into or retained in the present—for instance in memory, sedimentation, residues, affective colourations—and that same present is also suffused with anticipation, projection, and expectation of the future into which it continuously

Being born: Birth and Philosophy. Alison Stone, Oxford University Press (2019). © Alison Stone.
DOI: 10.1093/oso/9780198845782.001.0001

shades. The present, then, is this unfolding zone where something of the past endures and something of the future is foreshadowed, these two directions mingling with and qualifying one another. Unless past and future were already inside the present in this way, no present experience would even be possible; the present would be a mere durationless point too thin to contain any content.[1]

Now, one question about birth and temporality is how being born in the narrow sense of departing from the womb is experienced temporally. Yet, as we've seen, it is difficult to specify how we experience this departure at all. To be sure, attempts have been made: for Rank, one feels the pain of one's first separation from the mother in leaving her womb; for Irigaray, this is a dramatic loss of one's first home; and for Freud, this departure is traumatic because it transforms one's prior mode and conditions of experience so radically as to virtually overwhelm one's capacities for sense-making such as they are at this point. But in any case, I've surmised, infants do not long remember leaving the womb, because their powers of memory are very unformed at this point and are in flux, undergoing rapid development. Any fragmentary memories that do survive will later succumb, along with nearly all of our early lives, to infantile amnesia. So, leaving the womb is not something we can remember in later life. Fundamental as the event is for us as marking the point when we start to inhabit the shared world more unequivocally than we did before, this event is nonetheless irrecoverably lost to us.

Infantile amnesia gives human life a 'syncopated temporality', as Anne O'Byrne calls it (2010: 103).[2] I have forgotten nearly all of my earliest years, even though their impact lives on in my habits, emotional make-up, and personality. My capacity to understand my own reactions, motivations, and actions is proportionately limited: much of their rationale escapes me. I may narrate my life-story, but the narrative mode inevitably falls short of the era when I did not yet have either language or narratively structured memory. I know that the events of my life run back to my childhood and before it my birth, yet they defy retrieval and my birth structures my life as an absence, a vanishing point. In turn, insofar as the rest of my life unfolds from that point, inexplicable and indecipherable elements seep down through it.

Here we start to see some ways in which the temporal contours of human life overall are structured by our being born. The temporal shape of our lives is structured by birth in the particular guise it has for the human species, where we begin life very underdeveloped and pass through an extended developmental course over which our powers mature. In consequence our cognitive powers, including our powers of memory, develop in stages, and so they change systematically over the course of our childhood, resulting in infantile amnesia. Thus, first, because we are born, our lives become structured by a syncopated temporality, in which they run back into beginnings that are inaccessible.[3] That presupposes, second, that our lives are structured temporally as *having* beginnings, albeit ones to which we necessarily lose access. We are aware that we began, and that the events of our lives run back into this time of beginnings, despite not knowing what concretely occurred then.[4]

Because our lives have beginnings so that certain events come first for us, and because we begin life very underdeveloped, many of our initial powers develop and become shaped in the context of those first events, which are specially formative for us. Yet it is precisely the period of these formative events which we forget. Thus, another aspect of our syncopated temporality is that the events of our early lives remain active in our habits, emotions, behaviour, and selves, despite our inability to make these events the theme of our awareness. Our first years live on in us in the shape of psychical forces that we struggle to fathom, and of ingrained patterns of behaviour which we enact more or less unknowingly. Psychoanalytic thinkers have described this way in which we continually and unreflectively re-enact and repeat our past relationships, experiences, and histories under the category of 'transference', carrying-over (*Übertragung*). Plausibly, transference is crucial to lived experience having its affective richness and depth of meaning. It is by virtue of transference that things around us, whatever situations we are in, become coloured by their various connections and contrasts with past things encountered in previous situations. Some things around us stand out as salient because of these connections or contrasts, while others recede into the background. This, then, is a third way that being born structures lived human temporality: that we continually carry forwards our pasts without knowing we are doing so, in a tacit, bodily, affective, practical, and perceptual manner.

From this link between birth and transference, we see a way that being born structures the temporal quality of ordinary human experience as I described it at the start of this section. For it is through transference that a person's past is prolonged and retained into their present and so is already 'inside' the durational present. In addition, from the link with transference, we see a way that being born structures human life over time, by shaping how we carry our pasts forward on a long-term basis within our personalities and behaviours, through transference. Transference thus pertains both to the long-term temporal organization of human life and to shorter-term durational experience.

In all three of these connections between birth and temporality—syncopation, beginning, and transference—one's birth has a particular link with one's past. Suppose that, like Oedipus, I want to understand how I have come to be where I am at this point of my life. Towards that end, with help from others, I follow the string of events that has led me here as that string leads back in time, ultimately to when I was born. I might follow the thread further, into the events that preceded and led up to my birth. For example, Sartre begins his memoir *Words* by describing how, around 1850, a school-master in Alsace wanted his eldest son, Charles Schweitzer, to become a pastor. This marks the start of a chain of family events which eventually leads to the marriage of Anne-Marie Schweitzer with Jean-Baptiste Sartre, and so to their conception of the embryo, Jean-Paul Sartre. Up until Sartre was conceived, though, those were not events in *his* life-history, for he was not there yet. Rather, they were some of the prior events that had to occur for his life-history to begin when and where it did.

The link between a person's birth and their past goes beyond how I might narrate myself. In every situation in which I find myself, I have come here from how I made sense of and responded to my preceding situation, and so on back to my initial natal situation. In this way, situatedness is part-and-parcel of natality: being born into a natal situation, each subsequent situation I come into arises, however indirectly, from the one I came into at birth. So, my birth was not just one of many equally weighted episodes in my past. Rather, my birth is the taken-for-granted anchor to which my life-history is tethered, in that it is *from* my birth that this life-history has unfolded. Moreover, this means that my birth, although past, is never finished with or 'done and dusted'; its ramifications continue to unfold at every point in my life. Thus, although my birth is inaccessible to me, nonetheless it is presupposed in the structure of my experience—as I move through successive situations, each emerging from the one preceding it—that this flow of situations goes back to that concretely unknown but structurally necessary point, my birth. This is a fourth connection between birth and the temporal structure of human life: my birth is the necessary anchor-point to which my life runs back or, looked at from the opposite direction, out of which each of my life's successive events and situations flows down.

One might wonder whether I am suggesting that the past dominates the present and future. Yet Sartre and Heidegger, on whose work I have drawn, privilege other temporal dimensions, respectively the present and future. Sartre privileges the present on the grounds that the past only has any reality insofar as it is part of my present experience, into which the past figures as *my* past (1958: 110/153). *The* past—collective human and cosmological history—is something we can reconstruct only because we already have our individual pasts, which we unite to produce the sense of a single collective history (112/155). Thus, for Sartre, the priority of the present is the necessary condition of there being any past at all, either individual or, derivatively, collective. Still, although the present has priority over the past, for Sartre the present cannot exist without a past. As soon as I have conscious experience at all, I necessarily have a past, as part of my facticity, and so too as part of every situation I am in and to which I must decide how to respond. Without facticity I would have nothing to be conscious of, and without a situation I would have nothing about which to make free decisions. Yet the past is subordinate, although necessary, to the present, because it is *to* my present experience that this past is given; that past would not be there at all without anyone to whom it is presently given.

However, in Chapter 4, I suggested that one's past is sedimented into the way one makes sense of one's surroundings at every point and so into the possibilities that thereby arise. It is not that we freely negate these surroundings in interpreting and deciding how to act in them, as Sartre maintains. Rather, we make sense of our surroundings in ways that are already thickly ingrained with horizons of meaning that we have inherited and received. Concomitantly, there is givenness, not only in what surroundings I am in, but also in my ways of making sense of these surroundings and in my resulting possibilities. This does not mean that I have no agency, but that I exercise agency in how I relate together these strands that come from the past—how I conjugate them. So here the present has content insofar as the past comes forward into it. Even so, the past does not unilaterally prevail, for it is *in* my present surroundings that certain strata of the past become salient and I conjugate them in ways that shape how I apprehend my present circumstances. The net result is that rather than the past dominating the present, or being subordinated to it as Sartre holds, these two dimensions affect and animate one another.

For his part, Heidegger privileges the future: '*The primary phenomenon of primordial and authentic temporality is the future*' (1962: 378/329). This follows from his analysis of mortality. The possibility of my death is purely futural, since this possibility will never become present; for when I die, I will cease to be there to have present experience. To exist in view of the constant possibility of one's death is thus to exist in a mode that privileges the future. To exist in this way is to be alert to the possibility-status of the possibilities arising in my situation, and to the orientation towards future possibilities which is at work in all understanding (as when I use a hammer in-order-to realize some goal, and relate to it as for-hammering, etc.—that is, in terms of future possibilities).

Contra Heidegger, I suggested in Chapter 6 that I relate in advance to my death and the deaths of those whom I love based on the relationships between us that have already taken shape in, and come down from, our history together over time. That is, my past shapes how I anticipate death, so that I apprehend it as threatening not me, alone, but us, together. Moreover, our deaths are bound together such that I undergo a degree of death when those whom I love die. Consequently, (i) my death is not so purely futural as Heidegger holds, for there is an extent to which my death can be undergone in the present, strange as this might sound. Certainly, in mentally anticipating my death and those of others—expecting, fearing, dreading, worrying about, preparing for our deaths—I am adopting a futural orientation to our deaths. But (ii) this is an orientation that I adopt on the basis of my already-made (past) attachments to others and to the things we have already been valuing over time. It is because I already value certain things and relationships that I fear losing them because of death. Thus, the past shapes my concrete way of relating, futurally, to my death and those of others. From (i) and (ii), it transpires that the present, past, and future intermingle in our relations to death rather than the future having priority.

But if I anticipate death on the basis of my past and pre-existing relationships, so that the past shapes what I anticipate in the future and how I anticipate it, then perhaps this is indicative that the past does have priority over the future generally, specifying and filling out what I anticipate. One might argue, accordingly, that the past supplies my anticipations with what degree of content they have, whereas the past needs no reciprocal input from the future because it is already full of content itself (Gallagher 1999: 67–9). Yet although what has happened as a matter of fact is already fully given, things are less straightfoward with the past as a lived temporal dimension. In this regard, the past lives on for us by being re-enacted, carried forwards and—sometimes—remembered. Yet our present circumstances affect what we re-enact and bring forwards, depending on what has current relevance. Given that I could right now go out for a walk or keep working here on the sofa indoors, fragmentary memories of previous neighbourhood walks figure vaguely into the background of my awareness to motivate my possibility of taking a walk and give it content. But equally what I expect from a possible walk today affects which memories come forward. Seeing grey clouds out of the window, I expect rain, and this prompts memories of walks in the rain, making the possibility of walking unappealing. In such ways the anticipated future affects how the past figures into my experience, a phenomenon that psychoanalysts call *Nachträglichkeit*—'deferred action', 'after-action' or 'afterwardsness' (Laplanche 1999). The overall manner of this action is that depending on what I anticipate or expect, different parts of my past are called into my present experience, under different lights, to fill out my anticipation. Thus, it is precisely because the past serves to fill out the expected future that the former gets drawn forward selectively in light of the latter, in a reciprocal process.

Because the three temporal dimensions affect one another, lived temporality can be described as an organic unity, as the phenomenological psychoanalyst Hans Loewald has it:

> We encounter time in psychic life primarily as a linking activity in which ... past, present, and future are woven into a nexus .... The nexus itself is not so much one of succession but of interaction. Past, present, and future present themselves in psychic life not primarily as one preceding or following the other, but as modes of time which determine and shape one another ... There is no irreversibility on a linear continuum, as in the common concept of time as succession, but a reciprocal relationship whereby one time mode cannot be experienced or thought without the other and whereby they continually modify each other ... [and] interpenetrate.   (Loewald 1980: 143–4)

This enables me to address a possible concern that my view of our lives elapsing from birth to death presupposes a linear model of time as a succession of moments or 'nows', akin to mathematical points and following one another to yield the 'line' that is time—a model that is too simplified to fit human life.[5] In my defence, although I regard an individual's birth as their beginning, I do not see it merely as the first of a line of moments comprising their life, with all the moments fundamentally the same and each left behind as soon as the next comes along. On the contrary, one's natal beginning is never left behind, despite becoming forgotten; it flows down continuously into all that comes after it. Yet what comes afterwards affects how the beginning flows down and in what respects. Moreover, one's beginning is distinct in quality from all that comes after it, as the starting-point to which all the rest remains tethered. In this regard, and in the continuous action of temporal dimensions upon one another, we have a process that is more cyclical than linear and that involves not empty succession but qualitative difference and continual inter-animation.

The dimensions of lived temporality are interwoven and mutually constituting; within this, being born has particular links with the past. More specifically, each individual's own birth is linked with their past. However, the births of *others* as we experience and relate to them have a special connection with the future. This emerges from Arendt's thought. For her, as we know, whenever an individual is born, someone radically new appears, whose actions and story cannot be predicted or foreseen beforehand. Their sheer existence as a new subject is irreducible to all the causal interactions that have supplied the conditions of their appearance. Something in the birth of any new person—their first-person existence—goes beyond all that has happened already. In this regard, a person's birth stands to the past and present in the same way that the future does; both the one new-born and the future always harbour possibilities that go beyond existing states of affairs. As they harbour possibilities, they are open: they can go in different directions, between which choices will have to be made, whether by the new-born person regarding her own life or by human agents generally with respect to the future.

This is how the birth of someone other than me, rather than my own birth, presents itself. My own birth figures into my lived experience as the anchor-point of my past, the source of my givenness, and the point from which I began to receive all that I have inherited, before I ever made any choices. It was for those who existed before me, and who experienced my birth from their older standpoints, that I appeared as someone radically new. To myself, I do not appear radically new relative to what is already there, because for me nothing *was* there until I began to exist. By contrast, those who appear to me as radical newcomers are those who are born after me. Lisa Baraitser brings this out in her exploration of motherhood (2008). The child's existence interrupts the continuity of the mother's temporal experience, as the child's temporality extends into a future that is not the mother's own. This is because the child has his own temporally extended subjectivity: he can be expected to outlive his mother; he is oriented towards his own projects, not towards nurturing his mother's projects as she does with his; and as a child, he is unformed and open-ended, much more patently and completely a being of possibilities than his mother is.[6]

The births of others younger than us, then, have a special link with the future because they exemplify and attest to the openness of the future relative to the present and past. This provides a structural, existential basis for the common pattern for the birth of someone new to occasion intense hope in those anticipating and experiencing it. The new person's birth reminds us and demonstrates to us that the future remains open so that the world can be made better and renewed. Even if past hopes have been disappointed, new hopes can still spring forth, new possibilities for making life better. For example, Christopher Lebron in *The Color of our Shame* wrestles with whether 'America's race problems are so deeply embedded in our society...that no theory of justice [can] root them out' (2013: 156). But he ends by speaking about his son:

> He entered my life late in the project but at a time when I still had the opportunity to surrender to a kind of cynicism about people's capacity to be better. His inner beauty, perfection, and goodness are among the last and strongest influences on my hope that our society can achieve the goodness necessary to treat people decently.   (191)

However bad, unsatisfactory, or disappointing things presently are, then, the birth of someone new promises that things need not stay this way. We now see the world in light of its possibilities for future renewal, to which the new person's birth attests.

That said, we do not always find hope in others' births. Consider the escaped slave Sethe, the main character in Toni Morrison's *Beloved* (1987). When Sethe is about to be taken back into slavery along with her children, she tries to kill them to save them from enslavement, although she only manages to kill her 2-year-old daughter ('Beloved'). Enslaved, Beloved would have no chance of an open and better future; so Sethe judges it better for Beloved to be dead rather than having been born to a hopeless fate. Thus, the structural link between others' births and the open future can be broken by circumstances, such as slavery, which are so oppressive and entrenched that they seem hopeless and unchangeable. In such circumstances, it appears impossible for the future to be unlike the past and for the lives of newborn persons to be open and capable of going better than those of preceding generations. When all hope is taken out of someone's birth in this way, as with Beloved, it hardly makes sense for them to be born at all; the structural meaning of birth has been distorted.

As these considerations indicate, the births of others are also structurally connected to the sense of our societies having a future. Most simply, if new people stop being born then a society will die out, having no one to take it forward. P. D. James dramatizes this scenario in *Children of Men* (1992). In the dystopian England she depicts in 2021 AD, human beings have lost the capacity to reproduce; the last birth happened back in 1995. As existing generations age, the human species is gradually dying out. With this, hope is disappearing too. An utterly bleak atmosphere emanates from the society James depicts, whose once-cherished values and institutions—universities, museums, galleries, churches—have fallen into neglect and indifference or been ruthlessly repurposed to immediate pragmatic ends. The despot Xan Lyppiatt and his team govern unchallenged, for without new generations to come or a future for humanity, no one cares to defend democracy. What do political arrangements matter when soon the human race will be extinct anyway? Everything has become empty and pointless. More than that, people acquiesce in Lyppiatt's dictatorship because, without any radical newcomers arriving by birth to show that the future remains undetermined, people do not feel that society can be renewed, changed, or bettered. Because improvement looks impossible, people have no grounds to resist or oppose dictatorship.

Ultimately, the reason why England in *Children of Men* has lost all hope is because there is a structural link between the birth of others and the future, not only in terms of biological succession but also the existential attestation to open possibilities which new births provide. Or, at least, these births provide this attestation unless social circumstances become so oppressive that they close off any open future and so deprive new births of their meaning. Society, then, depends for its future on new births; but, recipro-cally, births can be stripped of their structural link with futurity and optimism if social conditions become bad enough.

However, James's view of birth, hope, and the future has been criticized by Lee Edelman from a queer-theoretical perspective. In *No Future*, Edel-man sees *Children of Men* as an expression of the wider prevailing ideology that he calls 'reproductive futurism' (2004: 11–13), an ideology that 'stakes its political claims on appeals to secure the future by protecting the... innocent Child' (Coffman 2013). The Child is not a real, empirical child but an imaginary figure. Tiny Tim from Dickens's *A Christmas Carol* and Little Eppie in George Eliot's *Silas Marner* are amongst its emblems—as well as the baby who, against all the odds, is born to Julian in *Children of Men* and heralds a possible return of the human species to a reproductive future. According to Edelman, contemporary political discussion makes pervasive appeal to the Child who must be defended so that the present can be perpetuated into the future, and temporal and generational continuity secured. But this horizon of thought and imagining has a constitutive outside, something that it must expel and banish outside of the political field. This is the queer: someone whose sexuality and pleasures are not oriented towards reproduction or the future but are purposeless, without issue, unproductive, empty, meaningless, doing nothing to help keep society going, destructive of social order, degenerating towards death. Exclusion of this figure pervades the whole social–political field, left as well as right, Edelman argues.

Edelman urges gay, lesbian, bisexual, and trans people to embrace this figure of the queer as the 'constitutive outside' of reproductive futurism. He claims that 'queerness ... figures ... the place of the social order's death drive' (2004: 3), drawing on a version of Freud's distinction between life and death drives. On Edelman's version, the life drives encompass energy that has been bound into desires for determinate objects, people, and ideas and therefore makes possible attachments, creativity, and social bonds. Conversely, the death drives encompass sheer psychic energy, unbound, unattached, and so operating purely as a force of negativity: excessive of any determinate desires, and therefore undermining any social bonds, attachments, or creative projects.[7] The 'death drives' denote that in sexuality which cannot be incorporated into social order but pulls against society, and which is embodied in queerness. Edelman celebrates the death drives in their pure negativity ('No future'), rather than valorizing life. Thus, for him, along with life, the very idea of the future must be rejected, as that idea is indelibly coloured by the longstanding association of the future with reproduction. Indeed, as we have seen, this is not merely a contingent association. Our belief that society has an open future is intimately bound up with our attitude towards new births, and new births need reproduction to bring them about. From Edelman's perspective, then, James espouses reproductive futurism because she takes it that hope, meaningfulness, and value are only possible if new individuals are born by way of sexual reproduction—a stance that renders marginal and undesirable those individuals who can't, don't, or choose not to reproduce.

One might object that Edelman's 'reproductive future' is precisely one that *reproduces* the social arrangements already in place: it is a closed, not an open future. But perhaps that is no genuine future at all. Certainly, we inevitably relate to the future by anticipating it in ways informed and filled out by the past and present. Yet it is in the nature of the future, if it is genuinely that, that it can always unfold otherwise than we expect: open possibility is inherent in and constitutive of the future. Insofar as the 'future' that Edelman opposes cannot exceed expectations, it seems after all to be merely a prolonged present. Edelman's target, then, may actually be reproductive *presentism*, an ideology and politics that would prevent the future from ever diverging from what is currently established. In that case, perhaps James's position does not fall under Edelman's critique of heteronormativity after all, but on the contrary dovetails with that critique. For James, the birth of new individuals is the condition of possibility for the creation of radically new ideas and practices. And given that most past and present social norms have been heteronormative, it is radically new ideas and practices which are needed if a non-heteronormative and queer-friendly society is to come about. So perhaps without new births we can have no hope of heteronormativity ever being overcome.

Edelman could reply that as long as birth and sexual reproduction are deemed necessary for newness, social change and any genuine future, then one set of possibilities is ruled out. This is the possibility that lives that are not centred around sexual reproduction, or that reject it, can be meaningful and valuable. In this key respect the future would remain tied down to the reproduction of the present, for the very conditions that are held to be necessary for society having an open future full of possibility rule out non-heteronormative and non-reproductive possibilities.

One might in turn reply to Edelman that, although new births are necessary for society to have a future, those births need not come about exclusively through heterosexual reproduction. All sorts of reproductive arrangements are possible, and assisted reproductive technologies have helped to expand the range of ways that individuals, families, and couples can have children. Again, it is in the open nature of the future that reproduction can always be practised in new ways that go beyond those that already exist. Edelman is sceptical, in the context of mainstream US gay and lesbian activism since the 1990s, which has pursued full inclusion in such existing institutions as marriage, the family, and the military. Edelman finds this goal of inclusion self-contradictory on the grounds that the institutions at issue rest on 'the absolute privilege of heteronormativity' (2)—amongst them reproduction, fundamentally defined in terms of heterosexuality for centuries. To include non-heterosexual people in reproduction is self-contradictory, for reproduction is so saturated with its traditional meanings that it is a constitutively heteronormative practice that can only be rejected, not expanded.

Edelman's rejection of the future, then, ultimately rests on his view that the past heteronormative meanings of reproduction saturate it so pervasively that they cannot possibly be changed or the nature and scope of reproduction transformed. But this view seems unnecessarily pessimistic, not only as regards reproduction, but also in its underlying assumptions about the nature of inherited meaning. As we've seen in previous chapters, inheriting the past as we do through birth does not condemn us to reproduce that past endlessly, without change. We inevitably modify what we inherit to some degree, and even when we nonetheless try to conserve an inheritance unchanged, (attempted) conservation is just one way of inheriting, not the only possible one.[8] In addition, the same individuals who are heirs are also, from the perspective of older generations, radically new arrivers in the world whose actions and lives cannot be predicted or anticipated. We therefore cannot anticipate the particular ways in which those newly born will inherit, and in inheriting modify, the cultures into which they come, including their practices of sex and reproduction.

So we need not succumb to Edelman's pessimism. The possibility of a non-heteronormative society remains open, despite the fact that the openness of the future and of societal possibility is connected with birth. Indeed it is because of this connection that a non-heteronormative future is always possible. For it is in the openness of those who are new-born that they can always change how sex, reproduction, and intimate relationships are understood and lived out.[9]

II. The Gift of Birth

I had no choice about when or where I was born, whom I was born as, or what natal situation I came into. All this was absolutely given to me by birth. But we may wonder whether these facets of my birth are given to me, not merely as contingent facts, but also in the stronger sense of being *gifted* to me by some agency or person. After all, people routinely talk about being given 'the gift of life', describe the conception or birth of a new individual as a 'gift', and use the expression 'giving birth'. But is 'giving' an empty word in such phrases or does it have substance?

Needless to say, the traditional Christian reply is that God gives us life as he creates each person's soul and infuses it into their embryonic body, either at or shortly after conception. Although some hold that the idea of life being a gift makes no sense outside of a religious framework, there are philosophers who give this idea a secular defence.[10] For Michael Hauskeller, this idea makes non-religious sense because a gift is something it is good to receive—and being alive is good—and because one can be grateful for the life one has received in general, without having to be grateful *to* anyone (2011: 67–8). But this last point is doubtful in view of the structure of the concept of gratitude (on which, see Manela 2015). Gratitude is a three-term relation in which C is or ought to be grateful to A for B, because A has given B to C. By implication, giving is also a three-term relation whereby A gives B to C. Conversely if C has come to have B but not *from* any agent A, then C's appropriate attitude is not gratitude but *gladness*, a two-term relation under which C is glad to have B, or that B (Manela 2015: pt. 1). So Hauskeller's proposed generalized gratitude is really gladness to be alive. Otherwise, if gratitude is in place, it is because my life or existence is a gift I've received *from* some person or agency. This seems to put pressure on how to make sense of my life being a gift without invoking God.

However, there is at least one obvious alternative candidate for the role of the one who gives me life—my mother—a candidate surprisingly rarely mentioned by anyone other than feminists. Lisa Guenther explores this possibility: that we are given existence by the mothers who gestate and bear us.[11] Others have forwarded similar ideas, but I'll focus on Guenther's version.[12] Appreciating its complexity requires us to turn first to a major influence on Guenther, Derrida and his thought about the gift, especially in *Given Time* (1992), where he responds to Marcel Mauss ([1925] 1990).

Mauss sets out his theory of the gift in opposition to the standard view that gift and exchange are opposites: that whereas exchange is of like for like, equivalent for equivalent, a gift is given freely and imposes no obligation to reciprocate on its recipient (Bernasconi 1997: 267). Mauss counter-argues that whereas modern societies have exchange economies, in 'primitive' or archaic communities, social bonds are typically sustained through gift economies. In these communities, gift-giving is a widespread and fundamental social practice, obliging recipients to respond to the gifts they receive in ways that maintain their social ties with the givers—ties of allegiance, friendship, gratitude, rivalry, etc. As recipients are expected to make this kind of formal or informal return for their gifts, the gift economy is after all, Mauss holds, a kind of exchange economy. In modern societies, exchange has been filtered out from the gift relations with which it was previously entwined. Yet informal relations of 'gift-exchange' still maintain the underlying fabric of modern social life.[13]

Derrida replies that Mauss continues, despite himself, to presuppose a distinction between gift and exchange (Derrida 1992: 37). Under this distinction there can only ever be a pure gift, fully distinct from an exchange, to the extent that a gift is unrecognized, invisible, and unmet with any gratitude (14).

For if we do have any reciprocation of, gratitude for, or even knowledge about a gift, then the relation is at least partially one of exchange—say, of services for gratitude, acknowledgement and loyalty. That much, Mauss's own studies show: that in practice gifts are generally impure, mingled with exchange relations. But this view presupposes a distinction between (pure) gift and exchange, albeit that in practice giving is impure and pure giving remains an ideal. As an ideal, though, it still has normative force and can remain an aspiration.[14]

Now, Guenther maintains that the mother's gift of existence to her child is pure in a Derridean sense because it cannot possibly be reciprocated. The one born cannot give existence back to his mother, because she is already alive by the time he comes into the world. Nor can he give her back anything equivalent to existence, as existence is total whereas anything else is finite. Moreover, the child cannot even recognize his mother's gift to him, at least not in its full magnitude, because he can remember neither being born nor receiving maternal care during infancy. By the time he becomes capable of exercising moral and practical agency, the greater part of his mother's gift has become invisible to him. But he cannot be grateful for what he cannot even recognize or comprehend. The mother's gift of birth satisfies Derrida's requirements for a pure gift: going unrecognized, unthanked, and being impossible to reciprocate.

What is given in this gift of birth is the child's very existence, for Guenther. But, she notes, this makes this gift very peculiar. Existence is not an object that one person can give to another; rather, someone must already exist to be able to be given an object of any sort. If A gives B existence, then, it seems that what A does is bring B into being in the first place: A creates or produces B. Yet someone's genetic and/or gestational mother is not his creator; saying that would misdescribe the nature of conception and gestation. Let's assume that my biological mother, rather than conceiving accidentally or against her wishes, positively decides to try to conceive. Even in that case, her decision is to allow insemination to take place, in hope that an unpredictable process of conception will then happen and that its consequences will unfold endogenously within her body. My mother does not 'create' the embryo that I am but only allows its formation and gestation to get under way. She makes her body available to host these processes. Thus, ultimately, what my mother gives me is welcome and hospitality, Guenther maintains (2006: 28).

Guenther argues that this pre-natal maternal giving continues postnatally when a new existent is welcomed into the world, as those around the newborn person accommodate and care for them whoever they are. Anyone who tenders this sort of welcome—be they male or female, a birth-mother or a social mother, etc.—is acting 'like a maternal body' (Guenther 2006: 11). Guenther intends this formulation, which she takes from Levinas ([1974] 1998: 67), to allow that many types of people can act 'like' maternal bodies without having to have female or maternal bodies. However, as it is *maternal* bodies that these individuals are to act like, the formulation may still merge child-caring, mothering, and gestating, while making trans fathers invisible by presupposing that all pregnant bodies are maternal ones. Then again, perhaps Guenther's formulation does justice to the fact that historically women and mothers have been the central birth-givers and child-carers, while allowing that men, fathers, and trans fathers can and increasingly do take part in gestation and childcare alongside ('like') women. After all, there is a real difficulty about how to acknowledge and remember women's historical primacy in regard to birth without reinforcing and perpetuating it; perhaps the 'like' in Guenther's formulation offers a solution.

Still, we might worry that the idea of maternity as welcome is romanticized.[15] Empirically, not all pregnant mothers feel welcoming towards their children. Children can be unwanted, unloved, or conceived against their mother's will. Many children have been conceived accidentally or without their parents deliberately seeking to have them. Given mothers' varied feelings and attitudes, pregnancy is experienced in correspondingly diverse ways, not all positive. Caroline Lundquist examines this, drawing on S, Slavenka Drakulić's fictionalized version of the experiences of pregnant women repeatedly raped in Serbian camps during the Bosnian war (Lundquist 2008). Lundquist finds that these women, conceiving against their will, felt invaded by their foetuses as if by an occupying army or a disease, a force they did not welcome but that seemed to be defeating and overpowering them.

One might reply that Guenther's view is not that mothers always or necessarily adopt an attitude of welcoming, but rather that at a bodily level pregnancy intrinsically expresses a welcoming orientation, at a level prior to consciousness. In a similar vein, Frances Gray replies to Lundquist that an absolute, non-empirical kind of hospitality inheres in pregnant flesh, and that the cases Lundquist describes are corruptions of this original hospitality, in which the welcoming that the maternal body is carrying out anyway becomes felt as unwanted and undesirable (Gray 2012). In further defence of this idea of the original hospitability of the pregnant body, we could appeal to Rosalyn Diprose's account of the pre-personal generosity of our bodies as a whole (2002). For Diprose, this generosity continually manifests itself in our intercorporeal relations with one another as they unfold in advance of reflection or conscious awareness on our part. As bodies, we continually participate in an anonymous corporeal field, affecting and being affected by other bodies, giving and receiving effects and affections. Although this occurs between all our bodies constantly for Diprose, we could say that this type of giving occurs in an especially intense, continuous, and close-knit way between a pregnant body and foetus. But this is pre-personal, not consciously intended, giving.

With all that said, this picture of maternal flesh may nonetheless remain romanticized. Consider, for instance, David Haig's alternative view that the foetus invades and manipulates the maternal body, which protects itself with counter-measures but becomes liable to develop illnesses, such as gestational diabetes, if these measures are insufficient (1993). On Haig's model, pregnancy involves a conflict that is only ever uneasily resolved. We may have doubts about Haig's model but, at the least, he reminds us both that 'pregnancy has commonly been viewed as a cooperative interaction' and that that view is not self-evidently true (Haig 1993: 495). So perhaps it is not the case that, underneath all our conscious attitudes and interpretations, pregnancy intrinsically expresses hospitality. Perhaps, rather, our interpretation of pregnancy as expressing hospitality has become so ingrained that it no longer appears to be the interpretation it is, and hospitality instead appears to be inherent in the maternal body. Arguably, though, this interpretation of pregnancy as hospitality covers over a more complex and difficult set of realities.

These considerations are meant not as decisive objections to Guenther's account but rather as notes of caution about ideas that being born is a maternal gift. Another strand of Guenther's account, to which I now turn, concerns the ethical implications of being born. For Guenther, the gift of welcome that is given to newborns, infants, and children imposes ethical obligations on those who receive it. We are commanded, silently and indirectly, to pass on to others the gift of welcome that we have received. Notably, the obligation is not to give welcome back to the same people who welcomed me (Guenther 2006: 58). Because those people are no longer natal newcomers, I cannot anyway return to them the same sort of welcoming (i.e. of a natal newcomer) which they gave me. Rather, my obligation is to pass the gift of welcome on to others who are natal newcomers relative to me, including any children I may have.

The pattern of obligations which Guenther identifies here can be under-stood in terms of Alasdair MacIntyre's picture of the ethical domain in *Dependent Rational Animals* (1999), while reciprocally Guenther's work allows us to deepen our appreciation of how natality figures into this picture. MacIntyre, who is informed by feminist care ethicists such as Kittay, argues that we only ever become capable of engaging in practical reasoning by virtue of relationships in which others—primarily our parents and families—care for and educate us, and through continuing relationships that sustain us in our already-acquired practical reasoning capacities. So, once we can deliberate about how we ought to act, we are already in debt to specific others (1999: 100). This debt places us under obligations which, therefore, precede and should guide our deliberations. What we have to deliberate about is how best to meet the obligations under which we already stand, prior to any conscious ethical reflection.

For MacIntyre, we are indebted for having received care, in material and emotional terms, as well as education, which includes informal encultur-ation in a culture or set of cultures. These debts obligate us to give care and spread enculturation in our turn. The obligations arising here are not strictly reciprocal such that, say, because my parents gave me a given type and quantity of care in my childhood I am obliged to return to them an exactly equivalent amount of that type of care. Strict reciprocity is ruled out here on at least four counts, MacIntyre argues. (i) Typically, it is not all of the same people who cared for and educated me (and it may not be any of them) whom I become obliged to care for and educate in turn. More typically, someone might be called on to care for her child having previously received care from her parents. (ii) That said, sometimes I *am* called on to care for the very same people who previously tended me (*pace* Guenther), say if my parents become infirm in their old age. Even then, what my parents' infirmity calls me to give them is not readily commensurable with what I received from them in my childhood. It is not obvious how one might measure a parent's care for a newborn baby against caring for an elderly and infirm father. (iii) Moreover, to attempt such measurements would be wrong, for we are called on to give whatever particular forms of care the other person needs from us. (iv) Accordingly, I may be called to give more care to others than I ever received myself—say, if my parents were very laissez-faire, whereas I have a wheelchair-bound daughter who needs a good deal of care from me. Conversely, I may have received more care than anyone else ever calls upon me to give.

Overall, then, by having received care and education from others—having been welcomed by them into life and culture, Guenther might say—I become obliged to give care and education to others in turn. I come under these obligations as a natal being, who begins life highly dependent and receptive to culture, which I come to inherit from the others around me and on whom I depend. But I do not become obliged to give care and education back to others in any prescribed measure; rather, what I am obliged to do is just to respond to the *particular* needs that others have without holding up any measuring-rod. This lack of prescribed measure does not mean that reciprocity is not at work at all. It is because I was given care in view of my particular needs that I become obliged to care for others in view of *their* particular needs. Because a degree of reciprocity is at work, we are not in the domain of the pure gift. But it is precisely because the gifts given here are impure that they function ethically and so sustain our relationships and social life (along the lines identified by Mauss).

However, we might wonder whether this picture misplaces the source of our obligations to care for others, tracing those obligations back to debts incurred when really they arise in a much more immediate way from people's needs. Perhaps another person's need immediately obliges me to respond to it, rather than my coming under that obligation only mediately, through having previously received care myself. For instance, Erinn Gilson says: 'Vulnerability carries with it...normative force; it *calls for response* and, moreover, for particular kinds of response... [namely] to try to prevent vulnerability from being turned into harm or being unequally distributed' (Gilson 2013: 15–16; my emphasis). Gilson says this against the backdrop of the broader view that we are all dependent and vulnerable beings, not only in childhood but also throughout our lives to varying degrees. Some feminist theorists of vulnerability then argue that an individual's vulnerability inherently and directly generates an ethical imperative to prevent that individual from suffering harm. Likewise, for some theorists of dependency such as Susan Dodds, an individual's dependency directly generates an imperative that people respond to it appropriately (2014: 182). It may further be argued that these imperatives are registered directly at an affective level, in our feelings that we must care for and help the person we are responding to—that we must try to prevent her dependency from resulting in her needs going unmet, her undergoing harm, or her powers being stifled.

If our dependencies and vulnerabilities have this immediate normative force, though, then that force applies wherever dependencies and vulnerabilities manifest themselves, to whom, and in whatever contexts. But to approach dependency and vulnerability in that way is tantamount to treating the human agents on whom they impose obligations as abstract individuals isolated from any relationships and relational histories. If we think of normative forces directly imposing themselves on individuals, then we seem to be assuming that the latter are free-floating, directly available to receive the impress of these forces, which only makes sense if we imagine individuals in abstraction from already-existing relationships.

In fact, we are always already relational beings. Consequently, who is obliged to give what to whom on any given occasion is always already structured by relationships which also shape people's levels of affective responsiveness to others. For example, earlier I mentioned a person's obligations to the ageing parents who cared for her as a child. But as that example presupposes, those obligations arise within an ongoing relationship—which also means that although many other ageing parents also have dependency needs and vulnerabilities, our individual does not have the same obligations towards them as she does to her own parents. This is not only because relationships mediate who is obliged to respond to whom and in what respects. Relationships further mediate who depends on whom in the first place, who is particularly vulnerable to being harmed by whom, who has a history of giving care to whom, whose needs are visible to whom, and so on. Relationships structure obligations partly because relationships already structure the dependencies and vulnerabilities that generate obligations.

And yet this structuring role of relationships may not be wholly to the good. First, our relationships may restrict our focus to our immediate circles, to the neglect of people outside them whose needs are actually greater. Indeed, our loved ones may actively discourage us from attending to the needs of people outside our circle, like the father that Patricia Williams describes who tells his daughter not to give money to a homeless woman (1991: 27).[16] Second, even internally our relationships are routinely structured in ways that prevent us from responding to some of the needs arising within them. Think of a distressed little boy who has injured himself but is not comforted because his parent thinks he must 'man up'. As this illustrates, our close relationships tend to be structured to reflect the power inequalities of the societies around them, here gender inequalities. These inequalities shape which needs go answered and unanswered, which responses are felt and not felt, within our everyday lives.

On the one hand, then, if our ethical lives were not organized relationally, it is not clear how well anyone could ever respond to anyone else's needs. Without any relational frameworks we would be pulled in all directions at once by a chaotic, confusing, overwhelming mass of needs pressing on us from all sides. On the other hand, relationships bring order to this chaos only by imposing limits on the scope and extent of our obligations and on our capacities to register obligations affectively. The question, then, is how to adjudicate that some given relational structuring of our dependencies and obligations is not merely necessary to making our obligations manageable but *wrongly* truncates the ethical domain. While this is clearly a huge issue, we might consider that the more our relationships are structured by inequalities of social power and the worse those inequalities are, the more those relationships do not merely limit our obligations to a level that prevents them from being over-demanding, but distort them. Such relationships concentrate our ethical attention too narrowly; they disfigure the shape of the ethical domain by, as it were, squeezing it too narrow in some places and too wide in others, reflecting the asymmetries of power which are driving these distortions.

This returns us to the question of how we can ever come to criticize our relationships along the preceding lines when we are always-already deeply attached to and encultured in the power inequalities that these relationships embody. After all, as we have repeatedly seen, these relationships and their inequalities form us long before we can criticize them and they even shape whatever powers for social criticism we may develop. While no one can ever escape their natal inheritance totally, though, there are various routes along which one may come to question, criticize, and turn against parts of one's inheritance, as I have noted earlier. The sets of power relations that shape any given individual's life are various and uneven, so that that individual can come to criticize some of these relations in light of values they have acquired under others. Our inheritances and attachments are always many and various, complicated and fissured, so that we can come to turn some of them against others. And to the extent that our relationships enable us to develop and maintain capacities for autonomous thought and judgement, we can come to apply those capacities even against the very relationships that have fostered them. These are not the only pathways along which one can learn to take a responsible and critical stance towards one's natal inheritance, but they indicate that there are various routes along which such a stance can become possible.

III. How Natality Structures Our Existence

I set out in this book to show how being born is a structuring dimension of our existence. Let me sum up some main ways in which this is so. This summary will be far from exhaustive of everything that we have covered, but hopefully it will help us to bring together and hold some of the threads of the inquiry together and take stock of the ground covered.

Initially I stated that for a human being, to be born is (i) to begin to exist at a certain point in time, by (ii) coming into the world with and as a specific body, and in a given place, set of relationships, and situation in society, culture, and history, while (iii) doing so by way of being conceived and gestated in and then leaving the womb. Furthermore, it is specific to the human species that a baby exits her mother's womb when her powers are so undeveloped that she effectively remains a foetus outside the womb for most of her first year of life. We therefore begin life highly dependent on care, and then we undergo a further extended period of dependency. That dependency shades in turn into various respects in which we remain dependent on others throughout life. Moreover, because we enter the world outside the womb while we are very immature and unformed, we are highly permeable by and receptive to the cultures which surround and bathe us when our powers are first forming. We begin to receive and inherit cultural horizons from the very first, long before we form any capacity to stand back critically from them. Thus, our natal dependency and receptivity mean that we also take on from the start the power relations of the social world into which we have come by birth. We may learn to criticize those relations later, but if so, this is along routes made possible by some of the same socio-cultural horizons and power relations which have shaped us.

Because of our dependency and receptivity, we attach with great affective intensity to our first care-givers, from whom we imbibe a good deal of our cultural horizons. In these ways, and because these relationships are our first ones—given that, being born, we are beginners—these relationships exert uniquely formative effects on us. They constitute our emerging selves, both our relatively thin senses of being selves-with-others and our concrete personality structures. Along this pathway our earliest relationships provide the templates on which we enter into later ones, although our selves are not thereby set in stone; rather, later relationships continuously re-form our already formed selves.

Under aspect (ii) of being born, we begin life situated within the world with respect to many variables, amongst them culture; gender, race, class and other social divisions; geography; history; body; and placement in a specific set of personal and wider relationships, including kin networks and generational differences. Our natal situations shape which sets of cultural horizons and power relations we begin straightaway to imbibe and to draw upon to make sense of the surroundings in which we find ourselves. Our natal situations also establish what these surroundings are. Thus, we are situated both as to what we have to make sense of and as to the inherited avenues along which we can make sense of it (we are sedimented sense-makers)—and as to the possibilities that arise from that conjunction. Through the choices we make amongst these possibilities, we come to move over time through successive situations, each flowing down from the one before it and so ultimately from our initial natal situation.

If there is an element of choice to the courses our lives take, nonetheless our original natal situation is absolutely given to us, unchosen. Hence, we begin as soon as we are born, and in being born, to *receive*. Passivity precedes and is the condition of activity. Insofar as the component elements of our natal situation are given to us, they make up our natal facticity, from which a dimension of givenness or facticity runs down through the rest of our lives. The net result is that not only our successive situations, but also our entire dimension of situatedness and facticity, flow down through our lives from birth. Our births are the temporal starting-points, necessarily presupposed in all experience, out of which our entire lives unfold.

Amongst the elements of the natal situation given to me at birth is the particularity of my body. It is as the body I am that I have the particular stream of first-person experience that I do. My being this particular first-person individual and none other is also something that is absolutely given to me by birth. My natal facticity thus includes the fact that I am me at all: there is no reason why I am born me; this is just a fact. By the same token it is radically contingent that I am me. This is not in that I might equally well have been born a different person; I could not have been, for then I would not have been me. Rather, the contingency is that there is no explanation for my leading the particular life I am. As such, my being me is groundless. Dimensions of contingency and groundlessness therefore flow down through my life from my birth, along with the rest of my facticity.

The inexplicability of my being me can occasion anxiety. So can other features of my natal existence. For one thing, there are always tensions, whether low level or acute and sharp, amongst the elements of my cultural horizon and the different relationships I am attached to: they all make obligating claims upon me, but I cannot simultaneously satisfy all their demands. It can also provoke anxiety that I am unable either to give a complete narration of my life-story going back to my birth or even to remember my birth or early years, although I must presuppose that my life and its story run back to them. This limits how far I can understand or regulate my own behaviour and reactions, given that the very experiences that have done most to form them are unavailable to my recollection. That we cannot remember our early years gives our lives a syncopated temporality, as we saw in this chapter. Yet across this syncopation our lives still run back, temporally, to our births, while looked at in the opposite direction we continually carry our past forwards, unknowingly, in the basic structures of our selves and in our habituated, ingrained patterns of response and behaviour.

This carrying-forwards shapes how we anticipate the future, including how we anticipate death. We anticipate it as natal beings, in light of our relational histories and attachments. From this perspective, death threatens us, and will befall us, together, and it is in this regard—as a shared rather than narrowly individual plight—that we feel fear and anxiety about the prospect of death.

Overall, human existence emerges in a new light when we take natality into account. Our dependency and relationality come into the spotlight, and mortality presents itself as a fate that we face together and not in individual isolation. We gain fresh perspective on some ways in which the temporal modes of our lived experience interpenetrate. Other aspects of the human condition—infantile amnesia, anxiety, our status as culture-making and culture-receiving beings, situatedness, contingency—turn out to hang together in specific ways through their connections with birth. Autonomy, critical reason, and agency step back; passivity, reception, and sedimentation step forward. In addition, by taking birth as our guiding thread, we have been able to acknowledge some difficult realities. Amongst them, there is no explanation for why we are each leading the particular lives that we are. To be born is to come into a world that contains an ineliminable dimension of mystery. And for us to be natal is for there to be an ineliminable aspect of mystery at the heart of each individual's own existence.

Notes

1. I'm restating Husserl's view that present perception intrinsically includes retention of the past and protention of the future alongside what he calls the 'primal

impression'. None of these three can occur without the others; instead, they comprise a single mental act Husserl [1893–1917] 1991). Amongst the many questions arising here is how the 'primal impression' differs from the 'now' conceived as a durationless mathematical point. One possible answer is that the mental act of retaining the past and 'protending' the future opens up a space of durational extension which creates room for sensory content to come into, enrich, and renew our experience.

2. This concept captures what Guenther calls 'the lapse of time between myself and my birth' (2006: 10).

3. We might wonder whether cognitive enhancement could enable us to remember all of our early years so that our lives would lose their syncopated temporality. My point, though, is just that so far that temporality *has* been syncopated, and on account of birth. As I suggested earlier regarding enhancement and new reproductive and genetic technologies generally, before we can assess how these might transform our existence, we first need to understand how being born has shaped our existence so far, as I am trying to do here.

4. One might ask, with Schües (2016), how we know that we underwent that early period at all when we cannot remember it. We know it on several grounds: (i) from what others tell us and (ii) from knowing that everyone begins life as an infant, including by observing others younger than us during their infancies. (iii) Having completed the transition from earlier to later memory systems, we generally remain aware that we used to be able to remember many early-life events that we can no longer access (indeed, I've watched this happen with my daughter). (iv) As adults, partial, fragmentary memories of our early years sometimes come back to us, and their very partiality makes us aware that there is more in them than we can recall. (v) We not infrequently become aware that we are engaging in behaviours, having feelings, or exhibiting dispositions which have their sources somewhere in our past experiences, even though we cannot pin those source-experiences down.

5. One articulation of the linear view is found in Hegel ([1830] 1970: vol. 1, §257, 229). Kristeva ([1979] 1986b) contends that the linear view is fundamental to modernity: it allows all events to be placed on a single time-line which therefore provides a uniform and universal measure of progress. I thank Anu Aneja for querying whether I've assumed that time is linear.

6. Baraitser is influenced by, amongst others, Levinas (1987: esp. 90–2), although Levinas's focus is paternity. Of course, tragically, sometimes children do die before their parents, but the nature of generational descent inclines people to expect otherwise.

7. I interpret Freud's life/death drives distinction differently, but what matters here is Edelman's interpretation, on which, see de Lauretis (2011).

8. As Derrida says, 'There is no backward-looking flavor in this reminder [about inheritance, *l'héritage*], no traditionalist flavor. Reaction, reactionary or reactive are but interpretations of the structure of inheritance' (1992: 54). And 'Inheritance is never a *given*, it is always a task'—that is, there are always choices to make about how to inherit.

9. There have been many other objections to Edelman: that his view of politics is reductive, ruling out any queer politics, taking all politics to be necessarily conservative and heteronormative, and embracing only an anti-politics. See Brenkman (2002), Doyle (2009), Halberstam (2008), Muñoz (2009), and Power (2009). Muñoz, in particular, upholds the possibility of a utopian future not reducible to the present.

10. For the defences, see Sandel (2007) and Hauskeller (2011); for the objections, see, for example, Anomoly (2013), and Kahane (2011).

11. Of course, one might prefer 'parents' or, given trans pregnancies, 'gestators'. But, again, feminist discussion of birth has focused on the mother, and I'm examining the discussion in the terms it has actually taken.

12. Some other variants of this line of thought are found in Cavarero (1995), Irigaray (1999), Protevi (2001: Ch. 3) and Reader (2017: Ch. 4).

13. The literature on Mauss is huge, as is Mauss-informed literature on the gift. One problem with Mauss's view is that he treats indigenous, pre-colonial societies as more 'primitive' than modern European ones. Thus, even though he seeks to vindicate gift-exchange and to argue that modern societies should acknowledge their reliance on it, Mauss still assumes that modern societies are the more advanced ones. Bracken (1997) locates Mauss's work in the context of actual colonial efforts then being made to outlaw and stamp out indigenous gift-exchange practices, specifically the Euro-Canadian 'potlatch ban' of 1884–1951.

14. John Milbank (2003) takes this in a direction that connects the gift with death. Only by dying for someone else can one give them a pure gift, one for which no return can possibly be made as one is no longer there to receive it. This is yet another way of privileging death over birth.

15. More broadly, some feminists have expressed doubts about associations between women and the gift (associations that are present, for instance, in Cixous's celebration of the 'feminine' gift economy—gratuitous, generous, profligate, luxurious, free from calculation—against the 'masculine' exchange economy; Cixous 1986; see also Bataille [1949] 1991). Morny Joy observes, critically, that women have often been expected to be 'all-giving': their giving of care to children and others has been both taken for granted and mandated (2013: 6). Thus, celebrating a feminine gift economy may romanticize a social reality that demands and exploits women's giving.

16. Care ethicists have therefore been accused of justifying parochialism when they hold that obligations arise within, and on the basis of, personal relationships (for this criticism, see, e.g. Tronto 1994: 111–12). The parochialism problem is especially pressing internationally, given the severe economic inequalities between formerly colonial and formerly colonized countries. If we are only to care for those in our immediate circles, then it seems that such inequalities can be of no concern to us—but they ought to be. That said, many recent care ethicists have developed the standpoint beyond its initial formulations precisely so as to avoid parochialism; see Keller and Kittay (2017).

Bibliography

Adorno, Theodor W. [1951] (1978) *Minima Moralia*. Trans. Edmund Jephcott. London: Verso.

Aeschylus (1953) *Oresteia*. Trans. Richmond Lattimore. Chicago IL: University of Chicago Press.

Agar, Nicholas (2004) *Liberal Eugenics*. Oxford: Blackwell.

Ainley, Alison (1988) Ideal Selfishness: Nietzsche's Metaphor of Maternity. In *Exceedingly Nietzsche: Aspects of Contemporary Nietzsche-Interpretation*, ed. David Farrell Krell and David Wood, 116–30. New York: Routledge.

Ainsworth, Mary D. Salter, Mary C. Blehar, Everett Waters, and Sally Wall (1978) *Patterns of Attachment*. Hillsdale NJ: Erlbaum.

Alcoff, Linda Martín (2006) *Visible Identities: Race, Gender and the Self*. Oxford: Oxford University Press.

Alcoff, Linda Martín (2007) Epistemologies of Ignorance: Three Types. In *Race and Epistemologies of Ignorance*, ed. Shannon Sullivan and Nancy Tuana, 39–58. Albany NY: SUNY Press.

Allen, Amy (1999) *The Power of Feminist Theory: Domination, Resistance, Solidarity*. Boulder CO: Westview Press.

Allen, Amy (2016) Feminist Perspectives on Power. *Stanford Encyclopedia of Philosophy* (Fall 2016 Edition), ed. Edward N. Zalta. At <http://plato.stanford.edu/archives/fall2016/entries/feminist-power/> (accessed 14 April 2019).

Anomoly, Jonny (2013) Review of Michael Hauskeller, *Better Humans?: Understanding the Enhancement Project*. *Notre Dame Philosophical Reviews* 2013.08.01.

Anzaldúa, Gloria (1987) *Borderlands/La Frontera: The New Mestiza*. San Francisco: Aunt Lute.

Appiah, Kwame Anthony (2016) There Is No Such Thing as Western Civilisation. *The Guardian* 9 Nov. (https://www.theguardian.com/world/2016/nov/09/western-civilisation-appiah-reith-lecture/) (accessed 14 April 2019).

Archard, David (1993) *Children, Rights and Childhood*. London: Routledge.

Arendt, Hannah (1958) *The Human Condition*. Chicago IL: University of Chicago Press.

Arendt, Hannah (1966) *Love and Saint Augustine*. Chicago IL: University of Chicago Press.

Arendt, Hannah (1978) *The Life of the Mind*. One-volume edn. New York: Harcourt.

Ariès, Philippe (1974) *Western Attitudes Towards Death from the Middle Ages to the Present*. Trans. Patricia M. Ranum. Baltimore NJ: Johns Hopkins University Press.

Assiter, Alison (2015) *Kierkegaard, Eve and Metaphors of Birth*. London: Rowman & Littlefield International.

Atkinson, Kate (1995) *Behind the Scenes at the Museum*. London: Doubleday.

Atwood, Margaret (1985) *The Handmaid's Tale*. London: Jonathan Cape.

Baier, Annette (1985) *Postures of the Mind.* Minneapolis MN: University of Minnesota Press.

Baraitser, Lisa (2008) *Maternal Encounters.* London: Routledge.

Bartky, Sandra (1988) Foucault, Femininity and the Modernisation of Patriarchal Power. In *Feminism and Foucault: Reflections on Resistance,* ed. Irene Diamond and Lee Quinby, 61–86. Boston MA: Northeastern University Press.

Barvosa, Edwina (2008) *Wealth of Selves.* College Station TX: Texas A&M University Press.

Bataille, Georges [1949] (1991) *The Accursed Share.* Trans. Robert Hurley. 2 vols. New York: Zone.

Battersby, Christine (1998) *The Phenomenal Woman: Feminist Metaphysics and the Patterns of Identity.* Cambridge: Polity Press.

Bauer, Patricia J. (1996) What Do Infants Recall of their Lives? *American Psychologist* 51.1: 29–41.

Bauman, Zygmunt (1992) *Mortality, Immortality and Other Life Strategies.* Cambridge UK: Polity Press.

Bauman, Zygmunt and Stanislaw Obirek (2015) *Of God and Man.* Cambridge UK: Polity Press.

Beatie, Thomas (2009) *Labor of Love: The Story of One Man's Extraordinary Pregnancy.* Berkeley CA: Seal Press.

Beauvoir, Simone de [1947] (1964) *An Ethics of Ambiguity.* Trans. Bernard Frechtman. New York: Citadel.

Beauvoir, Simone de [1964] (1966) *A Very Easy Death.* Trans. Patrick O'Brian. Harmondsworth: Penguin.

Beauvoir, Simone de [1949] (1972) *The Second Sex.* Trans. H. M. Parshley. Harmondsworth: Penguin.

Beauvoir, Simone de [1954] (1991) *The Mandarins.* Trans. Leonard M. Friedman. New York: Norton.

Beauvoir, Simone de [1946] (1995) *All Men are Mortal.* Trans. E. Cameron. London: Virago.

Beauvoir, Simone de [1944] (2004) Pyrrhus and Cinéas. Trans. Marybeth Timmermann. In Beauvoir, *Philosophical Writings,* ed. Margaret A. Simons, 77–150. Champaign IL: University of Illinois Press.

Becker, Ernest (1973) *The Denial of Death.* New York: Free Press.

Bell, Linda A. (1999) Different Oppressions: A Feminist Exploration of Sartre's *Anti-Semite and Jew.* In *Feminist Interpretations of Jean-Paul Sartre,* ed. Julien S. Murphy, 123–48. University Park PA: Penn State University Press.

Benatar, David (2006) *Better Never to Have Been.* Oxford: Oxford University Press.

Benatar, David and David Wasserman (2015) *Debating Procreation.* Oxford: Oxford University Press.

Benjamin, Jessica (1988) *The Bonds of Love: Psychoanalysis, Feminism and the Problem of Domination.* New York: Pantheon.

Benjamin, Walter [1919] (1996) Fate and Character. In *Selected Writings: Vol. 1, 1913–1926,* ed. Michael W. Jennings, 201–6. Cambridge MA: Harvard University Press.

Beresford, Meka (2017) 54 Transgender Men Have Given Birth in Australia This Year. *Pink News* 12 July. URL: http://www.pinknews.co.uk/2017/07/12/54-transgender-men-have-given-birth-in-australia-this-year/ (accessed 14 April 2019).

Bernal, Martin (1987) *Black Athena: The Afroasiatic Roots of Classical Civilisation. Volume I: The Fabrication of Ancient Greece 1785–1985.* London: Vintage.

Bernasconi, Robert (1997) What Goes Around Comes Around: Derrida and Levinas on the Economy of the Gift and the Gift of Genealogy. In *The Logic of the Gift*, ed. Alan Schrift, 256–73. London: Routledge.

Birmingham, Peg (2006) *Hannah Arendt and Human Rights.* Bloomington IN: Indiana University Press.

Biss, Mavis Louise (2012) Arendt and the Theological Significance of Natality. *Philosophy Compass* 7.11: 762–71.

Blattner, William (1994) The Concept of Death in *Being and Time. Man and World* 27.1: 49–70.

Blattner, William (2009) *Heidegger's* Being and Time. London: Continuum.

Bono, Paola and Sandra Kemp, eds. (1991) *Italian Feminist Thought: A Reader.* Oxford: Blackwell.

Bornemark, Jonna and Nicholas Smith, eds. (2016) *Phenomenology of Pregnancy.* Södertorn: Södertorn University Press.

Bortolotti, Lisa and Yujin Nagasawa (2009) Immortality without Boredom. *Ratio* XXII: 261–77.

Bostrum, Nick (2005) The Fable of the Dragon-Tyrant. *Journal of Medical Ethics* 31.5: 273–7.

Bovey, Alixe (2015) Death and the Afterlife. *British Library Newsletter* Apr 13. URL: https://www.bl.uk/the-middle-ages/articles/death-and-the-afterlife-how-dying-affected-the-living/ (accessed 14 April 2019).

Bowen-Moore, Patricia (1989) *Hannah Arendt's Philosophy of Natality.* New York: Palgrave.

Bowlby, John [1969] (1997) *Attachment and Loss: Attachment, Vol. 1.* London: Pimlico.

Bracken, Christopher (1997) *The Potlatch Papers: A Colonial Case History.* Chicago IL: University of Chicago Press.

Brant, Winnie (1997) The Gender Heresy of Akhenaten. In *Gender Blending*, ed. Bonnie Bullough, Vern L. Bullough, and James E. Elias, 215–26. New York: Prometheus Books.

Brenkman, John (2002) Queer Post Politics. *Narrative* 10.2: 174–80.

Brennan, Samantha (2006a) Is Death's Badness Gendered? *Dialogue* 45.3: 599–66.

Brennan, Samantha (2006b) Feminist Philosophers Turn their Thoughts to Death. *International Journal of Health Promotion and Education* 44.1: 34–7.

Brighouse, Harry and Adam Swift (2014) *Family Values: The Ethics of Parent–Child Relationships.* Princeton NJ: Princeton University Press.

Brison, Susan (2003) *Aftermath: Violence and the Remaking of a Self.* Princeton NJ: Princeton University Press.

Brison, Susan (2017) Relational Selves and Personal Identity. In *The Routledge Companion to Feminist Philosophy*, ed. Ann Garry, Serene J. Khader, and Alison Stone, 218–30. New York: Routledge.

Browne, Victoria (2016) Feminist Philosophy and Prenatal Death: Relationality and the Ethics of Intimacy. *Signs* 41.2: 385–407.

Bruckner, Donald W. (2012) Against the Tedium of Immortality. *International Journal of Philosophical Studies* 20.5: 623–44.

Buchanan, Allen (2011) *Beyond Humanity? The Ethics of Biomedical Enhancement.* Oxford: Oxford University Press.

Bulhan, Hussein Abdilahi (1985) *Frantz Fanon and the Psychology of Oppression.* New York: Plenum Press.

Butler, Judith (1990) *Gender Trouble.* New York: Routledge.

Butler, Judith (1993) *Bodies that Matter.* New York: Routledge.

Butler, Judith (1997) *The Psychic Life of Power.* Stanford CA: Stanford University Press.

Butler, Judith (2004) *Precarious Life.* London: Verso.

Butler, Judith (2005) *Giving an Account of Oneself.* New York: Fordham University Press.

Butler, Judith (2009) *Frames of War.* London: Verso.

Cahill, Ann J., Kathryn J. Norlock, and Byron J. Stoyles, ed. (2015) *Miscarriage, Reproductive Loss, and Fetal Death. Journal of Social Philosophy* 46.1: 1–157.

Callahan, Joan C. and Dorothy Roberts (1996) A Feminist Social Justice Approach to Reproduction-Assisting Technologies. *Kentucky Law Journal* 84.4: 1197–234.

Camus, Albert [1951] (1953) *The Rebel.* Trans. Anthony Bower. Harmondsworth: Penguin.

Camus, Albert [1942] (1975) *The Myth of Sisyphus.* Trans. Justin O'Brien. Harmondsworth: Penguin.

Camus, Albert [1942] (1982) *The Outsider,* including Camus's 1955 Afterword. Trans. Joseph Laredo. Harmondsworth: Penguin.

Camus, Albert [1947] (2001) *The Plague.* Trans. Robin Buss. Harmondsworth: Penguin.

Čapek, Karel [1922] (1999) The Makropulos Case. In *Four Plays,* 165–260. Trans. Peter Majer and Kathy Porter. London: Methuen.

Carel, Havi (2006) *Life and Death in Freud and Heidegger.* Amsterdam: Rodopi.

Carel, Havi (2007) Temporal Finitude and Finitude of Possibility: The Double Meaning of Death in *Being and Time. International Journal of Philosophical Studies* 15.4: 541–56.

Carel, Havi (2016) *Phenomenology of Illness.* Oxford: Oxford University Press.

Carey, Peter (1997) *Jack Maggs.* London: Faber & Faber.

Carlisle, Clare (2006a) *Kierkegaard's Philosophy of Becoming.* Albany NY: SUNY.

Carlisle, Clare (2006b) *Kierkegaard: A Guide for the Perplexed.* London: Bloomsbury.

Caruth, Cathy (1996) *Unclaimed Experience: Trauma, Narrative and History.* Baltimore NJ: Johns Hopkins University Press.

Casey, Edward (1987) *Remembering. A Phenomenological Study.* Bloomington IN: Indiana University Press.

Cavarero, Adriana (1992) Equality and Sexual Difference. In *Beyond Equality and Difference,* ed. Gisela Bock and Susan James, 32–47. London: Routledge.

Cavarero, Adriana [1990] (1995) *In Spite of Plato.* Trans. Serena Anderlini-d'Onofrio and Áine O'Healy. Cambridge, UK: Polity Press.

Cavarero, Adriana (1997) Birth, Love, Politics. *Radical Philosophy* 86: 19–23.

Cavarero, Adriana [1997] (2000) *Relating Narratives*. Trans. Paul A. Kottmann. London: Routledge.

Cavarero, Adriana [2007] (2009) *Horrorism: Naming Contemporary Violence*. Trans. William McCuaig. Columbia University Press.

Cavarero, Adriana [2014] (2016) *Inclinations: A Critique of Rectitude*. Trans. Adam Sitze and Amanda Minervini. Stanford CA: Stanford University Press.

CDC (2005) Health Disparities Experienced by Black or African Americans—United States. *MMWR Weekly* 54.1: 1–3. URL: https://www.cdc.gov/mmwr/preview/mmwrhtml/mm5401a1.htm (accessed 14 April 2019).

Champlin, Jeffrey (2013) Born Again: Arendt's 'Natality' as Figure and Concept. *Germanic Review* 88:2: 150–64.

Chanter, Tina (2001) *Time, Death and the Feminine: Levinas with Heidegger*. Stanford CA: Stanford University Press.

Chapman, Christopher N. (1989/2007) *Freud, Religion, and Anxiety*. Morrisville NC: Lulu.com

Chodorow, Nancy [1978] (1999a) *The Reproduction of Mothering*. Reprint edn with new preface. Berkeley CA: University of California Press.

Chodorow, Nancy (1999b) *The Power of Feelings*. New Haven CN: Yale University Press.

Christman, John (2009) *The Politics of Persons: Individual Autonomy and Socio-Historical Selves*. New York: Cambridge University Press.

Ciavatta, David (2017) Embodied Meaning in Hegel and Merleau-Ponty. *Hegel Bulletin* 38.1: 45–66.

Cixous, Hélène [1975] (1986) Sorties. In *The Newly Born Woman*, with Catherine Clément. Trans. Betsy Wing. Manchester: Manchester University Press.

Clack, Beverley (2002) *Sex and Death*. Cambridge UK: Polity Press.

Code, Lorraine (1995) *Rhetorical Spaces: Essays on Gendered Locations*. London: Routledge.

Coffman, Chris (2013) The Sinthomosexual's Failed Challenge to (Hetero)sexual Difference. *Culture, Theory and Critique* 54.1: 56–73.

Cohen Shabot, Sara (2017) Constructing Subjectivity through Labour Pain. *European Journal of Women's Studies* 24.2: 128–42.

Collins, Margery and Christine Pierce (1976) Holes and Slime: Sexism in Sartre's Psychoanalysis. In *Women and Philosophy*, ed. Carol C. Gould and Marx W. Wartofsky, 112–27. New York: Putnam.

Combahee River Collective [1978] (1983) The Combahee River Collective Statement. In *Home Girls: A Black Feminist Anthology*, ed. Barbara Smith, 264–74. New Brunswick NJ: Rutgers University Press.

Conly, Sarah (2016) *One Child: Do We Have a Right to More?* Oxford: Oxford University Press.

Cooper, Rachel (2015) How Might I Have Been? *Metaphilosophy* 46 (4–5): 495–514.

Craddock, Karen T. (2005) *Black Motherhood(s)*. Ontario: Demeter Press.

Craig, Katherine (2017) My Fellow White People. *The Guardian* 6 Sept. URL: https://www.theguardian.com/commentisfree/2017/sep/06/white-people-solution-problem-munroe-bergdorf-racist/ (accessed 14 April 2019).

Crenshaw, Kimberlé (1991) Demarginalizing the Intersection of Race and Sex. In *Feminist Legal Theory*, ed. Katharine T. Bartlett and Rosanna Kennedy, 57–80. Boulder CO: Westview Press.

Crews, Douglas (2003) *Human Senescence*. Cambridge UK: Cambridge University Press.

Cromie, William J. (2002) Long-Term Memory Kicks In After Age One. *The Harvard Gazette* Nov 7. URL: https://news.harvard.edu/gazette/story/2002/11/long-term-memory-kicks-in-after-age-one/ (accessed 14 April 2019).

Crosby, John F. and Marjorie E. Crosby (1976) Primal Birth Trauma: Rank, Janov and Leboyer. *Birth* 3.4: 171–7.

Cruise O'Brien, Conor (1970) *Camus*. London: Fontana.

Daoud, Kamel [2013] (2015) *The Meursault Investigation*. Trans. John Cullen. New York: Other Press.

Darley, J. M., and Batson, C. D. (1973) 'From Jerusalem to Jericho': A Study of Situational and Dispositional Variables in Helping Behavior. *Journal of Personality and Social Psychology* 27: 100–8.

Dastur, Françoise [1994] (1996) *Death: An Essay on Finitude*. Trans. John Llewellyn. London: Athlone.

Dastur, Françoise (2000) Phenomenology of the Event: Waiting and Surprise. *Hypatia* 15.4: 178–89.

DeCasper, A. J. and W. P. Fifer (1980) Of Human Bonding: Newborns Prefer their Mothers' Voices. *Science* 208.4448: 1174–6.

Deigh, John (1994) Cognitivism in the Theory of Emotions. *Ethics* 104.4: 824–54.

Dennett, Daniel (1991) *Consciousness Explained*. New York: Little, Brown & Co.

Derrida, Jacques (1992) *Given Time I: Counterfeit Money*. Trans. Peggy Kamuf. Chicago IL: University of Chicago Press.

Derrida, Jacques (1993) *Aporias*. Trans. Thomas Dutoit. Stanford CA: Stanford University Press.

Derrida, Jacques (1994) *Spectres of Marx*. Trans. Peggy Kamuf. London: Routledge.

Dick, Philip K. [1972] (2008) *We Can Build You*. New York: Harper.

Di Stefano, Christine (1991) *Configurations of Masculinity: A Feminist Perspective on Modern Political Theory*. Ithaca NY: Cornell University Press.

Dinnerstein, Dorothy (1976) *The Mermaid and the Minotaur*. New York: Harper & Row.

Diprose, Rosalyn (2002) *Corporeal Generosity: On Giving with Nietzsche, Merleau-Ponty, and Levinas*. Albany NY: SUNY Press.

Dodds, Susan (2014) Dependence, Care and Vulnerability. In *Vulnerability: New Essays in Feminist Ethics and Social Philosophy*, eds. Catriona Mackenzie, Wendy Dodds, and Susan Rogers, 181–203. Oxford: Oxford University Press.

Dolan, Frederick M. (2004) An Ambiguous Citation in Hannah Arendt's *The Human Condition*. *The Journal of Politics* 66.2: 606–10.

Donne, John [1624] (1999) *Devotions upon Emergent Occasions* and *Death's Duel*. New York: Vintage.

Doris, John (2002) *Lack of Character: Personality and Moral Behavior*. Cambridge UK: Cambridge University Press.

Doyle, Jennifer (2009) Blind Spots and Failed Performance: Abortion, Feminism and Queer Theory. *Qui Parle* 18.1: 25–52.

Dreyfus, Hubert (1991) *Being in the World: A Commentary on Heidegger's* Being and Time, Division I. Cambridge MA: MIT Press.

Drichel, Simone (2013a) Introduction: Reframing Vulnerability. *SubStance* 42.3: 1–27.

Drichel, Simone, ed. (2013b) *Vulnerability*. *SubStance* 42.3, issue 132.

Dunsworth, Holly M., Anna G. Warrener, Terrence Deacon, Peter T. Ellison, and Herman Pontzer (2012) Metabolic Hypothesis for Human Altriciality. *Proceedings of the National Academy of Sciences of the United States of America* 109.38: 15212–16.

Durst, Margarete (2003) Birth and Natality in Hannah Arendt. *Analecta Husserliana* 70: 777–97.

Edmunds, June and Bryan Turner (2002) *Generations, Culture and Society*. Milton Keynes: Open University Press.

Engels, Frederick [1894] (2000) Letter to Starkenburg. In *Marx and Engels Correspondence*, trans. Diana Torr. New York: International Publishers. URL: https://www.marxists.org/archive/marx/works/download/Marx_Engels_Correspondence.pdf/ (accessed 14 April 2019).

Ettinger, Bracha Lichtenberg (2006) *The Matrixial Borderspace*. Minneapolis MN: University of Minnesota Press.

Falque, Emmanuel [2004] (2013) *The Metamorphosis of Finitude: An Essay on Birth and Resurrection*. Trans. George Hughes. New York: Fordham.

Farrell Fox, Nik (2002) *The New Sartre*. London: Continuum.

Fineman, Martha (2008) The Vulnerable Subject: Anchoring Equality in the Human Condition. *Yale Journal of Law and Feminism* 20.1: 1–23.

Fink, Hans (2017) MacIntyre and Logstrup on Secularization and Moral Change. URL: https://ethicaldemand.files.wordpress.com/2017/04/fink-macintyre-and-logstrup-on-secularization-and-moral-change.pdf/ (accessed 14 April 2014).

Firestone, Shulamith (1970) *The Dialectic of Sex*. New York: Morrow.

Flax, Jane (1983) Political Philosophy and the Patriarchal Unconscious. In *Discovering Reality*, ed. Sandra Harding and Merrill B. Hintikka, 245–81. Dordrecht: Reidel.

Foley, James (2008) *Camus: From the Absurd to Revolt*. Durham UK: Acumen.

Fortin, Jacey (2017) L'Oréal Drops Transgender Model Over Comments on Race. *New York Times* Sept 2. URL: https://www.nytimes.com/2017/09/02/business/munroe-bergdorf-loreal-transgender.html/ (accessed 14 April 2019).

Foucault, Michel (1982) The Subject and Power. *Critical Inquiry* 8.4: 777–95.

Fox Keller, Evelyn [1978] (1983) Gender and Science. In *Discovering Reality*, ed. Sandra Harding and Merrill B. Hintikka, 187–205. Dordrecht: Reidel.

Fraser, Nancy (1989) Foucault on Modern Power. In *Unruly Practices: Power, Discourse and Gender in Contemporary Social Theory*, 17–34. Cambridge: Polity Press.

Fraser, Nancy and Linda Gordon (1994) A Genealogy of Dependency. *Signs* 19.2: 309–36.

Freud, Sigmund [1916] (1942) On Transience. In *Standard Edition of the Complete Psychological Works* [hereafter *SE*] vol. XIV, 305–7. London: Hogarth Press.

Freud, Sigmund [1901–5] (1953) *A Case of Hysteria, Three Essays on Sexuality and Other Works*. *SE* vol. VII. Reprint edn. New York: Vintage.

Freud, Sigmund [1919] (1955a) The 'Uncanny'. In *SE* vol. XVII, 217–56. Reprint edn. New York: Vintage.

Freud, Sigmund [1920] (1955b) *Beyond the Pleasure Principle*. In *SE* vol. XVIII, 3–65. Reprint edn. New York: Vintage.

Freud, Sigmund [1915] (1957a) Thoughts for the Times on War and Death. In *SE* vol. XIV, 273–302. Reprint edn. New York: Vintage.

Freud, Sigmund [1917] (1957b) Mourning and Melancholia. In *SE* vol. XIV, 237–58. Reprint edn. New York: Vintage.

Freud, Sigmund [1900] (1958) *The Interpretation of Dreams*. SE vols. IV and V. Reprint edn. New York: Vintage.

Freud, Sigmund [1926] (1959) *Inhibitions, Symptoms and Anxiety*. In *SE* vol. XX, 77–174. Reprint edn. New York: Vintage.

Freud, Sigmund [1933] (1960) Why War? In *SE* vol. XXII, 195–216. Reprint edn. New York: Vintage.

Freud, Sigmund [1923] (1961a) *The Ego and the Id*. In *SE* vol. XIX, 3–68. Reprint edn. New York: Vintage.

Freud, Sigmund [1924] (1961b) The Dissolution of the Oedipus Complex. In *SE* vol. XIX, 173–82. Reprint edn. New York: Vintage.

Freud, Sigmund [1930] (1961c) *Civilization and its Discontents*. In *SE* vol. XXI, 59–148. Reprint edn. New York: Vintage.

Freud, Sigmund [1894/5] (1962/2001) The Justification for Detaching from Neurasthenia a Particular Syndrome: The Anxiety Neurosis. In *SE* vol. III, 87–117. Reprint edn. New York: Vintage.

Freud, Sigmund [1915–17] (1963) *Introductory Lectures on Psychoanalysis Part III: General Theory of the Neuroses*. SE vol. XVI. Reprint edn. New York: Vintage.

Fullbrook, Edward and Kate Fullbrook (1993) *Sex and Philosophy: Rethinking de Beauvoir and Sartre*. New York: Continuum.

Gallagher, Shaun (1999) *The Inordinance of Time*. Evanston IL: Northwestern University Press.

Gander, Kashmira (2017) Anti-Natalism. *The Independent* Feb 7. URL: https://www.independent.co.uk/life-style/antinatalism-people-think-world-earth-better-off-if-humans-not-exist-humankind-extinct-a7565591.html/ (accessed 15 April 2019).

Gardner, Sebastian (2006) Sartre, Schelling and Onto-Theology. *Religious Studies* 42.3: 247–71.

Gardner, Sebastian (2009) *Sartre's* Being and Nothingness: *A Reader's Guide*. New York: Continuum.

Gatrell, Caroline (2004) *Hard Labour: The Sociology of Parenthood*. Maidenhead: Open University Press.

Gehlen, Arnold [1940] (1988) *Man: His Nature and Place in the World*. New York: Columbia University Press.

Gheaus, Anca (2012) The Right to Parent One's Biological Baby. *Journal of Political Philosophy* 20.4: 432–55.

Gilligan, Carol (1982) *In a Different Voice: Psychological Theory and Women's Development*. Cambridge MA: Harvard University Press.

Gilson, Erinn (2011) Vulnerability, Ignorance, and Oppression. *Hypatia* 26.2: 308–32.

Gilson, Erinn (2013) *The Ethics of Vulnerability*. New York: Routledge.

Glenn, Norbert (1977) *Cohort Analysis*. London: Sage.

Gómez-Robles, Aima, William D. Hopkins, Steven J. Schapiro, and Chet C. Sherwood (2015) Relaxed Genetic Control of Cortical Organization in Human Brains Compared with Chimpanzees. *Proceedings of the National Academy of Sciences of the United States of America* 112.48: 14799–804.

Gordon, Lewis (1995) *Bad Faith and Antiblack Racism*. New York: Humanity Books.

Goswami, Namita (2014) Europe as an Other. *Hypatia* 29.1: 59–74.

Gould, Stephen Jay (1977) *Ever Since Darwin*. New York: Norton.

Gray, Frances (2012) Original Habitation: Pregnant Flesh as Absolute Hospitality. In *Coming to Life: Philosophies of Pregnancy, Childbirth, and Mothering*, ed. Sarah LaChance Adams and Caroline Lundquist, 71–87. New York: Fordham University Press.

Green, Karen (1999) Sartre and De Beauvoir on Freedom and Oppression. In *Feminist Interpretations of Jean-Paul Sartre*, ed. Julien S. Murphy, 75–199. University Park PA: Penn State University Press.

Griffiths, Morwenna (1995) *Feminisms and the Self*. London: Routledge.

Grof, Stanislav (1988) *The Adventure of Self-Discovery*. Albany NY: SUNY Press.

Grosz, Elizabeth (2005) *Time Travels: Feminism, Nature, Power*. Durham NC: Duke University Press.

Guenther, Lisa (2006) *The Gift of the Other: Levinas and the Politics of Reproduction*. Albany NY: SUNY Press.

Guenther, Lisa (2008) Being-From-Others: Reading Heidegger after Cavarero. *Hypatia* 23.1: 99–118.

Guenther, Lisa (2012) Fecundity and Natal Alienation: Rethinking Kinship with Emmanuel Levinas and Orlando Patterson. *Levinas Studies* 7: 1–19.

Guenther, Lisa (2013) *Solitary Confinement*. Duluth MN: University of Minnesota Press.

Haag, Ernest van den (1963) *Passion and Social Constraint*. Piscataway NJ: Aldine Transaction.

Habermas, Jürgen (2003) *The Future of Human Nature*. Cambridge: Polity.

Haig, David (1993) Genetic Conflicts in Human Pregnancy. *Quarterly Review of Biology* 68 (4): 495–532.

Halberstam, Judith (2008) The Anti-Social Turn in Queer Studies. *Graduate Journal of Social Science* 5.2: 140–56.

Hamzelou, Jessica (2017) Artificial Womb Helps Premature Lamb Fetuses Grow for 4 Weeks. *New Scientist* 25 Apr. URL: https://www.newscientist.com/article/

2128851-artificial-womb-helps-premature-lamb-fetuses-grow-for-4-weeks/ (accessed 15 April 2019).

Han-Pile, Béatrice (2016) Foucault, Normativity and Critique as a Practice of the Self. *Continental Philosophy Review* 49.1: 85–101.

Hannan, Sarah, Samantha Brennan and Richard Vernon, eds. (2016) *Permissible Progeny? The Morality of Procreation and Parenting*. Oxford: Oxford University Press.

Haraway, Donna (1991) Situated Knowledges: The Science Question in Feminism and the Privilege of Partial Perspective. In *Simians, Cyborgs and Women*, 183–202. London: Free Association Books.

Hardimon, Michael O. (1992) *Hegel's Social Philosophy*. Cambridge UK: Cambridge University Press.

Harding, Sandra (1991) *Whose Science? Whose Knowledge?* Ithaca NY: Cornell University Press.

Harman, Elizabeth (2009) Critical Study: David Benatar, *Better Never to Have Been. Noûs* 43.4: 776–85.

Harris, Cheryl I. (1996–7) Finding Sojourner's Truth: Race, Gender, and the Institution of Property. *Cardozo Law Review* 18: 309–409.

Hartman, Saidiya (2007) *Lose Your Mother: A Journey Along the Atlantic Slave Trade*. New York: Farrar, Straus and Giroux.

Hartsock, Nancy (1990) Foucault on Power: A Theory for Women? In *Feminism/ Postmodernism*, ed. Linda Nicholson, 83–105. New York: Routledge.

Haslanger, Sally (2000) Gender, Race: (What) Are They? (What) Do We Want Them To Be? *Noûs* 34.1: 31–55.

Hauskeller, Michael (2011) Human Enhancement and the Giftedness of Life. *Philosophical Papers* 40.1: 55–79.

Haviland, William A, Harald E. L. Prins, Dana Walrath, and Bunny McBride (2017) *Anthropology: The Human Challenge*. 15th edn. Boston MA: Cengage.

Hegel, G. W. F. [1830] (1970) *Philosophy of Nature*. Trans. M. J. Petry. 3 vols. London: Allen & Unwin.

Hegel, G. W. F. [1807] (1977) *Phenomenology of Spirit*. Trans. A. V. Miller. Oxford: Oxford University Press.

Heidegger, Martin [1935] (1959) *Introduction to Metaphysics*. Trans. Ralph Manheim. New Haven CN: Yale University Press.

Heidegger, Martin [1927] (1962) *Being and Time*. Trans. John Macquarrie and Edward Robinson. Oxford: Blackwell. Cited with English pagination then, after a slash, German (using the 11th edn of 1967).

Heidegger, Martin [1927] (1967) *Sein und Zeit*. 11th edn. Tubingen: Max Niemeyer.

Heidegger, Martin [1961] (1991) *Nietzsche*. 2 vols. Trans. David Farrell Krell. New York: HarperCollins.

Heidegger, Martin [1929–30] (1996) *The Fundamental Concepts of Metaphysics: World, Finitude, Solitude*. Trans. William McNeill and Nicholas Walker. Bloomington IN: Indiana University Press.

Heidegger, Martin [1927] (2010) *Being and Time*. Trans. Joan Stambaugh. Rev. Dennis Schmidt. Albany: SUNY Press.

Heinämää, Sara (2010) Phenomenologies of Mortality and Generativity. In *Feminist Philosophies of Birth, Death and Embodiment*, ed. Schott, 73–153. Bloomington IN: Indiana University Press.

Held, Klaus [1992] (1993) Fundamental Moods and Heidegger's Critique of Contemporary Culture. Trans. Anthony Steinbock. In *Reading Heidegger: Commemorations*, ed. John Sallis, 287–303. Bloomington IN: Indiana University Press.

Held, Virginia (1989) Birth and Death. *Ethics* 99.2: 362–88.

Hempel, Jessi (2016) My Brother's Pregnancy and the Making of a New American Family. *Time* Sep 12. URL: http://time.com/4475634/trans-man-pregnancy-evan/

Hick, John (1976) *Death and Eternal Life.* London: Collins.

Hill Collins, Patricia (1990) *Black Feminist Thought.* New York: Routledge.

Hoagland, Sarah Lucia (1999) Existential Freedom and Political Change. In *Feminist Interpretations of Jean-Paul Sartre*, ed. Julien S. Murphy, 149–74. University Park PA: Penn State University Press.

Homiak, Marcia (2016) Moral Character. *The Stanford Encyclopedia of Philosophy* (Fall 2016 Edition), ed. Edward N. Zalta. URL: https://plato.stanford.edu/archives/fall2016/entries/moral-character/ (accessed 15 April 2019).

Honig, Bonnie, ed. (1995) *Feminist Interpretations of Hannah Arendt.* Pennsylvania PA: Penn State University Press.

Honig, Bonnie (2013) *Antigone, Interrupted.* Cambridge: Cambridge University Press.

Hook, Derek (2004) Fanon and the Psychoanalysis of Racism. London: LSE Research Online. URL: http://eprints.lse.ac.uk/2567

Howie, Gillian (2016) How to Think About Death. In *On the Feminist Philosophy of Gillian Howie*, ed. Victoria Browne and Daniel Whistler, 131–44. London: Bloomsbury.

Hrdy, Sarah B. (2000) *Mother Nature.* New York: Ballantine Books.

Husserl, Edmund [1936] (1970) *The Crisis of European Sciences and Transcendental Phenomenology.* Trans. David Carr. Evanston IL: Northwestern University Press.

Husserl, Edmund [1893– 1917] (1991) *Collected Works* Vol. 4: *On the Phenomenology of the Consciousness of Internal Time.* Trans. John Brough. Dordrecht: Kluwer Academic.

Huxley, Aldous [1932] (1994) *Brave New World.* London: Vintage.

Inwood, Michael (1992) *A Hegel Dictionary.* Oxford: Blackwell.

Irigaray, Luce [1974] (1985a) *Speculum of the Other Woman.* Trans. Gillian C. Gill. Ithaca NY: Cornell University Press.

Irigaray, Luce [1987] (1985b) *This Sex Which Is Not One.* Trans. Catherine Porter with Carolyn Burke. Ithaca NY: Cornell University Press.

Irigaray, Luce (1991a) *The Irigaray Reader.* Ed. Margaret Whitford. Oxford: Blackwell.

Irigaray, Luce [1980] (1991b) *Marine Lover of Friedrich Nietzsche.* Trans. Gillian C. Gill. New SYork: Columbia University Press.

Irigaray, Luce [1984] (1993a) *An Ethics of Sexual Difference.* Trans. Carolyn Burke. London: Athlone.

Irigaray, Luce [1987] (1993b) *Sexes and Genealogies.* Trans. Gillian C. Gill. New York: Columbia University Press.

Irigaray, Luce [1990] (1993c) *Je, Tu, Nous*. Trans. Alison Martin. London: Routledge.

Irigaray, Luce [1989] (1994) *Thinking the Difference*. Trans. Karin Montin. London: Athlone.

Irigaray, Luce (1995) '"Je – Luce Irigaray": A Meeting with Luce Irigaray'. Interview with Elizabeth Hirsch and Gary A. Olson. *Hypatia* 10.2: 93–114.

Irigaray, Luce [1983] (1999) *The Forgetting of Air in Martin Heidegger*. Trans. Mary Beth Mader. Austin TA: University of Texas Press.

Jacobs, Amber (2009) *On Matricide*. Ithaca NY: Columbia University Press.

James, P. D. (1992) *The Children of Men*. London: Faber & Faber.

James, Susan (2000) Feminism in Philosophy of Mind. In *The Cambridge Companion to Feminism in Philosophy*, ed. Miranda Fricker and Jennifer Hornsby, 29–45. Cambridge: Cambridge University Press.

Jantzen, Grace (1998) *Becoming Divine: Towards a Feminist Philosophy of Religion*. Manchester: Manchester University Press.

Jantzen, Grace (2004) Review of Clack, *Sex and Death*. *Theology & Sexuality* 11.1: 109–11.

Jantzen, Grace (2005) *Foundations of Violence: Death and the Displacement of Beauty*. London: Routledge.

Jantzen, Grace (2008) *Violence to Eternity: Death and the Displacement of Beauty Vol. 2*, ed. Jeremy Carrette and Morny Joy. London: Routledge.

Jantzen, Grace (2010) *A Place of Springs: Death and the Displacement of Beauty Vol. 3*. ed. Jeremy Carrette and Morny Joy. London: Routledge.

Johnson, Candace (2014) *Maternal Transition: A North-South Politics of Pregnancy and Childbirth*. New York: Routledge.

Jones, David Albert (2004) *The Soul of the Embryo*. London: Continuum.

Jones, Rachel (2012) Irigaray and Lyotard: Birth, Infancy, and Metaphysics. *Hypatia* 27.1: 139–62.

Joy, Morny, ed. (2013) *Women and the Gift*. Bloomington IN: Indiana University Press.

Kahane, Guy (2011) Mastery Without Mystery: Why there is no Promethean Sin in Enhancement. *Journal of Applied Philosophy* 28.4: 355–68.

Kant, Immanuel [1784] (1991) What is Enlightenment? In *Political Writings*, ed. Hans Reiss. Cambridge: Cambridge University Press.

Karen, Robert (1994) *Becoming Attached*. Oxford: Oxford University Press.

Kavka, G. S. (1982) The Paradox of Future Individuals. *Philosophy and Public Affairs* 11.2: 93–112.

Keller, Jean and Eva Feder Kittay (2017) Feminist Ethics of Care. In *The Routledge Companion to Feminist Philosophy*, ed. Garry, Khader, and Stone, 540–55. New York: Routledge.

Kierkegaard, Søren [1844] (1980) *The Concept of Anxiety*. Trans. Reider Thomte with Albert B. Anderson. Princeton NJ: Princeton University Press.

Kierkegaard, Søren [1843] (1983) *Repetition*. In *Writings VI: Fear and Trembling/ Repetition*. Ed. Howard Hong and Edna V. Hong. Princeton NJ: Princeton University Press.

Kierkegaard, Søren [1846] (1992) *Concluding Unscientific Postscript to* Philosophical Fragments, *Vol. 1: Text*. Trans. Howard V. and Edna H. Hong. Princeton NJ: Princeton University Press.

Kirkpatrick, Kate (2017) *Sartre and Theology*. London: Bloomsbury.

Kittay, Eva Feder (1999) *Love's Labor: Essays on Women, Equality, and Dependency*. New York: Routledge.

Kittay, Eva Feder (2011) The Ethics of Care, Dependence, and Disability. *Ratio Juris* 24.1: 49–58.

Kögler, Hans-Herbert (2007) Understanding and Interpretation. In *The SAGE Handbook of Social Science Methodology*, ed. William Outhwaite and Stephen P. Turner, 363–83. London: SAGE.

Krell, David Farrell (2015) *Ecstasy, Catastrophe: Heidegger from Being and Time to the Black Notebooks*. Albany NY: SUNY Press.

Kripke, Saul [1972] (1980) *Naming and Necessity*. Oxford: Blackwell.

Kristeva, Julia [1974] (1984) *Revolution in Poetic Language*. Trans. Margaret Waller. New York: Columbia University Press.

Kristeva, Julia [1983] (1986a) Stabat Mater. In *The Kristeva Reader*, ed. Toril Moi, 160–86. Oxford: Blackwell.

Kristeva, Julia [1979] (1986b) Women's Time. In *The Kristeva Reader*, ed. Toril Moi, 187–213. Oxford: Blackwell.

Kruks, Sonia (1995) Simone de Beauvoir: Teaching Sartre About Freedom. In *Feminist Interpretations of Simone de Beauvoir*, ed. Margaret A. Simons, 79–96. University Park PA: Penn State University Press.

Kulkani, Mangesh (1997) The Ambiguous Fate of a Pied-Noir: Albert Camus and Colonialism. *Economic and Political Weekly* 32.26: 1528–30.

Kyselo, Miriam (2016) The Minimal Self Needs a Social Update. *Philosophical Psychology* 29.7: 1057–65.

LaChance Adams, Sarah (2014) *Mad Mothers, Bad Mothers, and What a 'Good' Mother Would Do*. New York: Columbia University Press.

LaChance Adams, Sarah and Caroline R. Lundquist, eds. (2012) *Coming to Life: Philosophies of Pregnancy, Childbirth and Mothering*. New York: Fordham University Press.

Landau, Iddo (2017) *Finding Meaning in an Imperfect World*. Oxford: Oxford University Press.

Laplanche, Jean (1999) *Essays on Otherness*. Trans. John Fletcher. London: Routledge.

Laplanche, Jean [1999] (2015) *Between Seduction and Inspiration: Man*, trans. Jeffrey Mehlman. New York: Unconscious in Translation.

Laplanche, Jean and Jean-Bertrand Pontalis [1967] (1989) *The Language of Psycho-Analysis*. Trans. Donald Nicholson-Smith. London: Karnac.

Lauretis, Teresa de (2011) Queer Texts, Bad Habits, and the Issue of a Future. *GLQ* 17.2–3: 243–63.

Le Doeuff, Michèle [1989] (1991) *Hipparchia's Choice: An Essay Concerning Women, Philosophy, Etc*. Trans. Trista Selous. Oxford: Blackwell.

Lebron, Christopher J. (2013) *The Color of our Shame: Race and Justice in Our Time*. New York: Oxford University Press.

Lefkowitz, Mary K. (1996) *Not Out of Africa*. New York: Basic Books.

Lennartz, Norbert (2013) Review of *Quoting Death in Early Modern England: The Poetics of Epitaphs Beyond the Tomb*. *English Studies* 94.2: 241–2.

Levesque-Lopman, Louise (1983) Decision and Experience: A Phenomenological Analysis of Pregnancy and Childbirth. *Human Studies* 6.1: 247–77.

Levinas, Emmanuel [1961] (1969) *Totality and Infinity*. Trans. Alphonso Lingis. Pittsburgh PA: Duquesne University Press.

Levinas, Emmanuel [1979] (1987) *Time and the Other*. Trans. Richard A. Cohen. Pittsburgh PA: Duquesne University Press.

Levinas, Emmanuel [1974] (1998) *Otherwise than Being, or Beyond Essence*. Trans. Alphonso Lingis. Pittsburgh PA: Duquesne University Press.

Lispector, Clarice (1988) *The Passion according to G. H.* Trans. R. W. Sousa. Minneapolis MN: University of Minnesota Press.

Lloyd, Genevieve (1984) *The Man of Reason: 'Male' and 'Female' in Western Philosophy*. London: Routledge.

Lloyd, Moya (2015) The Ethics and Politics of Vulnerable Bodies. In *Butler and Ethics*, ed. Moya Lloyd, 167–92. Edinburgh: Edinburgh University Press.

Loewald, Hans W. (1980) *Papers on Psychoanalysis*. New Haven CN: Yale University Press.

Løgstrup, Knud Ejler [1956] (1997) *The Ethical Demand*. Ed. Hans Fink and Alasdair MacIntyre. Notre Dame IN: Notre Dame University Press.

Lublin, Nancy (1998) *Pandora's Box: Feminism Confronts Reproductive Technology*. Totowa NJ: Rowman & Littlefield.

Lucretius (2007) *On the Nature of Things* [*De Rerum Natura*]. Trans. Richard Jenkyns and Alicia Stallings. Harmondsworth: Penguin. Cited by chapter and line number.

Lugones, María (1989) Playfulness, 'World'-Travelling and Loving Perception. *Hypatia* 2.2: 3–19.

Lukács, György [1920] (1971) *History and Class Consciousness*. Trans. Rodney Livingstone. London: Merlin.

Lukes, Steven (1974/2005) *Power: A Radical View*. London: Palgrave.

Lundquist, Caroline (2008) Being Torn: Toward a Phenomenology of Unwanted Pregnancy. *Hypatia* 23.3: 136–55.

Lymer, Jane M. (2016) *The Phenomenology of Gravidity*. London: Rowman & Littlefield International.

MacAvoy, Leslie (1996) The Heideggerian Bias Towards Death. *Metaphilosophy* 27.1&2: 63–77.

Macdonald, Cameron Lynne (2010) *Shadow Mothers: Nannies, Au Pairs and the Micropolitics of Mothering*. Berkeley CA: University of California Press.

MacIntyre, Alasdair [1981] (1985) *After Virtue*. Second edn. London: Duckworth.

MacIntyre, Alasdair (1999) *Dependent Rational Animals*. London: Duckworth.

Mackenzie, Catriona (2017) Feminist Conceptions of Autonomy. In *The Routledge Companion to Feminist Philosophy*, ed. Garry, Khader and Stone, 515–27. New York: Routledge.

Mackenzie, Catriona and Natalie Stoljar, eds. (2000) *Relational Autonomy*. Oxford: Oxford University Press.

Mackenzie, Catriona, Wendy Rogers, and Susan Dodds, eds. (2014a) *Vulnerability: New Essays in Feminist Ethics and Social Philosophy*. Oxford: Oxford University Press.

Mackenzie, Catriona, Wendy Rogers, and Susan Dodds (2014b) Introduction: What is Vulnerability and Why Does it Matter for Moral Theory? In *Vulnerability*, 1–28. Oxford: Oxford University Press.

Macquarrie, John (1981) *Twentieth-Century Religious Thought*. London: SCM.

Manela, Tony (2015) Gratitude. *The Stanford Encyclopedia of Philosophy* (Spring 2015 edition), ed. Edward N. Zalta. URL: https://plato.stanford.edu/archives/spr2015/entries/gratitude/ (accessed 15 April 2019).

Mannheim, Karl [1927/28] (1952) The Problem of Generations. In *Essays on the Sociology of Knowledge*, ed. Paul Kecskemeti, 276–322. London: Routledge.

Marks, Elaine (1973) *Simone de Beauvoir: Encounters with Death*. New Brunswick NJ: Rutgers University Press.

Marks, Elaine (1986) Transgressing the (In)cont(in)ent Boundaries: The Body in Decline. *Yale French Studies* 72: 181–200.

Martin, Alison (2002) Report on 'Natality' in Arendt, Cavarero and Irigaray. *Paragraph* 25.1: 32–53.

Marvell, Andrew [1681] (2005) To His Coy Mistress. In *Complete Poems*, 50–2. Reprint edn. Harmondsworth: Penguin.

Marx, Karl (2000) *Selected Writings*. Ed. David McLellan. Second edn. Oxford: Oxford University Press.

Marx, Karl [1849/1891] (2017) *Wage Labour and Capital*. Bi Classics.

Matthews, Steve and Jeanette Kennett (2012) Truth, Lies and the Narrative Self. *American Philosophical Quarterly* 49.4: 301–15.

Mauss, Marcel [1925] (1990) *The Gift*. Trans. W. D. Halls. London: Routledge.

Mbiti, John S. (1971) *New Testament Eschatology in an African Background*. Oxford: Oxford University Press.

McCarthy, Rob (2016) *The Hollow Men*. London: Mulholland Books.

McConnell, Terrance (2014) Moral Dilemmas. *Stanford Encyclopedia of Philosophy* (Fall 2014 Edition), ed. Edward N. Zalta. URL: https://plato.stanford.edu/archives/fall2014/entries/moral-dilemmas/ (accessed 15 April 2019).

McDonagh, Eileen L. (1996) *Breaking the Abortion Deadlock*. Oxford: Oxford University Press.

McLean, Brian (2015) What's So Good About Non-Existence? *Journal of Value Inquiry* 49. 1–2: 81–94.

McLeod, Carolyn (2002) *Self-Trust and Reproductive Autonomy*. Cambridge MA: MIT Press.

McNeill, Will (2009) Rethinking the Possible: On the Radicalization of Possibility in Heidegger's Being and Time. *Theory@buffalo* 13: 105–25.

Meltzoff, Andrew N. and M. Keith Moore (1983) Newborn Infants Imitate Adult Facial Gestures. *Child Development* 54: 702–9.

Merchant, Carolyn [1980] (1990) *The Death of Nature: Women, Ecology and the Scientific Revolution*. New York: Harper & Row.

Merleau-Ponty, Maurice [1964] (1968) *The Visible and the Invisible.* Trans. Alphonso Lingis. Evanston IL: Northwestern University Press.

Merleau-Ponty, Maurice [1945] (2012) *Phenomenology of Perception.* Trans. Colin Smith. London: Routledge.

Meyers, Diana T. (1987) The Socialized Individual and Individual Autonomy. In *Women and Moral Theory,* ed. Eva Feder Kittay and Diana T. Meyers, 139–53. Totowa NJ: Rowman & Littlefield.

Meyers, Diana T., ed., (1997) *Feminists Rethink the Self.* Boulder CO: Westview Press.

Milbank, John (2003) *Being Reconciled: Ontology and Pardon.* London: Routledge.

Mills, Charles (1997) *The Racial Contract.* Ithaca NY: Cornell University Press.

Mills, Charles (2007) White Ignorance. In *Race and Epistemologies of Ignorance,* ed. Shannon Sullivan and Nancy Tuana, 13–38. Albany NY: SUNY Press.

Montagu, Ashley [1971] (1986) *Touching: The Human Significance of the Skin.* Third edn. New York: Harper and Row.

Moraga, Cherríe (1997) *Waiting in the Wings: Portrait of a Queer Motherhood.* Ithaca NY: Firebrand.

Morris, G. Shane (2016) Dear Media: It Is Not News When 'Transgender Men' Get Pregnant, *The Federalist* 7 Sept 2016, at http://thefederalist.com/2016/09/07/dear-media-not-news-transgender-men-get-pregnant/ (accessed 15 April 2019).

Morris, Katherine J. (2010) Introduction: Sartre on the Body. In *Sartre on the Body,* ed. Morris, 1–22. London: Palgrave.

Morris, Robert R. (1973) Anxiety: Freud and Theology. *Journal of Religion and Health* 12.2: 189–201.

Morrison, Toni. (1987) *Beloved.* New York: Vintage.

Moyzakitis, Wendy (2009) Exploring Women's Descriptions of Distress and/or Trauma in Childbirth from a Feminist Perspective. *Evidence Based Midwifery* 2.1: 8–14. URL: /https://www.rcm.org.uk/learning-and-career/learning-and-research/ebm-articles/exploring-women's-descriptions-of-distress (accessed 15 April 2019).

Mullin, Amy (2005) *Reconceiving Pregnancy and Childcare.* Cambridge: Cambridge University Press.

Muñoz, José Esteban (2009) *Cruising Utopia: The Then and There of Queer Futurity.* New York: New York University Press.

Murdoch, Iris [1961] (2001) *A Severed Head.* London: Vintage.

Murphy, Ann V. (2011) Corporeal Vulnerability and the New Humanism. *Hypatia* 26.3: 575–90.

Murphy, Julien S., ed. (1999) *Feminist Interpretations of Jean-Paul Sartre.* University Park PA: Penn State University Press.

Nagel, Thomas [1970] (1979) Death. In *Mortal Questions,* 1–10. Cambridge: Cambridge University Press.

Nagel, Thomas (1986) *The View From Nowhere.* New York: Oxford University Press.

Nelson, James Lindemann (1999) Death's Gender. In *Mother Time: Women, Aging and Ethics,* ed. Margaret Urban Walker, 113–29. Lanham MD: Rowman & Littlefield.

Nelson, Katherine (1993) The Psychological and Social Origins of Autobiographical Memory. *Psychological Science* 4.1: 7–14.

Nietzsche, Friedrich [1871] (1999) *The Birth of Tragedy and Other Writings*. Trans. Ronald Speirs. Cambridge: Cambridge University Press.

Nkrumah, Kwame (1966) *Neo-Colonialism: The Last Stage of Imperialism*. New York: International Publishers.

Noddings, Nel (1984) *Caring*. Berkeley CA: University of California Press.

Nsiah-Jefferson, Laurie and Elaine J. Hall (1989) Reproductive Technologies: Perspectives and Implications for Low-Income Women and Women of Color. In *Healing Technology: Feminist Perspectives*, ed. Kathryn Strother Ratcliff, 93–117. Ann Arbor MI: University of Michigan Press.

Nussbaum, Martha (2006) *Frontiers of Justice*. Cambridge MA: Harvard University Press.

Nye, Andrea (2015) *Socrates and Diotima*. New York: Palgrave Macmillan.

O'Brien, Mahon (2014) Leaping Ahead of Heidegger. *International Journal of Philosophical Studies* 22.4: 534–51.

O'Brien, Mary (1981) *The Politics of Reproduction*. London: Routledge.

O'Byrne, Anne (2010) *Natality and Finitude*. Bloomington, IN: Indiana University Press.

O'Reilly, Andrea (2004) *From Motherhood to Mothering*. Albany NY: SUNY Press.

Obedin-Maliver, Juno and Harvey J. Makadon (2016) Transgender Men and Pregnancy. *Obstetric Medicine* 9.1: 4–8.

Oksala, Johanna (2004) What is Feminist Phenomenology? Thinking Birth Philosophically. *Radical Philosophy* 126: 16–22.

Oksala, Johanna (2005) *Foucault on Freedom*. Cambridge: Cambridge University Press.

Oksala, Johanna (2017) Feminism and Power. In *The Routledge Companion to Feminist Philosophy*, ed. Garry, Khader and Stone, 678–88. New York: Routledge.

Oliver, Kelly (1995) *Womanizing Nietzsche*. New York: Routledge.

Oliver, Kelly (2011) Deconstructing 'Grown versus Made'. *Journal of Philosophy: A Cross Disciplinary Inquiry* 7.16: 42–52.

Oliver, Kelly (2018) *Response Ethics*. London: Rowman & Littlefield International.

Olkowski, Dorothea and Gail Weiss, eds. (2006) *Feminist Interpretations of Maurice Merleau-Ponty*. Pennsylvania PA: Penn State University Press.

Olsen, Eric (n.d.) Was I Ever a Fetus? URL: https://www.sheffield.ac.uk/polopoly_fs/1.101682!/file/FetusNew.pdf/ (accessed 15 April 2019).

Origen [c.220–230] (1936) *On First Principles*. Ed. W. D. Butterfield. Eugene OR: Wipf and Stock. Cited by book, chapter and paragraph numbers.

Ortega, Mariana (2001) New Mestizas, World-Travelers, and Dasein: Phenomenology and the Multi-Voiced, Multi-Cultural Self. *Hypatia* 16 3: 1–29.

Overall, Christine (2003) *Aging, Dying and Human Longevity*. Berkeley CA: University of California Press.

Overall, Christine (2012) *Why Have Children? The Ethical Debate*. Cambridge MA: MIT Press.

Parfit, Derek (1984) *Reasons and Persons*. Oxford: Clarendon Press.

Park, Shelley M. (2014) *Mothering Queerly, Queering Motherhood*. Albany NY: SUNY Press.

Parks, Jennifer (2009) Rethinking Radical Politics in the Context of Assisted Reproductive Technology. *Bioethics* 23.1: 20–7.

Partridge, Christopher (2006) *The Re-enchantment of the West* Vol. 2. London: Bloomsbury.

Pascal, Blaise [1670] (1958) *Pensées.* Trans. W. F. Trotter. New York: Dutton.

Patterson, Orlando (1983) *Slavery and Social Death.* Cambridge MA: Harvard University Press.

Pattison, George (2005) *The Philosophy of Kierkegaard.* Durham UK: Acumen.

Pattison, George (2013) *Heidegger on Death: A Critical Theological Essay.* Farnham: Ashgate.

Petherbridge, Danielle (2016) What's Critical about Vulnerability? *Hypatia* 31.3: 589–604.

Phillips, Stephen H. (2009) *Yoga, Karma, and Rebirth.* New York: Columbia University Press.

Piercy, Marge (1976) *Woman on the Edge of Time.* New York: Knopf.

Pilcher, Jane (1994) Mannheim's Sociology of Generations. *British Journal of Sociology* 45.3: 481–95.

Pizarro Obaid, Francisco (2012) Sigmund Freud and Otto Rank: Debates and Confrontations about Anxiety and Birth. *International Journal of Psychoanalysis* 93.3: 693–715.

Plato (1991) *Plato's Symposium.* Ed. R. E. Allen. New Haven CN: Yale University Press.

Plato (1993) *Republic.* Trans. Robin Waterfield. Oxford: Oxford University Press.

Plato (2001) *Apology.* In *The Trial and Death of Socrates,* ed. G. M. A. Grube, 20–42. Indianapolis IN: Hackett.

Poe, Edgar Allen [1845] (1986) The Facts in the Case of M. Valdemar. In *The Fall of the House of Usher and Other Writings,* 301–9. Harmondsworth: Penguin.

Portmann, Adolf [1942] (1969) *Biologische fragmente zu einem Lehre vom Menschen.* Third, expanded edn. Basel: Schwabe.

Power, Nina (2009) Non-Reproductive Futurism: Rancière's Rational Equality against Edelman's Body Apolitic. *Borderlands* 8.2: 1–15.

Protevi, John (2001) *Political Physics: Deleuze, Derrida and the Body Politic.* London: Athlone.

Pugh, Jonathan (2015) Autonomy, Natality and Freedom: A Liberal Re-Examination of Habermas in the Enhancement Debate. *Bioethics* 29.3: 145–52.

Quijano, A. (2000) Coloniality of Power, Eurocentrism, and Latin America. *Nepantla: Views from South* 1.3: 533–80.

Radford, Colin (1975) How Can We Be Moved by the Fate of Anna Karenina? *Proceedings of the Aristotelian Society,* Suppl., 49: 67–80.

Rank, Otto [1924] (1973) *The Trauma of Birth.* New York: Harper & Row.

Rawlinson, Mary (2016) *Just Life.* Albany NY: SUNY Press.

Reader, Simon (2017) *The Ethics of Choosing Children.* New York: Palgrave Macmillan.

Reynolds, Jack (2005) *Understanding Existentialism.* Durham: Acumen.

Rich, Adrienne (1976) *Of Woman Born: Motherhood as Experience and Institution*. New York: Norton.

Ricoeur, Paul [1965] (1986) *Fallible Man*. Trans. Charles A. Kelbley. New York: Fordham University Press.

Ricoeur, Paul [1985] (1990) *Time and Narrative* Vol. 3. Trans. Katherine Blamey and David Pellauer. Chicago: University of Chicago Press.

Ricoeur, Paul [1990] (1995) *Oneself as Another*. Trans. Katherine Blamey. Chicago: University of Chicago Press.

Roberts, Dorothy (1993) Racism and Patriarchy in the Meaning of Motherhood. *Journal of Gender and the Law* 1.1: 1–38.

Roberts, Dorothy (1997) *Killing the Black Body: Race, Reproduction, and the Meaning of Liberty*. New York: Vintage.

Roberts, Dorothy (2009) Race, Gender and Genetic Technologies. *Signs* 34.4: 783–804.

Rogers, Wendy (2014) Vulnerability and Bioethics. In *Vulnerability*, ed. Catriona Mackenzie, Wendy Rogers, and Susan Dodds, 60–87. Oxford: Oxford University Press.

Rolls, Alastair C. and Elizabeth Rechniewski, eds., (2005) *Sartre's Nausea: Text, Context, Intertext*. Amsterdam: Rodopi.

Rothman, Barbara Katz (1986) *The Tentative Pregnancy: Prenatal Diagnosis and the Future of Motherhood*. New York: Viking.

Rubin, Henry S. (1998) Phenomenology as Method in Trans Studies. *GLQ* 4.2: 263–81.

Ruddick, Sara (1989) *Maternal Thinking*. Boston: Beacon Press.

Sacks, Mark (2005) Sartre, Strawson and Others. *Inquiry* 48.3: 275–99.

Sadedin, Suzanne (2014) War in the Womb. *Aeon* 04 Aug. URL: https://aeon.co/essays/why-pregnancy-is-a-biological-war-between-mother-and-baby/ (accessed 15 April 2019).

Said, Edward (2004) *Culture and Imperialism*. New York: Vintage.

Salamon, Gayle (2010) *Transgender and Rhetorics of Materiality*. New York: Columbia University Press.

Salamon, Gayle (2014) Phenomenology. *Transgender Studies Quarterly* 1.1–2: 153–5.

Salecl, Renata (2004) On Anxiety. London: Routledge.

Salvador Dalí [1942] (1993) *The Secret Life of Salvador Dalí*. Trans. Haakon P. Chevalier. New York: Dover Press.

Sandel, Michael (2007) *The Case Against Perfection: Ethics in the Age of Genetic Engineering*. Cambridge MA: Harvard University Press.

Sartre, Jean-Paul [1943] (1958) *Being and Nothingness*. Trans. Hazel E. Barnes. London: Routledge. Cited with English pagination first then, after the slash, French (*L'être et le néant*. Paris: Gallimard).

Sartre, Jean-Paul (1964) *Words*. Trans. Irene Clephane. Harmondsworth: Penguin.

Sartre, Jean-Paul [1938] (1965) *Nausea*. Trans. Robert Baldick. Harmondsworth: Penguin. Cited with English pagination first then, after the slash, French (*La nausée*. Paris: Gallimard).

Sartre, Jean-Paul [1961] (1967) Preface to *The Wretched of the Earth*, by Frantz Fanon. Trans. Constance Farrington. Harmondsworth: Penguin.

Sartre, Jean-Paul [1971] (1981) *The Family Idiot: Gustave Flaubert 1821–1857*. Trans. Carol Cosman. Chicago IL: University of Chicago Press.

Sartre, Jean-Paul [1983] (1984) *The War Diaries of Jean-Paul Sartre: Nov. 1939 to Mar. 1940*. Trans. Quintin Hoare. New York: Pantheon.

Sartre, Jean-Paul [1945] (2001a) *The Age of Reason*. Trans. David Caute. Harmondsworth: Penguin.

Sartre, Jean-Paul [1946] (2001b) Existentialism and Humanism. Trans. Philippe Mairet. In *Sartre: Basic Writings*, ed. Stephen Priest, 25–46. London: Routledge.

Savulescu, Julian (2006) Justice, Fairness and Enhancement. *Annals of the New York Academy of Sciences*. 1093: 321–38.

Schechtman, Marya (2000) *The Constitution of Selves: Version 2*. Ithaca NY: Cornell University Press.

Schelling, F. W. J. [1809] (2006) *Philosophical Investigations into the Essence of Human Freedom*. Trans. Jeff Lowe and James Schmidt. Albany NY: SUNY Press.

Schott, Robin May (2010a) Introduction: Birth, Death and Femininity. In *Birth, Death and Femininity*, ed. Schott, 1–22. Bloomington IN: Indiana University Press.

Schott, Robin May, ed. (2010b) *Birth, Death and Femininity*. Bloomington IN: Indiana University Press.

Schües, Christina (1997) The Birth of Difference. *Human Studies* 20: 243–52.

Schües, Christina (2002) The Meaning of Natality. In *Metafizik ve Politika— Metaphysics and Politics: Martin Heidegger & Hannah Arendt*, ed. S. Yazicioğlu Öge, Ö. Sözer, and F. Tomkinson, 181–223. Istanbul: Boğaziçi University Press.

Schües, Christina (2014) Improving Deficiencies? Historical, Anthropological, and Ethical Aspects of the Human Condition. In *The Human Enhancement Debate and Disability*, ed. Miriam Eilers, Katrin Grüber and Christoph Rehmann-Sutter, 38–63. New York: Palgrave Macmillan.

Schües, Christina (2016) *Philosophie des Geborenseins*. New expanded edn. Munich: Alber. Original edition 2008.

Scully, Jackie Leach (2014) Disability and Vulnerability. In *Vulnerability*, ed. Catriona Mackenzie, Wendy Rogers, and Susan Dodds, 204–21. Oxford: Oxford University Press.

Scuro, Jennifer (2017) *The Pregnancy [does-not-equal] Childbearing Project: A Phenomenology of Miscarriage*. Totowa NJ: Rowman and Littlefield.

Secomb, Linnell (1999) Philosophical Deaths and Feminine Finitude. *Mortality* 4.2: 111–25.

Shakespeare, Tom (2006) *Disability Rights and Wrongs*. London: Routledge.

Shakespeare, William [1597] (1984) *Romeo and Juliet*. Ed. G. Blakemore Evans. Cambridge: Cambridge University Press.

Shakespeare, William [1599–1602] (2003) *Hamlet, Prince of Denmark*. Ed. Philip Edwards. Updated edn. Cambridge: Cambridge University Press. Cited by page then act, scene and line numbers.

Shildrick, Margrit (2002) *Embodying the Monster: Encounters with the Vulnerable Self.* London: Sage.

Simms, Eva M. (2008) *The Child in the World: Embodiment, Time, and Language in Early Childhood.* Detroit MI: Wayne State University Press.

Sizer, Laura (2006) What Feelings Can't Do. *Mind and Language* 21.1: 108–35.

Skidmore, Emily (2017) *True Sex: The Lives of Trans Men at the Turn of the Twentieth Century.* New York: New York University Press.

Smuts, Aaron (2011) Immortality and Significance. *Philosophy and Literature* 35.1: 134–49.

Söderbäck, Fanny (2014a) Introduction: Why Birth? *philoSOPHIA* 4.1: 1–11.

Söderbäck, Fanny, ed. (2014b) *Birth. philoSOPHIA* 4.1.

Söderbäck, Fanny (2018) Natality or Birth? Arendt and Cavarero on the Human Condition of Being Born. *Hypatia* 33.2: 273–88.

Söderbäck, Fanny (2019) Birth. In *The Bloomsbury Handbook of Twenty-First Century Feminist Theory*, ed. Robin Goodman, 59–79. New York: Bloomsbury.

Staehler, Tanja (2007) How is a Phenomenology of Fundamental Moods Possible? *International Journal of Philosophical Studies* 15.3: 415–33.

Staehler, Tanja (2008) Unambiguous Calling? Ethics and Authenticity in Heidegger's *Being and Time. Journal of British Society for Phenomenology* 39.3: 293–313.

Staehler, Tanja (2012) Introduction to *Existentialism*, vol. 1. 4 vols., ed. Staehler. London: Routledge.

Staehler, Tanja (2016a) Passivity, Being-With and Being-There: Care during Birth. *Medicine, Health Care and Philosophy* 19.3: 371–9.

Staehler, Tanja (2016b) Who's Afraid of Birth? Exploring Mundane and Existential Affects with Heidegger. *Janus Head* 15.1: 139–72.

Stapleton, Karyn and John Wilson (2017) Telling the Story: Meaning Making in a Community Narrative. *Journal of Pragmatics* 108: 60–80.

Stephens, Julie (2012) *Confronting Postmaternal Thinking: Feminism, Memory and Care.* New York: Columbia University Press.

Stern, Daniel N. (1985/1998) *The Interpersonal World of the Infant.* London: Karnac.

Stone, Alison (2006) *Luce Irigaray and the Philosophy of Sexual Difference.* Cambridge UK: Cambridge University Press.

Stone, Alison (2007) *An Introduction to Feminist Philosophy.* Cambridge UK: Polity Press.

Stone, Alison (2011) *Feminism, Psychoanalysis, and Maternal Subjectivity.* New York: Routledge.

Stone, Alison (2017) Europe and Eurocentrism. *Proceedings of the Aristotelian Society*, Suppl., 91.1: 83–104.

Strickler, Jennifer (1992) The New Reproductive Technology: Problem or Solution? *Sociology of Health and Illness* 14.1: 111–32.

Summerscale, Kate (2008) *The Suspicions of Mr Whicher.* London: Bloomsbury.

Svenaeus, Fredrik (2017) Phenomenology of Pregnancy and the Ethics of Abortion. *Medicine, Health Care and Philosophy* 21.1: 77–87. Jul 1. DOI: 10.1007/s11019-017-9786-x.

Svendsen, Lars (2007) *A Philosophy of Fear*. Trans. John Irons. London: Reaktion.

Taylor, Charles [1976] (1982) Responsibility for Self. In *Free Will*, ed. Gary Watson, 111–26. Oxford: Oxford University Press.

Tepl, Johannes von [c1401] (1969) Der Ackermann aus Böhmen. URL: http://www.hs-augsburg.de/~harsch/germanica/Chronologie/15Jh/Tepl/tep_tod.html

Tolstoy, Leo [1886] (2012) *The Death of Ivan Ilyich*. New York: Vintage.

Toombs, S. Kay (1995) The Lived Experience of Disability. *Human Studies* 18: 9–23.

Trivers, Robert L. (1974) Parent–Offspring Conflict. *American Zoology* 14: 249–64.

Tronto, Joan (1994) *Moral Boundaries: A Political Argument for an Ethic of Care*. New York: Routledge.

Tuana, Nancy (1993) *The Less Noble Sex: Scientific, Religious and Philosophical Conceptions of Women's Nature*. Bloomington IN: Indiana University Press.

Varga, Somogy, and Charles Guignon (2017) Authenticity. *Stanford Encyclopedia of Philosophy* (Fall 2017 Edition), ed. Edward N. Zalta. URL: https://plato.stanford.edu/archives/fall2017/entries/authenticity/ (accessed 15 April 2019).

Waldenfels, Bernhard (2011) *Phenomenology of the Alien*. Trans. Alexander Kozin and Tanja Staehler. Evanston IL: Northwestern University Press.

Walrath, Dana (2006) Gender, Genes and the Evolution of Human Birth. In *Feminist Anthropology*, eds. Pamela L. Geller and Miranda K. Stockett, 55–70. Philadelphia PA: Pennsylvania University Press.

Warnke, Georgia (2001) Intersexuality and the Categories of Sex. *Hypatia* 16.3: 126–37.

Warren, Mary Anne (1989) The Moral Significance of Birth. *Hypatia* 4.3: 46–65.

Webber, Jon (2010a) Bad Faith and the Other. In *Reading Sartre*, ed. Jon Webber, 180–94. London: Routledge.

Webber, Jon, ed. (2010b) *Reading Sartre*. London: Routledge.

Weinberg, Rivka (2016) *The Risk of a Lifetime: How, When, and Why Procreation May Be Permissible*. Oxford: Oxford University Press.

White, Sheldon H. and David B. Pillemer (1989) Childhood Amnesia and the Development of a Socially Accessible Memory System. In *Functional Disorders of Memory*, ed. John F. Kihlstrom and Frederick J. Evans, 29–73. Hillsdale, NJ: Erlbaum.

Whitford, Margaret (1991) *Luce Irigaray: Philosophy in the Feminine*. London: Routledge.

Wiley, Tatha (2002) *Original Sin: Origins, Developments, Contemporary Meanings*. New York: Paulist Press.

Wilkinson, Stephen (2016) *Choosing Tomorrow's Children: The Ethics of Selective Reproduction*. Oxford: Oxford University Press.

Williams, Bernard (1973) The Makropolus Case: Reflections on the Tedium of Immortality. In *Problems of the Self*, 82–100. Cambridge UK: Cambridge Books Online.

Williams, Patricia J. (1991) *The Alchemy of Race and Rights*. Cambridge MA: Harvard University Press.

Winnicott, Donald [1971] (2005) *Playing and Reality*. London: Routledge.

Withy, Katherine (2012) The Methodological Role of Angst in *Being and Time*. *Journal of the British Society for Phenomenology* 43.2: 195–211.

Withy, Katherine (2014) Situation and Limitation: Making Sense of Heidegger on Thrownness. *European Journal of Philosophy* 22.1: 61–81.

Yeomans, Christopher (2017) Towards an Immanent Conception of Economic Agency. *Hegel Bulletin* 38.2: 241–65.

Young, Iris Marion [1980] (2005a) Throwing Like a Girl. In *On Female Body Experience*, 27–45. Oxford: Oxford University Press.

Young, Iris Marion [1984] (2005b) Pregnant Embodiment. In *On Female Body Experience*, 46–61. Oxford: Oxford University Press.

Zahavi, Dan (2014) *Self and Other: Exploring Subjectivity, Empathy and Shame.* Oxford: Oxford University Press.

Index

Printed and bound by CPI Group (UK) Ltd, Croydon, CR0 4YY